Dim Sum Strategy

Bite-Sized Tools to Build Stronger Brands

Peter Wilken

First Parafine Press Edition 2019

Hardcover ISBN: 978-1-950843-02-2
Paperback ISBN: 978-1-950843-03-9
E-Book ISBN: 978-1-950843-04-6

Parafine Press
3143 West 33rd Street, Cleveland, Ohio 44109
www.parafinepress.com

CONTENTS

"Give us the tools, and we will finish the job."
Sir Winston Churchill

This is a book for anyone interested in building a stronger brand and a stronger business. Whether you're a young entrepreneur, an established CEO, a CBO, the owner of a private company, part of a corporate team building an established brand, or simply interested in building your own personal brand, the principles of brand-building and brand maintenance are applicable across the board.

Our world has changed. Consumers have more information, more channels, more power, more brands, and more choice, but less time, less loyalty, and less trust.

What is a brand? How do you build a strong brand in this changing landscape? Brands are more than logos and advertising. They're a promise. A commitment that creates an expectation. They exist as perceptions and are 'owned' by the customer. Brands are organic entities—living, changing, and in need of constant nurturing. The best way to build enduring brands in this constantly changing world is to integrate business, brand, and communications, with the brand at the centre.

Strong brands have relevant, differentiated, and compelling promises that they keep. Your promise is the over-arching commitment you make to your stakeholders. Consistent delivery of desired experiences is the heart of what makes great brands great. At The Brand Company in Hong Kong, we developed an approach we called Brand Centered Management™ (BCM). Based on timeless principles that are as relevant today as they were yesterday, it is both a philosophy and a process to help build businesses in a consistent, brand-centric way. It is a right-brained, creative way of approaching business strategy.

The medium or delivery mechanisms may change, but the principles of brand-building remain the same. A motivating and credible promise is essential for a brand whether it's communicated in a newspaper, a website, or a Facebook message. Don't be fooled by the wonderment of new media; yes, it's important to stay abreast of new ways of connecting with your target audience and getting your message successfully delivered to them. But it's still just a means to an end—the content of the message and how it is interpreted is what's important—more important than the messenger that delivered it.

The Risk of Brand Mismanagement Is Real

Brands are mismanaged every day.

In my thirty years of advertising and brand consulting, I have witnessed companies and people making the same mistakes over and over again. Few companies will admit to not having a strategy for their brand, but even when they have one it is often ill-defined. Branding and brand-building are often confused. Refreshing your logo or visual identity is often mistaken for brand building.

Neglecting your brand increases the risk of lost opportunity, competitive incursion, irrelevancy and obsolescence. Innovation and creativity are overused words that are under-delivered in kind. Easy to say; hard to do.

So, what's the solution?

What companies often fail to recognise is that effective brand-building means positioning your brand in people's minds. Defining the target and territory you want to own is essential. Regular strategic review of your brand helps keep it strong and healthy.

Strategy is all about choice; what you choose to do and, just as importantly, what you choose not to do. The Brand Centered Management™ approach provides a disciplined structure and process within which creative freedom is encouraged. It is agnostic; it works with a wide range of tried and tested strategic tools to illuminate, inspire and help 'lift the mist' in order to make good choices each step of the way.

The result is a greater awareness of current perceptions of your brand and an enduring strategic platform on which to build its strength going forward. It also engages the team and encourages them to pull together behind a focused strategy that aligns brand, business and communication.

Tools as a Dim Sum Meal

I collected the strategic tools I used at workshops to solve customer problems in a file labeled the 'toolbox'. The beauty of the Brand Centered Management process is that it is eclectic in accommodating all sorts of strategic tools. Over the years I've developed and collected dozens.

Tools are what differentiate higher-thinking species. They help perform tasks that without them are extremely difficult, if not impossible. And they unlock new ways of thinking and doing things that might never have happened without them. It took the aardvark eons to evolve a long sticky tongue to reach the ants inside an ants' nest. It took chimpanzees considerably less time to figure out a stick could do the same job.

Dim Sum Strategy captures some of the most useful strategic tools, tips, ideas and insights that I've encountered throughout my career. I've curated the ones that I most frequently return to, the ones that have resonated with my clients. Then I've boiled them down to the bare essence—just enough to get a solid understanding and to be of immediate value within minutes of reading.

I've tried to present them like a Dim Sum meal. They are mostly bite-sized, in a wide variety of flavours. Some are more substantial, but all are easy to digest. Some will be familiar old favourites, others something new you've not tried before. Most are the result of collaborations with colleagues in the agencies and consulting companies I've worked with, some are my own and some the works of better minds than mine. For the latter, I have given attributions and references wherever possible for those interested in searching for more detail. I have provided little more than a researcher could find through an internet search other than provide relevance and context. My hope is that it will raise awareness of these valuable strategic tools amongst a new generation of leaders and influencers.

I would be surprised if some concepts are not familiar to you already and, simultaneously, disappointed if some are not new to you. I hope you'll find them insightful and can apply them to your business and personal life.

Each is a timeless tool. A constant. Something that has stood the test of time and will likely continue to do so. I've tried to keep each one short, but there should be enough information to grasp the concept and apply it straightaway. The intention is to introduce each tool—an appetiser if you like—not a comprehensive philosophy or step-by-step instruction manual.

For those who like order and plan to read it cover to cover, the book is structured as the Brand Centered Management process is, from Discovery through to Delivery. If you want to test your knowledge of your business and your brand or question the value of reading this book, go to the Brand Health Check on page 49. If you're interested in defining your brand you can jump to the section on Definition and Brand DNA development. Or if you just want to browse the content list and cherry-pick tools that intrigue you, that's fine too; you should get something out of every tool in its own right, although each is richer in the context of the whole.

Throughout the book I've added sidebars to highlight relevant points or anecdotes.

With that in mind—dig in!

It's a well-worn cliché that change is constant. What is less well known is there is also constant in change. The next generation of young leaders can do worse than learn some of the timeless lessons it takes a career lifetime to learn.

Years of practice have made me an active listener. I listen to what is *not* said as much as to what is.

When I was based in Singapore working with Ogilvy & Mather as it was then in a regional role in the Silver Kris lounge (we travelled so much around the region we named our office after the Singapore Airlines hospitality suite) my boss and mentor was a wise man called Ranjan Kapur. During an annual appraisal he gave me some excellent advice: "If you really want to know what people think about you, listen to what they *don't* say." He then went on to list a number of attributes that I clearly had room for improvement in, but delivered in a kind way that I absorbed. It became a life lesson that I've applied ever since to myself, others and brands.

What are you *not* hearing about your brand or business? Read on, and maybe you'll finally hear it.

BRAND-CENTERED MANAGEMENT™

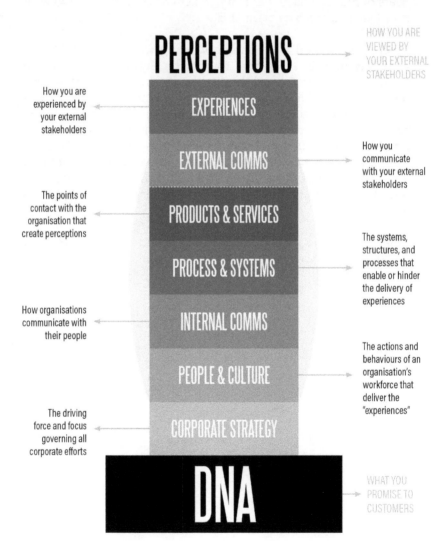

PERCEPTIONS → HOW YOU ARE VIEWED BY YOUR EXTERNAL STAKEHOLDERS

How you are experienced by your external stakeholders ← **EXPERIENCES**

EXTERNAL COMMS → How you communicate with your external stakeholders

The points of contact with the organisation that create perceptions ← **PRODUCTS & SERVICES**

PROCESS & SYSTEMS → The systems, structures, and processes that enable or hinder the delivery of experiences

How organisations communicate with their people ← **INTERNAL COMMS**

PEOPLE & CULTURE → The actions and behaviours of an organisation's workforce that deliver the "experiences"

The driving force and focus governing all corporate efforts ← **CORPORATE STRATEGY**

DNA → WHAT YOU PROMISE TO CUSTOMERS

What makes great brands great? I can tell you now, but you won't believe me.

We all instinctively know—but tend to ignore—the simple truth that adults cannot be told what to think. Classroom environments may work for young brains where open-minded innocence and clean mental cupboards eagerly store information unhindered by skepticism, self-interest and alternative agendas. Adults, on the other hand, struggle to learn that way. They need to experience things for themselves.

So bear with me and let's play a little word game.

Romance

I will often start seminars by writing this word in big letters. Then I tell the audience that I am thinking of a city in the world. What is it?

Paris. Without hesitation I hear Paris.

Often a Florence or a Venice get an honourable mention—it would appear the Italians are challenging the French for animal magnetism—but there aren't that many other cities on the radar for this particular attribute. Paris is head and shoulders above the rest, even for people who've never been there.

The last time I went to Paris, though, it was far from romantic. Taking my then 16- and 8-year-old sons to Euro Disney (my wife had brilliantly orchestrated herself out of this particular pleasure) turned out to be a soulless affair pitched in a flat grey field somewhere on the outskirts of the city. My eldest son's bags hadn't arrived at Charles de Gaulle airport, nor had they turned up at the Disneyland resort hotel, so given the eclectic choice of Disney character merchandise available he settled for Donald Duck boxers and a T-shirt, as any trend-setting 16-year-old would.

We quickly gave up on our Disney adventure and caught the Metro down to the West Bank, admiring the wall to ceiling graffiti and narrowly avoiding being assaulted by a posse of Paris Saint Germain fans by keeping our 'roast beef' mouths firmly shut. Not a femme fatale in sight. Not even a woman, in fact.

Romantic? Definitely not! So how come Paris still holds this magic?

Well, this little snapshot experience is not really being fair to the city. Our trip wasn't planned to be a romantic getaway, and the rest of the trip was fabulous for what it's worth. When most people come to Paris, they already start with the mindset that it's going to be a romantic experience and to an extent the perceptions are then tuned-in. So powerful is the ownership of this particular intangible attribute that one can see past everything else—the 'mistakes' if you like—while the positive experiences reinforce the perceptions. This is a mark of a powerful brand. Believers are prepared to forgive them if they are honest and, on the whole, deliver on their promise.

And through this filter, the city is truly magnificent and romantic. The iconic images of the Eiffel Tower, the Seine, the artistic West Bank, the Louvre, Maxim's, French accents, the amazing food, the champagne. All of it is indelibly etched in people's minds. That territory is owned by Paris.

What's more, it's been a consistent theme for nearly a century. So much so that we're attuned to Paris being 'the right answer' to the question of the most romantic city in the world — even if we've never experienced it for ourselves.

So what about this next one...

Safety

What car company owns this word? Think about it.

Not everybody says the same thing, but nearly always there's a few people in the audience that without prompting automatically say 'Volvo'. One of Sweden's largest export brands alongside ABBA and Ikea, Volvo is certainly a sizable brand. But how have they managed to acquire this highly desirable attribute of safety ahead of all other brands?

Well, Volvo have been safety conscious from the outset, building cars with passenger safety cages since the 1940s and pioneering design safety through car accident research. In 1927, Volvo's founders Gustaf Larsson and Assar Gabrielsson articulated clearly their intention for the company:

"Cars are driven by people. The guiding principle behind everything we make at Volvo therefore is—and remains—safety."

So from the start, safety was a core brand attribute for Volvo. But the word itself became welded to Volvo in people's minds through the powerful Crash Test Dummies advertisements produced by Bartle Bogle Hegarty in the late 1980s. Remember the dummies that send a Volvo crashing through second-story showroom plate glass windows, smashing in slow motion on the ground below to demonstrate the crumple zone? Remember the tag line, 'tested by dummies, driven by the intelligent'?

Now, I imagine the safety aspect of the car was originally highlighted as a strength because it was one of the few attributes the company excelled at. Volvos have never been the fastest, the most stylish, the most prestigious or the most aspirational of cars. But they have always been solidly built and safe.

And because safety has been a central belief for Volvo's founders, critically, they deliver it in the product. Safety has been a consistent theme for 70 years.

So when management occasionally get distracted by research that tells them their cars are boxy and not as stylish as BMW or Mercedes and orders a sleek redesign and relaunch, their faithful audience reminds them: "Volvo's not stylish, it's safe!"

Don't get me wrong, markets evolve and it's not good enough to be safe alone if your car is ugly. But the corollary for Volvo is that a good-looking design is not the differentiator for the brand. Their loyal customers are primarily looking for safety, and that's what they believe Volvo owns.

When you own a word or territory in the mind like this, it becomes an incredibly powerful force. People perceive Volvo to be the safest car even when it is beaten in safety tests by other brands. It's not what you say you are, or even what you are, but *what people perceive you to be* that defines your brand.

Overall, Volvo have not just been talking about safety and claiming it for themselves, they've been *delivering* it through the cars they make and the design innovations they've pioneered or adopted.

Let's try another one.

Driving Experience

Okay, so how about this? Who owns Driving Experience?

BMW of course! Why? Because they've been consistently banging the 'Ultimate Driving Experience' drum for forty years or more. It's in everything you see about BMW and everything you hear. A bold claim that they mostly live up to.

I've owned a BMW. The company was one of our clients and I believe one must honour a client's products. It was a terrific car, especially the engine, which never missed a beat. It was a pleasure to drive for sure, but was it the 'ultimate driving experience' compared with, say, a Mercedes? Or a Bentley? What about a Ferrari?

Honestly, it's hard to tell. It would be very difficult to prove that their driving experience was any more 'ultimate' than many competitive cars these days. The point, though, is that the faithful Beemer drivers believe it to be so. Perception exists only in the mind; it can never be rationally proven. What constitutes 'ultimate' for one driver is not the same for another. The concept, however, is ownable—and BMW have it.

Now, try this one.

Everything We Do Is Driven By You

Okay, you're in the part of your mental store-cupboard where you placed car-related memories—who owns 'Everything we do is driven by you?'

Do you know?

Even with the help of being in the automotive category headspace, people find it difficult to remember. What if I told you this was supported by a multi-million dollar advertising campaign over several years—does that help?

This is the perfect demonstration of the difference between a tagline and a positioning.

A positioning is what you stand for in someone's mind—literally a position or a territory in their hearts and minds that you own. The longer you've been there and the more distinctive and important a territory it is, the more powerful the brand.

A tagline is simply a catchy phrase or hook designed to stick to the brand like a burr sticks to a jacket. After much repetition it can penetrate thick skulls and become an attribute and can even reinforce a positioning. But for every memorable 'Just do it!' there are a thousand taglines that lie in the mountains of unattached, unassociated, forgotten ones.

There are many stimuli that can evoke the image of a territory, of which a tagline or catch-phrase may be one. It could also be a piece of music or an iconic image, a colour combination or even a smell. The hard part though, is owning and building the positioning—that plot of real estate in the mind—that these stimuli remind you of.

Oh, and the answer was Ford. By all accounts an automotive brand most of us are aware of. Do Ford own the belief that they are the company that is genuinely and sincerely driven by you (the customer's) wishes?

Clearly not.

Reliability

Any guesses?

Until recently, the most popular answer would have been Toyota. Toyota is the world's No.1 car company, and their success stems from their reputation for making affordable, reliable cars. They may not be as prestigious as a Mercedes or as fun to drive as a BMW, but they are well-built.

Or at least that was the perception of the company until the issue of faulty accelerator pedals and uncontrolled acceleration was exposed around 2009. After decades of success based on providing quality, reliability and value, Toyota lost its way.

What happens when you're the brand leader in a highly competitive and fragmented sector, where protecting brand share is becoming increasingly difficult, let alone growing it? What happens when shareholders demand the same high dividends they've become used to year in and year out? The answer is you try to increase profit by reducing costs.

Saving a few dollars on a slightly cheaper component may not sound like much, but when you sell millions it adds up to millions of dollars. So quality is sacrificed. A perfectly good accelerator pedal is replaced by a cheaper component that sometimes gets stuck in the floor mat—with fatal consequences. After a global recall of 6.5 million cars and an appearance before a congressional hearing to demand an explanation into the crisis, Chairman Akio Toyoda must have reflected that perhaps the cost-cutting exercise wasn't such a good idea.

It's a cliché and a truism that the trust that takes years to build can be destroyed in seconds. The biggest damage to Toyota was lost reputation. The perception that Toyota is dedicated to quality, if not lost forever, was certainly dented. This is not a mission to knock Toyota or anyone else; in fact, I've purposely chosen examples where the crisis has abated and been well managed. The VW diesel emissions test scandal is a more recent case and serves as proof that mistakes that undermine the trust of consumers are made time and again, even by some of the largest and best run organisations.

So how do these giants recover? The answer lies in just how close to the problem the individual relating to the brand is.

People humanise their experience with brands. Each of us live in our own brain and the perceptions within it. For the people directly impacted by these accidents, I doubt there will ever be a way back. To well-informed new customers who do their research, I suspect it will be difficult to persuade them the brand has a competitive advantage in quality over their rivals. For a thirty-year Toyota brand loyalist with a good dealer and a trouble-free relationship with the brand, they are likely to forgive and even willfully forget. They will dismiss the mistake as an aberration.

In the days when large corporations could largely control the public perception of their customer base, it was possible to overcome problems behind a curtain and emerge the other side smiling to an unknowing public. Even when problems did become public—and let's face it, every business encounters problems at some time—handled properly, with an honest and open account of the situation, most customers accepted a reasonable argument and could forgive the occasional genuine mistake.

The digital age has changed this dynamic. The consequences of bad corporate decisions can be discovered and amplified almost immediately. Companies have to deal with real-time information (and misinformation) from a morass of media sources. Facebook, Twitter, Instagram, YouTube, and blogs accelerate the epidemic. Suppression of awareness is almost impossible—a virus can 'go viral' in an instant.

Recently a domestic US airline was called to account by returning US military personnel who, disgusted by being hit with excess baggage charges for the equipment they were bringing home after serving abroad, posted a YouTube video that provoked instant outrage. The airline rescinded its policy within a matter of hours.

When it comes to brands, we are likely to fit them into mind maps that match our own beliefs. We look for experiences and brands that reinforce our own beliefs. Sometimes it takes a dramatic shock that shakes the foundations of trust to the core before people will change their minds.

Powerful brands can be forgiven mistakes, even lies, if they volunteer the truth and seek forgiveness. Their brand loyalists and advocates will want to forgive them most of the time. But if the truth has to get dragged out of you through law courts and congressional hearings, there's little chance of forgiveness.

Okay, let's keep moving. The previous examples demonstrate ownership over words within a market, but what about ownership over a market itself? Take one of my favourite examples.

Chocolate

Now if you're in North America, the response is likely to be Hershey's. But if you're British or Australian it's Cadbury's. Both are dominant chocolate families that have become institutions in their respective countries. The Hershey bar and Hershey's kisses have been around for over a century, as has Cadbury's Dairy Milk and Bourneville. These brands have become deeply woven in the fabric of multiple generations. Loyalty or preference to one or the other runs high.

Hershey's and Cadbury's would make up 80-90 per cent of the first names mentioned. If we've got some Swiss in the audience, perhaps a Lindt or a Nestle too. Occasionally, Godiva gets thrown out by an upmarket chocaholic. But mostly it's Hershey's and Cadbury's, in equal proportion depending on what side of the Atlantic your chocolate roots come from.

When you consider there are literally hundreds of chocolate brands out there, it's perhaps surprising that these two emerge as such dominant mainstream forces. Then again, it's not so surprising when you understand how brand categories form in our minds. (More on this later.)

Now what if I add a single descriptor?

Triangular Chocolate

Everybody says Toblerone. One simple descriptor and suddenly there is no uncertainty who owns that particular attribute. Toblerone does— and nobody else.

This is one of the most powerful examples of owning a territory in the mind. When I say Toblerone, most people think of that heavy shiny gold triangular bar you see in airport duty free shops—big, heavy, triangular bars that can keep even the most voracious chocaholic busy for days. Whether through accident or design, the triangular shape of Toblerone is a brilliant piece of marketing differentiation. The fact that it is integral to the brand's origins—the shape mimicking the triangular peaks of the Swiss Alps—suggests this was no accident. It also makes ownership of the attribute more credible and harder for competitors to claim for themselves. (Belgium, for one, would have a struggle finding mountains to mimic!)

So what happens when a new marketing team gets hold of a brand like this? Inevitably, someone queries the wisdom of staying triangular. Perhaps they're looking to change things up a little, to keep things fresh. How about we do something different for the Christmas promotional season this year? Maybe we'll make them round, wrap them in foil, and put them in bags. It'll be brilliant!

This line of thinking is how you can destroy your key differentiating property in an instant. Does anyone think of Toblerone round and in a bag? I doubt it. Fortunately, this particular promotion wasn't a long-lasting experiment. Most every variant—be it white, dark or fruit and nut—still comes in the familiar triangle shape.

Why? Because Toblerone owns triangular chocolate. It's that simple. This principle works in other markets, too. Try this one.

Watch

Most people tend to name the brand of watch they are currently wearing: Omega, IWC, Tag Heuer, Seiko, Citizen and so on. Normally it's the luxury brands you hear first, but sometimes it's the popular affordable ones like Swatch or Fossil.

What happens when I add a descriptor?

Gold Watch

Rolex. Easy. Nine out of ten times that will be the answer.

Rolex has collared the gold retirement watch. It is the expensive, prestigious gift that recognises and symbolises a lifetime of achievement.

There are plenty of other gold watches out there that could do just as good a job, but Rolex owns this territory. And the longer you've owned the top of the hill and built your fortress with ramparts to defend against invaders, the harder it is to dislodge you.

What about a different descriptor?

Sports Watch

Who owns this?

Tag Heuer most likely. Tag Heuer have conspicuously associated themselves with the world of sports since the late 19th century. Pioneers in accurate stopwatches and time trip features for cars and aircraft, they have advertised across a spectrum of sports, particularly in motor racing.

(Interestingly, Rolex have been active sponsors of prestigious golf tournaments for decades and yet Tag Heuer still has more sporting pedigree and association.)

Because watches have been with us for close to two hundred years, it's a highly fragmented category. In order to find their own niche, brands have had to look further and stretch harder to reach small pockets of white space. Even being a Swiss watch isn't sufficient to differentiate. Over two centuries there are scores of brands claiming the foundation attributes of heritage, fine craftsmanship and superior mechanisms traditionally associated with Swiss watchmakers.

So how do they stand apart from each other? Like branches on a centuries old oak tree, they push out in different directions looking to own their own spot in the sunshine. Breitling base their positioning around aviation. It's masculine, mechanical, typically with leather or alligator straps and large round faces and multiple complications. By way of contrast, Cartier, is more feminine, typically with a smaller rectangular face, and more delicate metallic strap. The brands try to move away from each other like magnets repelling. As the space gets more crowded and cramped, the distances between them may be compressed, but the force to keep apart becomes ever stronger the closer they are squeezed together.

What's happening now as the Millennials abandon wearing watches altogether because they can carry the time with them on their mobile devices? The world comes full circle. Dominant digital brands are trying to expand their franchise into the now empty space. Apple, struggling to find another niche screen size between laptops, iPads, and iPhones, has now expanded into watches. Fitbit has already rapidly found a niche in the health-monitoring sub-category. It's found a new purpose for wearing a band around your wrist that, conveniently, also tells the time.

Your Brand?

So, what word does your brand own?

Most often I find it's hard for my clients to pinpoint a single word. Even for some very large multinational, household name brands. There is an awkward silence.

Now it doesn't mean that your brand isn't well known or successful if you don't own a word. It just implies the boundaries of your territory are perhaps not as well defined as they might be. Perhaps it's a young brand still cementing itself. Perhaps it's a complex brand with multiple attributes, although this becomes increasingly untenable. If you stand for everything, you stand for nothing. Or perhaps your brand falls into the largest category: having no clearly defined territory at all.

Most every brand has to work hard and constantly to keep their 'battle lines' of demarcation sharp. Knowing clearly where those lines of when you're 'in' and, perhaps even more importantly when you're 'out' are the mark of a strong brand.

To this last point, the temptation to stretch the appeal of your brand to target segments beyond their natural reach is all too prevalent. Marketing Directors keep trying to stretch the blanket to be able to throw it over a larger crowd of customers. Most times it's better to target the right customers you want under your blanket.

The ultimate success in owning a word is when your brand name defines a category. Hoover used to define vacuum cleaners years ago, and if they'd kept abreast of technology developments they still would. The fact that Dyson has since usurped them demonstrates a golden rule of brand-building—even if you're 'king of the hill', changing environments and the law of entropy means you have to constantly improve to stay there.

Polaroid is another that enjoyed a brief period of defining instant photos. Many will remember that clunky black or grey camera box with the special film roll that you wait a couple of minutes to process then peel back to reveal the photograph. It capitalised on a powerful human drive for instant gratification but succumbed to digital photography.

Google began in 1996 when Larry Page and Sergey Brin were PhD students at Stanford University. It was incorporated in 1998 and within two decades Google has not only defined the search engine category, it has become a verb. The Oxford English Dictionary defines 'To Google' as "to use the Google search engine to obtain information on the Internet".

You know you've made it when your brand name not only defines the category but the active verb of a newly formed action or behavior, too. As 'hoovering' to the British used to mean vacuum cleaning, to much of the world 'Googling' means searching for something on the Internet.

Of course Google is now a ubiquitous behemoth that is beginning to test the boundaries of its elasticity. The end users in the real world define these boundaries more than anyone in the boardroom. For example, Instagram has become the Facebook for young teens and pre-teens; they have a lexicon of codes and meanings intentionally designed to actively exclude adults. By doing this they strengthen the 'you're in our club' affinity.

What are the brands you have a strong personal affinity for? What brands would you actively advocate for? What brands have disappointed you and do you actively avoid?

I normally ask my audience these questions at the beginning of my talk. I ask them to think about this as I'm talking and be ready to volunteer some thoughts at the end. It's never a disappointing discussion. Inevitably it ends up concluding that the strongest brands treat us like intelligent human beings. They don't insult our intelligence. They aspire to it.

Own a Territory in the Mind

The size of the territory a tiger controls depends on the type of tiger (i.e. Bengal, Sumatran or Amur), its age, its fitness, and whether it's male or female. Habitat and prey density are determining factors too. A dominant male Amur or Siberian tiger may control a territory of over 800 square kilometers while his Bengal counterparts may control less than one quarter of that space. Females territories are also much smaller, sometimes a tenth of the males. Why? Because their needs and aims are different. The males are looking to maximise encounters with fertile females and find prey. The females want to minimise conflict with other tigers while maximising food resources for feeding cubs.

Either way, territories are carefully staked out and marked by scenting, scratching, and vocal warnings. Only the fittest adults in their prime can control large territories. Aging males are constantly challenged by younger males to take over their territory, with the best territories being the most in demand. When the habitat grows and competition decreases, the entire population (category) prospers. The reverse happens under adverse conditions.

The parallels between nature and brand-building are apparent. Darwinian principles apply to brands in the same way as they do to the natural world.

The strength of a brand can be related to how dominant it is within its defined territory. Strength can be measured in different ways—dominance, longevity, the ability to command a premium, the ability to withstand a crisis or survive a drought for example. It is not an exact science. Is it better to live longer in want than shorter in prosperity? I think most would agree the aim is to 'have it all'— health, wealth and longevity.

The key to success is defining clear boundaries that can be owned and defended within the power you possess. A tiger stalking a territory of nearly 1,000 sq km is going to have a tough time protecting the far reaches of his estate from competitive incursion. He expends energy and resources covering vast distances to defend his territory and protect what he owns—time that could be spent hunting, eating or reproducing. A smaller territory may have fewer opportunities to meet other females but is easier to defend. The longer a territory is owned, the stronger the scent marks, the deeper the scratches, the clearer the demarcation of boundaries becomes—often this is enough alone to deter competitors from challenging dominance.

In the same way, dominant brands have marked out their territory and presented a considerable barrier to entry for new challengers by owning territory in the mind of its customer's. The longer that territory has been held and the more consistently it has been reinforced over time, the harder it is for another brand to displace it from that customers mind. The strategy for newcomers is more likely to be to carve out a small corner of an expansive territory that can be taken over and held. Or better, discover fruitful, unclaimed land that they can make their own. Define new territories (categories) and own them.

Most successful brands share common characteristics. Great brands are:

- Distinctive
- Singular
- Consistent
- Own or define a category
- Own or define a key time, occasion or experience
- Have strong personalities
- Differentiate on *emotional* platforms
- Own and protect 'territories in the mind'

Distinctive brands stand apart from their competitors. They look different, feel different, smell different, sound different, or taste different. Perhaps most importantly, they make their brand loyalists *feel differently* towards them. Distinctive brands aren't afraid to not appeal to everyone. In fact, some actively alienate certain types of customers in order to appeal to their loyal customers.

Strong brands also tend to be singular—that is, they do one thing extremely well for their brand users. What they do well may involve more than singular action or emotion. For example, a large retail grocery brand can appeal to its loyal customer group through the environment it creates, its friendly service, and the selection of brands they offer. But on all these fronts, they deliver the experience better than any other.

In my workshop groups I use this exercise to illustrate the point about focus. Try catching three tennis balls thrown at the same time. Often people drop all three because they don't know which one to look at. But when I throw one ball at them hard, they can catch it one-handed. Focus is key. A singular message is easier to 'catch'. It's easier to demarcate your territory and therefore easier to own and defend that territory.

Strong brands are also consistent. They deliver consistent experiences time and again. Loyal users are confident that the experience they know and love will be repeated when they return. How many of us go back to the same restaurants and order the same dishes we know and love? We expect the taste, the presentation and the service to be the same and are disappointed if it's not.

It's no different with brands. Strong brands set up an expectation—the promise of a consistent repeat pleasurable experience—and then deliver against it. Every time they do so, they add another layer of strengthening reinforcement. When that foundation becomes trust, even the occasional aberration will be forgiven if dealt with openly and honestly. But if the consistent experience becomes one of disappointment then the trust will rapidly erode. Even the strongest brand cannot afford to be complacent.

Brand leaders reinforce their singular messages consistently. They say the same thing over and over again in different ways. They don't literally repeat the same message rote—a sledgehammer approach that rapidly bores, then irritates—they find interesting ways to communicate the same underlying promise to keep it engaging and fresh.

I can hear voices interjecting at this point: *What about innovation? What about constantly striving for better?* Well, innovation and consistency are not mutually exclusive. If your brand is known for innovation and design (think Apple) then brand users have a higher expectation for development. Even then, the reality is, they easily differentiate between 'tweaks' to existing products or platforms (how many iPhone iterations are there left?) and the truly innovative product developments that are much rarer. Think about evolutions of car models. Characteristic grilles tell you it's still a BMW, Jaguar, Mercedes, Chrysler or whatever, sometimes spanning several decades. It's expected that the brand will stay abreast of technological advancements while retaining familiarity with certain aspects. Similarly, Burberry retain their classic plaid pattern but use it in innovative ways. We see it spread from the original raincoat to T-shirts, handbags, umbrellas and even doggie-wear.

The strongest brands define their own category. It is unusual for a pioneer brand that defines a category to lose perceptual ownership of that category. Prime-mover advantage is so great for those that win the race and have the financial and legal muscle to protect it. Tupperware, Velcro, and Post-It notes are good examples. Ski-doo, Jacuzzi, and Zamboni are winter sport examples; their names symbolise the category and dominate perceptions so much they mask competitors. I hear my ice hockey parent friends calling the ice-cleaning machine a Zamboni even as it passes by with the name Olympia emblazoned on it!

Owning an Occassion

As pumpkins are to Halloween or turkeys are to Thanksgiving, certain brands are to an occasion or event. They become an integral part of a time of day, an event or a special occasion. Associations built up by repetition over time become habitual, then characteristic of the brand. Heinz tomato soup is still the first thing I return to after an illness; it may be Campbell's chicken noodle soup for others. Owning a time or occasion is a way of diversifying or specialising. It narrows the field of context and makes it easier to define a territory, then own it through association.

Occasions are more commonly associated with product categories than brands themselves. Special occasions are toasted with champagne. Engagement rings invariably contain a diamond. Breakfast is when we eat the most eggs. Chances are though, that if you're the brand leader in the product category you'll be top of mind when that occasion comes around. So Moet & Chandon doesn't own every special occasion, but when the moment calls for champagne, chances are it's one of the first brands you'd consider.

Strong Personalities

Strong brands have strong personalities. They're not wishy-washy. You know exactly who they are when they walk into a room. Like people with strong personalities they may be complex. They may change with mood and occasion, but they still have instantly recognisable behaviours and characteristics. Mass market brands with broad appeal tend to adopt more universally acceptable traits. Brands at the extremes can be more exclusive or even intentionally divisive.

Strong brands keep their promises every time. They DO before they SAY—that is they deliver first, then speak after. They do this without boast. Better still, they have a third party say it for them. Isn't an unsolicited endorsement from a third party much more powerful than pointing out your own merits?

I've always bluntly told my clients: "One ounce of action is worth ten tons of bullshit". Tangible results will always beat the promise of tangible results.

Strong Foundations

The taller you want your building to stand, the deeper you have to dig your foundation. As with architecture, the strongest brands have the strongest foundations.

I've seen entire cities spring up in less than 15 years. I recall looking out of the thirtieth story window of the Spaceship Hyatt building at the surrounding towers in Shanghai and remembering when the spot on which I stood was completely flat without a single building on it. A little more than a decade later it was a bustling high-rise metropolis. Dubai could tell the same story. These are sturdy structures, built to last. The pyramids and other ancient monuments have proven that buildings built on solid foundations of stone can stand for millennia.

If you want your brand to stand tall for a long time, it needs to be built on strong foundations. It helps to have the tenure of centuries, as companies like Hovis, Coca-Cola, Cadbury, Marmite, and Dunlop do. These brands have been around for multiple generations, building stronger and wider foundations. But they are subject to the same pressure of continuing to present relevant propositions to their customers in an increasingly competitive environment. Globalisation, technology and the information age have made it much easier for brands to reach wider audiences, across a bigger geography, faster than ever before. Let me qualify that—it's much easier for interest groups or 'tribes' that share the same interests to connect—be it in luxury yachts, model airplanes, holidays in the West Indies, computer games or expensive shoes—to find each other and share thoughts. Brand affinity or antipathy can be amplified quickly. Malcolm Gladwell's 'tipping point' of influencers is reached in a fraction of the time it once was.

The rate of change of brand dominance is accelerating. Twenty years ago most of the top 10 brands in the world would have been the same top 10 brands of fifty years ago. The big oil companies like Shell and Esso (Exxon) topped the rankings with familiar names like Coca-Cola, McDonald's, Kodak, and Sony. In 2015, half of the top 10 brands weren't in the top 10 a decade before—including the No. 1 brand by value then, Apple.

Even in the last two years we've seen shifts in the top 10. Google edged out Apple from the top spot in the 2017 rankings. The top five spots are now occupied by technology giants including Microsoft, Amazon, and Facebook. Chinese internet and gaming company Tencent broke into the top 10 for the first time, displacing 'old school' Top 10 stalwarts Marlboro and Coca-Cola. These so-called ecosystem brands, through technology, have mastered the art of maximising the opportunity presented by the online relationships they own with their customers. They use data and insight to exploit multiple touchpoints with their customer base. Importantly though they also *deliver*. Apple's products are aesthetic in design and functional. Amazon's back-end logistics are simply astonishing, with next day delivery in major markets now commonplace.

What's important to understand is that entire categories have emerged in a relatively short period of time.

A 'steady as she goes' approach in such a dynamic landscape isn't sufficient to hold on to your ranking. Marlboro increased their value by $7Bn in the last two years yet slipped out of the top 10 rankings. Oil giants ExxonMobil and Shell, table-toppers in recent memory, are now 57th and 58th in ranking respectively. Technology and the Internet have created brands and businesses that were largely unknown fifteen or twenty years ago. Google was founded in 1998. It took them less than twenty years to become the top ranked brand in the world. Facebook, Alibaba and YouTube are other examples. Apple had computers but not iPhones or iPads. Mobile telephony has created new telecom service providers. Mobile applications or Apps have sprouted like wildfire for every interest one can imagine.

By the time you're reading this, the ranking and makeup of the top 10 brands will have changed again. In all probability there will be a newly emerged category that none of us would have foreseen. Despite the scale and speed of change, there are constants in the way in which these new behemoth brands succeed.

At The Brand Company, the brand consulting company in Hong Kong I set up with partners James Stewart and Ian Henry, we used to run an annual brand survey in which the characteristics of desired brands were assessed. Consistently, the top ranked attributes were 'quality products and services' and 'delivers on promises', the two being closely related.

Great brands have relevant promises that they deliver against consistently—every place, every time. They know the territory in the mind they want to own. They define it, build it, and protect it. They have a story to tell, but they focus on delivering the experience before talking about it—they DO before SAY. When they do talk, they are consistent in their messaging. The different faces of their brand are harmonised; corporate brand, product brand, brand personality and brand identity. They tend to tap into deep-rooted, emotional needs.

When they do this consistently, they create interest groups of like-minded people that share values and value the brand experience. They convert users into loyalists, loyalists into advocates, and advocate into evangelists. As a result, they can build leadership positions, sometimes defining their category. They can command significant premiums and withstand crises.

It sounds easy. The reality is different. There are many problems brands and brand-builders encounter every day that prevent them from following this path.

Branding vs. Brand-Building

When I say I'm a brand guy the common reaction is *Oh that's great... we just did a re-branding exercise, revamped the logo, freshened up the look.* Visual Identity is an executional end product for sure, and a tool in the brand-building arsenal, but it's not what I mean by brand-building.

Brand-building is owning a territory in the mind. It is positioning your brand to create or take over that space in people's minds. A space that is uniquely yours. A space that stands for something that over time has a special place in the hearts and minds of your users. A space that carries value when it comes to making purchasing decisions.

Branding, or making your look and feel reinforce your positioning, may be a part of brand-building, but it's not brand-building in itself. This is at the heart of the problem of brand-building today: Too much attention is paid to the 'superficial packaging' of the logo and visual identity as opposed to the substance of the experience delivered. *What you SAY is far less important than what you DO.*

As I constantly remind my clients, one ounce of substance is worth ten tons of talk. It's such a basic concept to grasp and yet so many marketers get it wrong. In the same way, many confuse any publicity with *good* publicity. Believe me, getting your name out there is only good if the message is a desirable one.

For so many marketers it seems the rule is this: "If I say this loud enough and often enough people will believe me... heck, I'll even begin to believe it myself". This boastful approach of making exaggerated claims only serves to undermine the brand when the experience fails to deliver against expectations. It is far better to manage expectations and then exceed them.

How do we feel when someone struts into a room, chest puffed out and loudly claiming they're the best? Unless they're parodying themselves, we think of them as arrogant, conceited or even offensive. Yet, this is still how so many marketers pitch their brands in advertisements—in a self-congratulatory, loud, boastful way. I'd go further than that to say it's almost expected of marketers to assume this approach. Because it's accepted category practice, many of them feel that's how they must behave, or risk not being seen as a serious player.

It's not surprising so many people are annoyed or frustrated by advertising interruptions. But people don't hate advertising. They hate *bad* advertising.

I can't promise the advice in this book will guarantee you'll produce messages people will love—but it will certainly improve the chances of creating stronger brands and better communications. And perhaps more importantly, it will remind everyone that the communication part should come *after* the hard groundwork of delivering against the promise has been done.

This is the biggest challenge. Companies satisfy themselves with *branding* instead of **brand-building** and think the job is done. They invest large sums of money in changing the 'packaging' of the brand—the logo, identity and advertising—without changing the *substance* of the brand experience.

You can't fool customers. Well, at least not all of them all the time, and not for long. Take me for example. Some time ago my doctor told me I had to be kinder to my liver and lose some weight. So what's the first thing I did? Go out and buy some new clothes and tell people I'm lighter and healthier? No. I started exercising and went on a six-month liver-cleansing diet. That's what makes the difference. The clothes and the boasting come after the hard work, not before it.

It's not difficult to understand why companies go the short-cut route. It's easy to churn out an ad campaign and a new identity. It's also something tangible. You can see a design and review an ad, and the board can see where their money is going.

Changing the product or service is much harder. Changing the way staff think and behave, or the product portfolio you're offering is time-consuming and expensive. But it's these harder-to-make changes that affect the brand experience in ways that make the difference between genuine brand-building and just 'branding'. The substance of what brands DO rather than the packaging of what they SAY.

As with people, it sometimes takes a crisis to bring out the best (and worst) in brands.

Who remembers the Ford vs Firestone debacle? It's well into a second decade since the problems of tread stripping off Firestone tyres on Ford Explorers occurred, causing a flood of complaints. In the most severe cases vehicles flipped, leading to 88 tragic deaths by 2001. The two companies had a business relationship spanning nearly a century and yet, as *Newsweek* reported, "crisis management experts aren't likely to write flattering case studies about how either company handled it". Acrimonious finger-pointing brought both companies down to a base level that did credit to neither.

Some basic human values apply here. Even the strongest of partnerships get tested. When they are, it pays to support each other, to accept responsibility for a shared fate, and navigate the consequences together. A distasteful public spat is like a squabbling couple at a party—it's rare either comes out of it with dignity or an enhanced reputation.

Sometimes you can do the right thing and still get it wrong. Perrier's benzene contamination in the early 1990s is now a textbook PR case. Despite apparently doing the right thing in recalling its entire stock after trace elements of benzene were found in a just a few bottles in North Carolina, Perrier lost credibility when they claimed it was an isolated incident, the result of a cleaner's improper use of a solvent when cleaning filling machinery. They were also perceived to have downplayed the scale of the problem, recalling only the North American product at first.

Instead of the recall reassuring customers of their commitment to purity—the promise of the brand—the incident made consumers question the purity of the product. The result was a significant loss of market share, decline in share value and hundreds of jobs lost. Within two years, Perrier had been acquired by Nestle.

Johnson & Johnson forever enhanced their reputation as a pharmaceutical company to be trusted through the way they handled the case of tampering with their leading painkiller brand Tylenol in 1982. In a tragic case, seven people died after an unknown suspect laced tablets of Tylenol with cyanide.

Johnson & Johnson put people before profit. As soon as the association with the deaths was made, they made announcements warning the public of the danger. They made an immediate recall of the product—31 million bottles across the country. Much later they re-introduced the product in a triple-seal tamper-proof packaging, accompanied by a price discount promotion and a massive PR push to medical professionals to reassure them. Johnson & Johnson credit their quick and correct behavior to their mission statement and an understanding that their responsibilities were to the consumers and medical professionals using their products. They could have diverted attention towards the culprit (the case remains unsolved), but instead they took responsibility at great financial sacrifice to themselves in the short term. In the long-term their enhanced reputation has been justly rewarded with recovered brand leadership and enduring patronage.

In short, there are no short cuts to brand-building. You have to take the medicine, do your time.

I'm not saying design, identity and advertising aren't important. There is no doubt that they are. They can define or reposition a brand, and occasionally they create the brand itself. Communications can generate interest, awareness and trial, but they should not be mistaken as a substitute for the experience itself.

Polarisation of the Role of Brand and Marketing

It appears to me that the importance on the brand at the boardroom table is moving in two opposite directions. For one, it is taking precedence, with the significance of the brand being embraced at the highest level of the organisation. For these organisations, the role of CBO (Chief Brand Officer) is often aligned with the role of CEO (and indeed sometimes is one and the same person). The brand informs the actions of all parts of the organisation.

For others, concerns about the brand have been moved away from the boardroom. What used to be the domain of the chairman or owner, who had direct control over his or her 'name', has gradually been pushed down the hierarchy and often out of the boardroom altogether.

If the brand is central to owning the place in the hearts and minds of customers, it follows (at least in my simple logic) that the brand should be at the heart of corporate strategy and the domain of the CEO.

But these companies are in the minority. As it stands now, brand is most often the responsibility of the marketing department. Marketing is often riveted to sales as well, in which the operational side of sales dominates politically and financially.

As the roles in organisations specialise, the marketing team typically controls communications, although it may be spun off into its own department in larger organisations. With this division of labour, it becomes more and more challenging for organisations to speak with one voice, as responsibility for messaging is divided between multiple parties.

Is the role of marketing slowly being devalued? My observation over the years, at least from an agency perspective, is that it has become compartmentalised and less strategic; more tactical and even administrative. In the agency world, the 'added value' strategic planning departments were amongst the first to feel the pressure on resource and costs. Specialist brand strategy companies grew and lured this expensive talent away, or clients hired them.

Paradoxically, while there appears to be growing recognition of the importance of brands in determining the fortunes of companies, the role of marketing in many traditional companies is being moved further away from the centre of power. How many CEOs come from a marketing background? Not so many. The majority come from finance and operations, or have technical backgrounds like computing or engineering.

That trend is reversed in places like Silicon Valley, where creative companies are led by brand-centric founders. Apple, Google, Amazon, Facebook, Pixar, Tesla have all been driven by intuitively brand-oriented founders and the brand is central to what the organisation does.

So perhaps we're seeing a polarization with younger, creative organisations placing greater emphasis on the brand and making it central to what they do, while older, more traditional organisations move it away from the centre into a more functional role.

For the tradtional companies with devolved marketing departments reporting to a board of directors, there is also less continuity in the role—in Europe, the average tenure of a marketing director is now 21 months. That is just about long enough to sort out the mess the last incumbent made, or reap their successes and muck it up for the next person!

When I first started, agencies were smaller, all-round inventive enterprises. Flamboyant founders led them. They had more distinctive differences, and dealt with CEOs to solve *business* problems, not just communication problems. Clients went to agencies to deal with the smartest thinkers—people who could provide strategic solutions to improve their business. Communications were almost a by-product of business solutions.

In thirty years, the scene has changed dramatically; the traditional agencies are larger, less differentiated and—despite all protestations to the contrary—are largely seen by clients as 'the guys that do the ads'. They are more commoditised than differentiated and more executional than strategic. Client organisations have hired smart marketing minds for themselves. They rely less on traditional agencies for strategic input (they have specialists and management consultants for that) and focus more on the execution.

Diversification and fragmentation into specialised disciplines; media, social media, CRM, interactive, digital, P.R., design, brand consultancy, management consultancy and so on has brought multiple areas of expertise to bear, but has fragmented stewardship of the brand. At the time when clients need greater continuity and experience in developing their brands, the general trend is the opposite.

So what's the answer?

Putting the brand back in the boardroom is one solution. Make it central to everything the company does and says. Make it integral to the CEO's success. In those instances where the brand is integral to the organisation, it is engrained in the culture and intuitively informs every action of every employee. In this way, the problem of managing communications to ensure consistency of messaging is solved because everyone intuitively acts and communicates in a desired way.

Another answer is to let the process of natural selection unfold. Those companies that are investing in brand-centered approaches, I predict will be at a strategic advantage. The younger Millennial leaders and even more so the Gen Z leaders coming behind them, are more entrepreneurial and experiential than their predecessors. A brand-centered philosophy is likely to sit easily with them.

Then, I believe we will see the role of CBO, Chief Brand Officer, being recognised and elevated.

Counting Only the Things that You Can Count

Another major problem is the issue of paying for the intangible benefits of branding. I believe this stems from a common strategic mantra of *measure, measure, measure*. I am all for setting goals and parameters to monitor progress and performance, but this shouldn't come at the expense of sacrificing the emotional intangibles that are difficult to measure yet hugely significant.

I believe the most significant decisions we make in life are made with the heart, then justified by the head. If you're a little skeptical try asking yourself these questions:

- How did you choose your life partner?
- How did you decide what career to pursue? What job to take?
- What made you choose to live where you do?

Almost without exception, these are emotional decisions made by the heart that we later rationalise with our heads.

Given the major issues facing brands—mistaking branding for brand-building, devaluing the role of brands and focus on measuring tangibles rather than assessing intangibles—it is worth considering if there is a root cause.

Here's a thought. If you accept that we all have two sides of our brain, with one side dominant over the other, the majority of us would have a left-brain bias. If you're right-handed, as most of us are, you're already carrying a natural left-brain tendency. Our default mode is analytical, logical, linear, numerical and verbal, as opposed to right-hemisphere brainers, whose natural world is more intuitive, emotional, spatial, visual and physical.

Which side do most CEOs prefer?

I'd suggest that *the vast majority of CEO's are 'left-brainers'*. They've typically risen from the rational world of finance, operations or manufacturing. The emotional world of brands is not a naturally comfortable place for them, so they are eager to hand it off to the marketing team

Still, while CEOs may be a cause of failure to build brands, there are often other forces at play.

The 3 Reasons Brands Fail

Why do brands fail? If you know the common causes you can work to avoid making the same mistakes. There are three reasons why brands fail, and they're all based around broken promises:

1. They make irrelevant promises.
2. They over-promise.
3. They are inconsistent in delivery of their promise.

Irrelevant Promises

An irrelevant promise is like offering a product nobody wants. It happens quite often that a product people once wanted very much becomes irrelevant to them. Nokia used to be one of the most powerful telecom brands in the world. They made the neatest, durable, compact handphones when the age of cellphones was dawning.

Their problem was that they owned the hardware, not the benefit of having a portable device that connects people to other people and the information and entertainment they seek. When a better, newer, different hardware option arrived in the form of the iPhone, Nokia suddenly became unfashionable and irrelevant. Apple's brilliance in launching the iPhone was not only to deliver excellence in design, but to own the software and platform for delivering applications (apps) too. In other words, they own the benefits beyond the hardware.

There are many examples of brands becoming irrelevant through technology advancement, often because they have tied themselves to a tangible product format rather than an emotional benefit. The Polaroid instant camera made irrelevant by digital image technology. Blockbuster video rentals made irrelevant by online brands like Netflix. If Blockbuster had stayed true to its brand mission of delivering home movie experiences wouldn't it have been a natural extension to deliver the same benefit, just through a different medium? With foresight, the board of Blockbuster would have 'done a Netflix' and used the brand familiarity and equity they had to continue their franchise.

Of course, in the real world that is much easier said than done. Imagine suggesting to the board of Blockbuster that they dismantle the extensive retail network they've spent years building up across the continent. This is why so many companies find it so difficult to embrace jump-shift change. And why brands can become irrelevant in a relatively short period of time.

When I was advising Kodak in the mid-1990s, their focus was on a global launch of a new product format called Advantix, designed to provide a smaller, more convenient photographic format. Already by that time, digital imaging was on the horizon and I asked a high-level executive why they were spending vast sums of money in outdated technology when they had a chance to take their powerful brand promise—to help you reflect and enjoy special memories through images—and spearhead the digital revolution.

"Impossible, Peter," he replied. "The bulk of our profits come from sales of silver nitrate through processing traditional photographic prints".

Kodak would have had to sacrifice its biggest cash-cow in order to make the brand relevant to consumers and a continued success. Unfortunately they didn't see it, or weren't prepared to do so. Instead, they sacrificed one of the most potentially rewarding brand promises ever to their competitors.

Not so many people 'Keep it with Kodak' anymore—they keep it in digital format on their computers, or on their iPhones.

The lesson for all? Technology is an enabler, a means to an end to deliver a benefit, not an end in itself.

If you're a baker, a 'fresh out of the oven' proposition becomes irrelevant in a matter of hours. Coffee shops display the time the pot was made to show how fresh it is and start another rather than serve cold coffee. There is a time period for some brands when the need is raised and the importance of sating that need elevated. You may not think of throat lozenges until you have a rasping sore throat, then you'll go out of your way to find one. The minute your sore throat has gone, with it goes the imperative to consider a purchase.

So relevance is time and need-based. If that relevance diminishes for whatever reason, so will the health of the brand.

Over-Promising

More common than irrelevance is *over-promising*—raising expectations and then failing to deliver against them.

How many times do we experience that? Hotels that promise paradise when in fact they're still 'soft-launching' and drilling the foundations of the new wing next to your bedroom! Banks that promise they listen, airlines that they care, beauty products that they will change your life. The list goes on.

How do you feel when someone breaks a promise? Whether it's a little one like a promise to turn up on time and being 10 minutes late, or a big one like breaking a marriage vow—it's a negative experience and it takes something away from the relationship.

Ultimately, broken promises result in broken relationships in brands as in humans—whether it's slow death by a thousand cuts or a fatal shot to the heart.

Why do folks tend to have such little respect for politicians? Because they consistently make promises they fail to deliver. Even if they are sincere in what they're saying and circumstances beyond their control are the reason, by raising expectations that are not matched by reality they disappoint their constituents and diminish themselves.

Brands are the same as people in this regard. If someone makes a promise to you that they break, then you lose trust and respect for them. Depending on how important the promise is, you may choose to forgive and forget—as many loyal customers with a healthy bank account of goodwill towards a brand will do—or you may not. It might be a promise, such as fidelity, that once broken is very difficult to mend. Relationships end.

There's a subtle difference between putting your best foot forward and creating unrealistic expectations. How many of us have experienced the hotel stay where the amazing bedroom and vista advertised isn't anything like the room and view you get when you arrive? How many of us cherry-pick that one great shot for our Facebook home page and are still using it ten years later? The burgers on the display boards always seem to look better than the ones you're served.

It's so important to manage expectations properly in order not to fall beneath them. Far better to set modest expectations and exceed them than raise expectations and fall short. The latter is seen as boastful or even deceitful.

If you say you can deliver your pizza within half an hour of ordering, you'd better be sure you can. If you say your trains run on time to within two minutes of schedule, you'd better be able to deliver. If you do, you will earn trust for your brand. If you don't, you may never be able to gain trust in the future.

Inconsistent Delivery

Consistency of delivery is just as important, if not more so. Western travellers to foreign countries will go to McDonald's because they can be assured that they'll be able to get the same Big Mac anywhere in the world. McDonald's imposes incredibly strict protocols and quality measures on their franchisees to ensure this consistency is maintained whether you're in Tokyo or Toronto.

Heinz tomato ketchup is a good example of how this can go wrong. As a heavy user of the brand I can attest to my disappointment when suddenly I cannot find my beloved glass ketchup bottle, with the thick red sauce that you have to bang the bottom of the bottle to get out. More and more, the glass has been replaced by plastic bottles with easy shut lids. This might be a small aesthetic difference — except that they've changed the formula too, so it's easier to squirt through the nozzle. What! Mr. Heinz, you've just destroyed the essence of what I've enjoyed and become accustomed to for over 40 years! It doesn't look the same, taste the same, or deliver the same consistent experience that's made me a loyal brand devotee for decades. To be fair, Heinz clearly do understand their customers because they have preserved the old original glass bottle for 'heritage' customers like myself in many retail outlets and restaurants.

Now, for sure, brands have to develop and constantly improve. But for your core loyalists, consistency of experience is vital to their continued patronage. An Audi loyalist can evolve with the technology and advancements over the years by changing models every few years without changing brand allegiance. With good brand management, these loyal users are carried with the brand on the development journey, each step being joined to the last by recognisable bridges. Brands must keep up with the times and the competitive nature of the category. Consistency in this case means delivering the same benefits with the same values in evolved forms.

More often than not brands fail to deliver consistently because they over-estimate their ability to execute; they believe they can deliver a consistent experience too widely. It's possible if you're manufacturing something simple to operate within high specific tolerances—even though something as basic as a Kit Kat appears to differ from one market to another; it's much more difficult if you're providing a service or anything that involves any form of human interaction.

My advice is not to try to do too much. Go back to your most profitable customers and the high potential interest groups for future growth, then identify the two or three most meaningful brand experiences for them and concentrate on delivering consistent experiences in these areas to those people.

What happens when brands break their promises?

What happens when they say one thing on their website:
"Welcome to Standard Chartered Bank's people pages. Our people are our greatest asset. We have a clear people agenda, set out in our roadmap, designed to contribute to our development as a high performance organisation."

And contradict it with their actions:
"StanChart sacks 200, blaming tight loan market," reads a 2004 South China Morning Post article, while simultaneously reporting, "The Asia-Pacific focused bank is anticipating a rise of 28% in pre-tax core profits for the year reaching £1 billion"

Trust? What trust? Standard Chartered bank called their people their greatest assets, but didn't hesitate to sack 200 of them during a billion-dollar profit increase.

The result of course was ridicule and condemnation from the press:
"We go faster – you go further" and "We stand strong – you stand out" are two of Standard Chartered's global advertising slogans …"We let you go faster" and "You get out" might be more appropriate after the bank, coming from a fat year, laid off 200 staff yesterday, wrote the *South China Morning Post*.

Now I don't mean to single Standard Chartered Bank out for criticism. The reality is this could have been one of any number of banks. But it looks astonishing when it's presented as coldly as this, doesn't it? How can brands get it so wrong?

One of the reasons this happens, I believe, is because large organisations lose their individual conscience. They become accountable to the law, eventually, but lose the one-on-one *human* accountability. Good individuals can do bad things in bad organisational systems or cultures. They may genuinely be ignorant of what's happening, or be shielded by the anonymity of the collective 'company'.

United Airlines spent millions of dollars over several years to encourage people to "Come fly the friendly skies"—while simultaneously being voted the rudest airline in the United States. I'm sure United's CEO did not intentionally set out to lie to or deceive their customers. It's more likely that under constant pressure for financial growth and performance—and often distanced from the real world of doing business with customers on the ground—companies like United lose their desire and ability to keep their promises *before individuals do.*

I'm not advocating the opposite extreme either. Suddenly baring everything 'warts and all' would be foolhardy and might well significantly damage the brand reputation. British Rail, well known at one time for union strikes and irregular train services, tried to strike a more positive—and honest—note in a campaign: "We're getting there." The British public treated this with a derisory laugh: "Yes mate, but you've got a bloody long way to go!"

Or worse, the story of Gerald Ratner who almost single-handedly ruined his family's low-cost jewellery business by stating: "I can sell it for £4.95 because it's total crap…it costs less than a prawn sandwich and probably won't last as long!"

The answer isn't necessarily to give people more information than they need to know. The answer is simply to be human.

The desire to grow, to develop and to stretch is natural. Without it, the world would be a dull, less exciting place. I'm all for creating interest, excitement and innovations that move the world forward. Within this, make sensible promises that are meaningful, attainable and reflective of the reality of the experience.

Why do the transgressions of some large brands appear to go unpunished? I don't believe management teams intentionally go out to make mistakes or to deceive or disappoint their customers, except in the rarest of cases. But it does seem to happen with alarming regularity.

The Exxon Valdez oil spill, Shell's oil spill in the Gulf of Mexico, Toyota's sticking accelerators, VW's diesel emissions scandal, the Firestone tyres v Ford Explorer dispute, Korean Air in the 90s. How come these brands are still around if the law of survival of the fittest applies?

With strong brands that have built up a reservoir of goodwill, forgiveness is not uncommon. Brand loyalists will forgive one or two mistakes in the context of years of good experience. If it becomes habitual, enough to make them think the personality of the brand has permanently changed, then not.

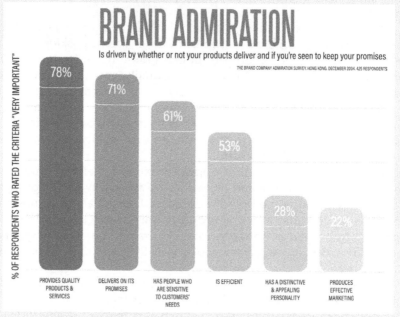

BRAND ADMIRATION

Is driven by whether or not your products deliver and if you're seen to keep your promises.

THE BRAND COMPANY ADMIRATION SURVEY, HONG KONG, DECEMBER 2004, 425 RESPONDENTS

% OF RESPONDENTS WHO RATED THE CRITERIA "VERY IMPORTANT"

78%	71%	61%	53%	28%	22%
PROVIDES QUALITY PRODUCTS & SERVICES	DELIVERS ON ITS PROMISES	HAS PEOPLE WHO ARE SENSITIVE TO CUSTOMERS' NEEDS	IS EFFICIENT	HAS A DISTINCTIVE & APPEALING PERSONALITY	PRODUCES EFFECTIVE MARKETING

For many of these companies their sheer scale is a symbol of success. Even multi-billion dollar fines mean little to them when they have the means to pay them within a year or less. Then they have political muscle too. They are huge employers and taxpayers. Some of these brands are so large and so closely linked with the fabric of nation, government and society (think big energy companies, automotive and airlines) that they do have protective security nets under them that allow them to survive crises when others wouldn't.

Even with these measures though, pressure eventually tells. The forces of Darwinian principles begin to show with pressure on government budgets, privatisation and increasing public awareness.

Interestingly, Millennials are much less trusting of large organisations than previous generations. Bigger doesn't necessarily mean better to them; if anything the opposite.

Nobody escapes the consequences of broken promises forever.

Organisations with founders who live by a set of beliefs and values that they uphold tend to shine in contrast to their less scrupulous peers. Apple, Google, Amazon, Facebook and Netflix are relative newcomers alongside established names like Walt Disney, Coca-Cola, General Electric and Johnson & Johnson in Fortune's annual rankings of the most admired companies in the world.

The brand admiration survey conducted by the Brand Company surveyed 1,928 respondents and over 100 brands in Hong Kong, Shanghai and Beijing. Although this was conducted many years ago now, I suspect the findings are as valid today as they were then.

The consistent finding is that having 'quality products & services' that do what they say they're going to do, and being perceived to be delivering against promises are the two most important criteria for driving brand admiration. Having a distinctive personality and effective marketing isn't unimportant, but it's nowhere near as important as the top two.

Southwest Airlines is the classic textbook example of this. Southwest focused on delivering their promise of providing low cost, safe and reliable air transport (an unusual combination and clearly differentiating). Only *after* they'd become the best at delivering this did they talk about 'giving people the freedom to fly'. While their competitors have struggled or collapsed, they've consistently been voted onto *Fortune* magazine's ten best companies and had decades of consecutive profit.

What about Starbucks? They built a world-beating brand without spending a dollar on advertising. They re-defined the coffee drinking experience and made it interesting and accessible to millions of people. They did it through the products, the service and the ambience. Sure, their product is also beautifully packaged with a very distinctive logo. And with new competitors crowding the category, communications help clarify their promise and differentiate the brand. But by delivering a consistent, quality experience *first*, they're doing it the right way around.

Consciously or not, companies like Southwest and Starbucks follow a Brand Centered Management approach, delivering a relevant, differentiating, compelling and credible promise to stakeholders *consistently.*

Putting Your Brand at the Centre of Your Business

Brand Centered Management™ is both a trademarked process and a philosophy. It puts the brand at the centre of your business to inform corporate strategy and every aspect of business that leads towards the customer experience. At its best, it intuitively informs the behaviour of organisations.

If your brand is what you wish to stand for in your customer's mind, why wouldn't you want to make this central to everything your business DOES and SAYS?

The Brand Centered Management approach we developed at The Brand Company in Hong Kong at the turn of the millennium was the guiding philosophy that led that small company to be one of the most successful brand consultancies in Asia. It was forged by a clash of cultures between the three founders, one a successful young entrepreneur, another an accomplished marketer, and the third the head of a prominent advertising agency. We also had a terrific team of young brand specialists from a variety of different fields including brand consultancy, HR, design, strategic planning and research.

We spent countless hours crafting what became known as Brand Centered Management, or BCM. We all agreed that organisations appeared to confuse branding with brand-building. They tended to use the word brand as a verb (to brand) rather than a descriptor. To brand something was essentially to claim ownership by slapping your logo on a product. Re-branding was just doing a makeover of your logo or brand identity.

A brand to us is a perception in the mind. That perception in the mind of a customer, a prospect or an employee is the entirety of what the organisation is to them. It could mean the world to them, or it could mean nothing. You could be central to their everyday life, hugely engaging and enriching, or irrelevant. Your image could be distinctive and carved in sharp relief, or fuzzy and unclear.

Too often clients use communication and design agencies alone to solve brand dilemmas, when these need to be solved by integrating all the strategies, systems, structures, processes, people and policies across the whole spectrum of business.

A Brand Centered Management approach integrates brand, business and communication. It aligns people and organisations around the desired perceptions or territory in the mind they want to own. Money spent on the 'quick fix' tasks of *branding*—a new logo and advertising campaign—without paying attention to the brand positioning and delivery of the brand experience is a waste.

Brand-building is a total process. It involves not just marketing and communications but also HR, product development, customer service, operations, and finance. And most importantly, it must be **championed by the CEO**.

> The human brain learns from experience in order to shortcut solutions. If it recognises a familiar pattern it can instantly access the place where that memory is stored and trigger all the associations that expand that small piece into a 'whole image'. It's almost like an instantaneous series of jumping to conclusions that shortcut to a predictable conclusion. Every time that conclusion is right, those associations are reinforced and the linkages become stronger and more automatic.
>
> Disruption occurs when an expected pattern, especially one that has been reinforced over years, is suddenly broken. Suddenly, when in the past A + B = C it now = X. Predictability is thrown out of the window and uncertainty takes its place. As we race to try to 'understand the rules' of the new game, as is human nature, there is a level of excitement for some, but for most it's an unsettling period characterised by doubt and anxiety.
>
> Without such energy saving mechanisms we'd have to learn everything as if it were new, experienced for the first time. And this is why delivering consistent experiences is so important in imprinting brands in the mind. Every time a consistent, positive experience is received it reinforces the strength of the perception and the territory in the mind that brand occupies.

When we talk about brands as future desired perceptions, this becomes a central beacon to inform and guide organisational behaviour.

If your brand is what you want to be perceived as in the minds of your customers, why wouldn't you want to use this to direct your organisation's thinking and behaviour? Wouldn't it help if everything your organisation does and says reinforces that desired perception?

The BCM tools on which this book is based were developed over years of experimentation and refinement until we felt we had created the most efficient models. They needed to be insightful, to add value in a different way. We also designed them to be uncomplicated, easy to understand and use. Over the years of use we gradually improved them until they ran smoothly like a well-tuned engine.

We started with defining the components of what made up the nucleus of the brand. We worked backwards to break down brands into the fundamental elements, the raw genetic material that made one brand distinctive over another. The concept of the brand as a molecule was explored and the notion of the Brand DNA stuck.

The heart of the DNA is your promise—your over-arching commitment to your stakeholders. Placed at the centre of the organisation it informs the corporate strategy that is the driving force and focus that governs all corporate effort.

This echoes outwards from the centre as in the model shown above.

When thinking about how to illustrate the concept of BCM with the Brand DNA at the centre, we were inspired by the image of a Matryoshka doll. These Russian 'nesting dolls' have a small solid doll in the centre inside a larger doll, which itself sits inside a larger doll and so on. The DNA acts in the same way, sitting at the centre of everything an organisation does and affecting every layer or face of the organisation as it moves outwards to the customer experience.

So here's the thinking behind the model, follow along with me:

The Brand DNA, the heart of which is what you promise to your customers, informs corporate strategy. Corporate strategy in turn is the driving force and focus of all action for the organisation. It begins with directing the actions and behaviours of the workforce that deliver the experience to customers. This in turn is influenced by how organisations communicate with their people. The structures, systems and processes then enable or hinder the delivery of the products and services produced by the organisation.

The products and services delivered by the organisation are where the external stakeholders (or customers) typically meet the brand. The dotted line in the model here marks the point that divides the internal world of the organisation from the external world of the customer. I ask clients: 'Where does your customer shake hands with your brand?' This is the critical point of first impression.

Collectively the actions and behaviours of the workforce, how the organisation communicates and the structures, processes and systems they employ are the culture of the organisation.

External communications may be initiated internally by the organisation, but are received externally by stakeholders, both staff and customers. External communications cannot be controlled entirely by the organisation. Traditional media, social media, competitors and other influences all contribute to the noise of communication about the brand. The boundaries between internal and external communications are becoming increasingly blurred with the diversification of media touch points. It is increasingly difficult to manage the message to staff of large organisations when the formal channels of communication such as presentations, speeches, memos and meetings are usurped by Twitter, Snapchat, Facebook and instant access to online information.

How your customers *experience* the product or service you offer overrides what you say about it anyway. You may say you have the best hotcakes in town, but it's the taste experience that will play a larger part in determining whether or not people like it. I say a larger part, because the total experience is what creates perception. I put it that more people eat caviar than like it because they receive the message it is aspirational, expensive and sophisticated.

The final layer of the onion is the sum of all these activities and experiences that comprise how external stakeholders perceive the brand.

Hold that thought for a moment. The DNA is an expression of a desired perception for the brand. The external perception of stakeholders is the current perception of the brand. The two are inextricably linked by a feedback loop of constant research and monitoring to align current perceptions with desired perceptions.

It also means that although the brand DNA is something that organisations can create and control, it is informed by external stakeholders—in other words it is a customer-led strategy. It obeys the basic laws of marketing in that it is driven by perceived customer needs and wants.

The 4 Ds Process

Brand Centered Management™ follows a four-step process – the Four Ds.

The tools you'll encounter throughout the rest of this book are classified into four sections that correspond to these Four Ds: Discovery, Definition, Direction and Delivery.

Discovery is about discovering current perceptions of your brand; the environment and the challenges and opportunities it faces.

Definition is about determining what you want to stand for in your customers' minds, then articulating it through your Brand DNA to enable you to replicate consistent experiences.

Direction is the goals you set and the strategic choices you make to achieve them, as guided by your Brand DNA.

Delivery is the countless ways in which you execute against your plan to bring your Brand DNA to life every day.

Discovery tools help you discover more about yourself, your brand and the environment it operates within. It sets the context for brand-building. Definition tools help you define your brand positioning. Direction tools are strategic planning tools that help set the course you

wish to steer and make the necessary choices you will have to make along the way. And Delivery tools are enablers to help execute plans.
The chart below gives you a sense of the process.

THE 4Ds PROCESS

DISCOVERY

DATA COLLECTION
ANALYSIS AND INSIGHT
BRAND OPPORTUNITY

Competitive Review
In-depth Interviews
Desk and Internet Research
Discovery Report

DELIVERY

IMPLEMENTATION
MEASUREMENT
REFINEMENT

Communication Cascade
Project Teams
Third Party Partnerships

DEFINITION

DNA

DNA Development
Workshop

DIRECTION

GOALS
STRATEGIES & ACTION PLANS

Four Pillars Workshop
7-Step Strategic Ladder

Part 1: Discovery

As the name suggests, discovery is all about discovering more about yourself, your brand, your organisation and the environment you operate in. I prefer the word discovery to research because it implies probing into previously unexplored areas or looking at old information in new ways to gain insight.

Too often clients want to dive into the 'fixing' part without having done their homework. As every great chef will tell you, the best meals from the greatest kitchens start with the preparation: sharp knives; clean pots; fresh ingredients sliced, diced, and ready.

Discovery is the preparation for developing strategy. It's more than gathering facts. It's asking better questions. It's processing raw data into information, information into knowledge, and knowledge into insight. It's good to separate the yolks from the egg, to have the butter cut and weighed, the lemon squeezed, the salt, cayenne and parsley ready. It's better to have Hollandaise sauce ready to pour.

The discovery process covers the Four Cs:

• Company – the organisation, the heritage and evolution of the brand

• Customer – the brand customers, stakeholders and customer segments

• Currents – the social, technological, economic and political macro-environment and trends

• Competition – the competitive frame

DIM SUM STRATEGY

There are no hard and fast rules to how broad or how deep you go with a Discovery process. It varies according to time, budget and need. We employ a variety of methods including a quick strategic health check, semi-structured interviews, buddy-group interviews, desk and Internet research, and commissioned research if required.

I favour in-depth qualitative interviews. It gives you rich data and identifies the main issues and opportunities quickly, accurately and at low cost. Quantifying things can always come later... with a number of interviews you can begin to get a true feel for the importance and urgency of an issue too. I use a Discovery Questionnaire template (see below) that was forged over many years by a collective group of brand specialists at The Brand Company in Hong Kong. We found these questions, with minor modifications to suit customer needs, cover the information we need in a MECE (Mutually Exclusive, Collectively Exhaustive) way.

MECE or Mutually Exclusive, Collectively Exhaustive is a McKinsey thinking tool that is a professional way of saying "cover everything that's important in the shortest way possible." A MECE list is often short—no more than three or four points—but it addresses the essential items without repetition or exclusion.

Patterns emerge quite quickly when you use the same set of questions with different customer segments. It does rely on the skill and experience of the interpreter. Being able to actively listen beyond the questions (listen to what I mean, not what I say) is a real skill that allows a good interviewer to know when to prompt or probe and when to stay silent to let responses flow.

I favour qualitative research. It's called in-depth research for good reason. The secret is having the right questions and the skill to interpret a collective response. Knowing when to filter out irrelevant 'white noise' without losing the quiet voice or hidden gem of an insight. Not over-reacting to extreme comments good or bad, but not underplaying the significance of small details sometimes too.

We determine your brand strengths and weaknesses and category opportunities and threats, from different stakeholder perspectives. We present a comprehensive Discovery Report, based on face-to-face interviews with stakeholders within the company, that distils findings into the key challenges and opportunities for the brand. I like to make these visual and use verbatim, quoting the words used by respondents in clusters that make a point.

42

The secret to a good Discovery Report is to use verbatims. It is difficult to 'shoot the messenger' when verbatims are used collectively to make a point. I present clusters of verbatims under a headline word or point. I use this technique for each of the Discovery Questionnaire questions; What Springs to mind, Strengths, Challenges etc.

Responses often reflect broad agreement on issues. Occasionally, issues polarise responses and these are often the interesting, contentious issues where a decision needs to be made one way or another (left or right? black or white? yes or no?).

What is interesting is to see the similarities and differences to responses between different stakeholder groups, and sometimes within the same group, to the same question. Patterns emerge pretty quickly. Everyone feels that character development is pivotal to a boy's education, nobody thinks there's a place for bullying. Some issues polarise respondents, such as strategic integration of girls into an all boys school. Some issues are highly relevant to one or two stakeholder groups and not at all to others.

Condensing this into a clear picture takes practice. Discovery Reports help clear the mist by laying out a schematic picture of the key issues and opportunities for the brand. I like to think of it as identifying planets and patterns in a solar system where each planet is a concept, a challenge or an important issue to address. The number of planets varies as does the size and proximity to the centre of the system (the brand). Some planets are micro-planets on the outer fringe; others are Jupiter-like monsters with multiple moons and a powerful gravity that consumes all other issues within a certain radius.

When drafting a Discovery Report we share it first as a group of five or six of us internally to interrogate it, identify patterns and apply the wisdom of multiple minds. Alternative lenses and fresh perspectives from other brand strategists provide objectivity and make the finished Discovery Report robust.

The Discovery Report is then shared with the client problem owner and leadership team for comment and refinement if necessary. Then it becomes a useful historical source to return to and an excellent way of bringing people up to speed quickly on the brand.

The Discovery Questionnaire

I must emphasise, that while it looks like just a simple bunch of questions below, the process of distilling these down to the essential ones has been far from simple. Having presented creative concepts and finished work many times, there is always an element of Pied Piper about the reveal. Once shown it can never be taken back, and the world is changed a little bit forever.

Sometimes it's useful to remind an audience waiting for the 'answer' that they don't know it until you show it to them. "What am I about to tell you?" is a legitimate question. I ask it sometimes before a Discovery presentation: "Jot down on a piece of paper the key points you think I'm going to make".

It's true, much of what will be revealed will be familiar. But what most people forget is that you may have illuminated a handful of points from many thousands of others lying in the litter of leaves that they could also claim to have heard before. And what about things they've not heard before, would they have selected those in advance?

With that in mind, I present the Discovery Questionnaire:

1. Who are your key customers, now and in the future?

2. What role do you play in these customers' lives?

3. How is the brand/organisation perceived by your customers?

4. What are the major strengths of the brand?

5. What are the major weaknesses of the brand?

6. What is the single most important challenge the organisation/ brand faces?

7. What is the key promise the brand makes to its customers?

8. And what is the main benefit customers get from delivering against this promise?

9. How well do you deliver your promise?

10. What needs to be done to help your people deliver your promise every day, everywhere?

11. Do they have the tools to deliver it? (If not, what do they need?)

12. How would you describe the culture or spirit of your brand? (think 'how business is done around here')

13. How would you describe the ideal culture or personality if different from above?

14. Who do you see as your main competitors and why?

15. Do any competitors own a distinctive positioning in the category? If so, please describe.

16. How does your brand promise differ from your main competitors' promises?

17. How should the brand position itself relative to these competitors?

18. What are the most important products and services you offer? What lies behind their importance?

19. What would you like the organisation to Continue, to Stop and to Start?

20. You're the Chairman, we're giving you a magic wand to change things and granting you three wishes...what are they?

Of course these questions can be modified and personalised for each client. Not every question needs to be asked. Once an area has been illuminated beyond reasonable doubt as a Discovery process unfolds, it is better to use the interview time to probe areas of darkness. A certain amount of repetition is useful to act as reinforcement, but if you ever do conduct an interview process use your common sense to conduct the session to get the most out of the time available.

A Discovery Process is an ongoing one. It doesn't begin and end with the qualitative Discovery Questionnaire above. The tools in the following section can help you probe deeper into what your brand really represents, and where you want it to go.

Johari's Window

WHAT THIS TOOL DOES

Johari's Window is a useful tool for improving self-awareness at both a personal and a corporate level. While it is used more commonly for 'soft skills' and interpersonal relationship development, it can also be useful applying it to leadership teams and their businesses.

Johari's Window was devised by two American psychologists, Joseph Luft and Harry Ingham, in 1955 (the name is a combination of Joe and Harry). Johari's Window has four panes. They represent windows or lenses on your world based on four dimensions: what you know about yourself, what you don't know about yourself, what others know about you, and what others don't know about you. It can be useful to get people thinking about the model at a personal level first, perhaps with a facilitator illustrating by example what a 'dark area' of unknown to self but known to others is. Then they can apply the concept to the organisation as a whole.

Area 1 is the open or free area where both you and others know. For example, everyone knows I'm married and live in Vancouver. Everyone knows that Coca-Cola makes soft drinks.

Area 2 is the blind area where other people know things about you that you don't know yourself. It might be a pleasant thing, like your doctor giving you positive health test results. Or it could be less pleasant, like your clients knowing that their business has been taken over and that major changes are coming that will affect your company.

Area 3 is known by you but not by others. It could be something personal, such as a feeling about a coworker that you keep buried. Or you may have discovered a secret to the success of a competitor that they have no idea you know.

And area 4 is the 'dark' area—the unknown space where you don't know what you don't know and others don't either. You don't know and others don't know that a cure for cancer is going to be announced tomorrow.

The blind spots in areas 2 through 4 are the key insight of Johari's Window. Many organisations are so deeply involved in their own category or world that just having them conceive that there are dark spaces out there is a step forward.

Real life examples of Johari's Window at work abound. During World War II, Alan Turing and the team of code breakers at Bletchley Park solved the German naval cipher. The Germans had invented a brilliant machine called Enigma that created codes that were supposedly unbreakable. With 15,000,000,000,000,000,000 potential combinations, one would be inclined to agree. Instead of applying traditional code breaking techniques, Turing's team produced what was the precursor of the first digital computer. In effect, they built a machine to beat a machine. So from the early days of the war, British intelligence could read German naval messages. They knew important information that others did not—Area 3 of Johari's Window.

While the visualisation shows the four windows as equal in size, in reality they can vary drastically for each individual or organisation. The faint lines in the graphic represent a more likely distribution of areas. Most are likely to have larger open or shared areas and smaller hidden 'dark' areas.

I have found that organisations with the largest open areas are the ones that are most transparent and comfortable with their identity. They tend to display attributes that one would associate with extroverts: confidence, candor, accessibility, sharing, and inclusiveness. They tend to be more liberal in their outlook and more open to creative ways to bring success in the future.

By contrast, organisations with large hidden areas tend to be more secretive, more guarded with knowledge they hold, and less trusting. Their management structures are more rigid and hierarchical. They tend to be more conservative in their outlook and more inclined to hold on to tried and trusted methods that have brought them success in the past.

Neither is right or wrong; they're just different. How open would you want the National Security Agency to be? How open would you like Silicon Valley to be?

I often use Johari's Window at the beginning of client relationships. Not to discover hidden secrets; more to have them reflect on their own personal and organisational window frames. Expanding your open or shared area can be a liberating experience.

Increasingly, in this age of nearly universal access to information, the protected hidden areas are shrinking. Governments can no longer hide in fog or behind curtains; they are held accountable in real time. News can no longer be suppressed or controlled as easily when there are millions of input channels—although the challenge of filtering, editing and distributing is greater as a consequence. 'Fake news' is a relatively new term that describes a modern phenomenon of obfuscation, distraction and clutter.

Having a portion of yourself hidden can be a good thing, though. Not everyone wants to expose themselves to the embarrassing transition years of adolescence. It's good to be able to experiment behind closed doors and fail without the world seeing. That's how we all—people and brands—grow. Johari's Window can help you better understand what you are hiding from yourself. It can provide a useful framework to decide what to share with the world and when; and also how others may be doing the same.

	KNOWN BY SELF	UNKNOWN BY SELF
KNOWN BY OTHERS	1 OPEN / FREE AREA	2 BLIND AREA
UNKNOWN BY OTHERS	3 HIDDEN AREA	4 UNKNOWN AREA

JOHARI'S WINDOW

Brand Health Check

WHAT THIS TOOL DOES

Brand Health Check is a comprehensive strategic report on the strength and vitality of your brand. It employs carefully curated questions in a structured framework developed through decades of collective experience handling brands. Structured questions allow for insightful discovery and illumination of issues and opportunities. It is a powerful diagnostic tool that requires skilled interpretation.

Most CEOs would like to think they know their brands well—and many do—but in my experience many executives are more familiar with their financial spreadsheets than they are with the brand experiences that drive these financials.

Is your brand being managed to maximise business profitability? How well do you understand the health of your brand? Take the Brand Health Check and find out.

The Thinking Behind the Brand Health Check

How did the Brand Health Check come about? When we formed The Brand Company in Hong Kong at the turn of the millennium, we were a small but diverse group of brand experts with different backgrounds. We managed our own portfolios of clients and collaborated in shared forums to exchange knowledge and solve problems.

Over time, we found we were all doing some form of diagnostic discovery questionnaire with our new clients, each with something a little different. We set about developing a single questionnaire that covered the most important aspects of our customers' brands in relation to their business, within a structure that followed our philosophy of brands as being central to the management of businesses.

The result is the Brand Health Check that follows. It is a comprehensive yet succinct set of questions that go deep and spread wide quickly. Perhaps most importantly, the questions follow a structure that leads into prescriptive solutions to problems in much the same way as a doctor would diagnose and prescribe remedies to a patient. Many are common occurrences that can be easily remedied, some require specialist help and treatment over time, a few require surgery.

The Brand Health Check covers nine stakeholder areas moving

from outside the organisation to its heart. It follows the customer journey with the brand from where they first meet it (their initial perceptions and experience) all the way to the corporate strategy and the brand that informs everything else.

Each section follows a logical sequence. Corporate strategy is informed by the brand and in turn drives internal communication, people and culture within the organisation. This in turn influences process and systems that deliver the products and services that are supported by external communications and drive the customer experiences and perceptions of the brand. There is an invisible membrane between the internal processes and the external products and services that divides 'inside' the organisation from 'outside'. Products and services are where customers most directly and most often experience the brand.

It is no coincidence that the questions about the brand at the centre of corporate strategy and the questions about customer perceptions at the far extremity are similar. The brand is a perception. It is, in essence, a desired positioning in the mind of customers.

Good questions have the power to illuminate and unlock. Good questioners do so without embarrassing those being questioned; to most of these questions there are no rights or wrongs, only perceptions.

Customer Perceptions

'Perception is reality' is the oldest cliché in the book, but is so true. How you are perceived can be based on something as solid as decades of experience or as flimsy as second-hand comments overheard at a dinner party. We are wired to make broad impressions from whatever pieces of information we have on hand. It's not something humans can switch off. It's a primitive part of what makes us human.

Whodunits never get old because they use this trick to their advantage. We are given snippets of information, a few pieces of the jigsaw puzzle, from which our minds extrapolate to create an image of the 'whole'. The mind works automatically to fill in the gaps (or jump to conclusions without completing all the exhaustive research). That perception may change as more pieces of the jigsaw puzzle reinforce or contradict assumptions. But once the whole picture is revealed, it's difficult to see any other solution. One becomes 'blinded by the right answer'—which is why so many people find it hard to contemplate the notion of more than one right answer, or even 'better right answers' (as we were always encouraged to look for in advertising).

Look quickly at the shape below. What do you see?

Pretty much everyone sees a circle. The truth though is that's it's an incomplete circle. The 'law of good form' completes the circle automatically for us.

The answers to these questions unlock the core perceptions of your brand. They are mostly open-ended and may need prompting with suggestions.

How is your brand currently perceived?

What are your strengths and weaknesses relative to competitors?

What does your brand stand for? Against?

Do you have a clear promise? (If so, what?)

Is it differentiating, relevant, compelling and credible?

Are you living up to your promise everywhere, every time?

Customer Experiences

Experiences are the next rung up the ladder; they're most likely what has formed the perceptions uncovered above. It's important to understand how well the brand owners understand their customers' experience of their brand. Very few of them live their customers' lives or experience their brands in the way ordinary customers do. Experience implies physical use of a product or a service. It's a firsthand account of how an offering performs against expectations.

That said, it's important to understand that a perception of a brand is not limited by actual experience. Far from it. How many children who've never visited Disneyland still want to go? They've seen TV ads and heard stories from friends and relatives. They likely know a dozen Disney characters and movies. These pre-experience perceptions conjure a powerful image in their minds of what a visit to Disneyland would be like and can play a powerful role in determining the actual experience. The power of suggestion, positive or negative, is very real.

Still, the actual physical experience of the product or service can reinforce or override a predisposed perception. Think about visiting a restaurant for the first time. You've heard reports from a friend that it's great, but your experience is they kept you waiting for a table, the waiter was rude, the food so-so and expensive, and to top it all off the service tip was automatically added to the bill (which always gets my goat). Your personal experience is likely to override the 'going-in' perception you had from your friend's endorsement.

It's not straightforward. The same product can elicit different experiences depending on a myriad of criteria such as price, mood, context, current brand patronage, peer pressure, timing and so forth. The questions below are the right ones to ask, but there is still a skill in interpreting the answers in order to determine what's relevant and important from what's not.

Do you understand your customer experience?

Is it constantly monitored and improved according to desired performance measures?

How does it differ for different customer segments?

Does it reflect your desired brand experience?

Is it consistent across all customer touch points?

How can you improve your customer experience?

External Communications

At The Brand Company, we felt it important to distinguish between external communications directed to stakeholders outside the organisation and internal communications directed towards employees.

Perhaps an even more important distinction is between formal and informal communications. Formal communications are 'controlled' or managed. They are paid-for advertisements, formal speeches, presentations, meetings, brochures, literature, websites and managed corporate social media messages. Informal communication is what I refer to as 'water cooler' conversations. These are unstructured, not paid for and very difficult to control or manage.

Informal communications are harder to control but much more influential. They are the interpretation of formal messages that come without all the corporate filters and with all the 'real life' bias of perceptions and misperceptions.

There is in-built scepticism about commercial messages. The self-interest in selling something—even if it's just an idea—is the lens through which any paid-for message is invariably viewed. Consumers are wising up to the disguised paid-for messages such as product placement in films and advertorials accompanying paid-for space. But if your message aligns with existing perceptions about your brand, it is much more likely to make an impact.

Does what you SAY reflect the reality of what you DO?

Does it do this in an engaging way that 'justifies the intrusion'?

Do your marketing communications have a compelling
creative idea?

Does your visual identity reflect the brand promise and brand architecture?

Are you consistent in your look and feel across all channels?

Products and Services

There's an invisible dividing line between products and services and external communications. This marks the boundaries of corporate influence or control. Although all good companies have their product and service offerings informed by customers, ultimately it's the organisation that decides what products it offers.

Case in point, Toblerone recently launched a version of their famous mountain bars with a large gap between the chocolate peaks. They made the choice (incorrectly, it would seem) to change the form of the product to lower the chocolate content rather than raise the price of the existing one. 'Britons do mind the gap' as the BBC article says, spoofing the London Underground announcements that warn passengers alighting from trains to mind the gap. "Give us a shorter bar with the same chunky blocks if you have to," say some consumers.

The point is, ultimately the brand owners decide the product and service offering that then informs external communication, experience and perception. You may feel companies also control external communications and for some channels they do. Increasingly though, they have less and less control of external messaging despite tenacious attempts to manage social media. The court of public opinion holds sway, right or wrong.

Of course, innovation doesn't come without risks and companies should be applauded for constantly looking for ways to innovate and improve too, even if sometimes, acknowledging mistakes is part of moving forward.

Do your products and services do what you promise they'll do?

Do you have the right number and type of products/services to achieve your goals?

Do your products and services satisfy important customer needs that relate to the core promise of the brand?

Are you constantly looking at innovative ways to improve your product and service offering?

Processes and Systems

Investigating the processes and systems behind the development of products and services can help identify forces that help or hinder the customer's experience. The intention here is not to do a full-blown TQM (Total Quality Management) or ISO-type analysis of systems. Rather, these questions can elucidate some of the obvious blockages and bottlenecks in the processes that may be preventing the company from delivering the brand promise in the most efficient way.

When consulting with clients at The Brand Company, we looked for the 25% of change that can make 75% of the difference relatively easily. Processes and systems are typically more established the larger and older the company is. The issues faced by small, entrepreneurial start-up (or infant) companies are very different from those faced by larger, older bureaucracies. But no matter the size, if you are not delivering on your brand's promise, it is imperative to find out why.

What processes are hindering your ability to deliver your promise?

What systems can you implement to enable you to deliver more efficiently…faster, higher quality, more consistently?

What 25% of change will generate 75% of the benefit?

People and Culture

Next, let's explore the culture and people within the organisation. How are things done around here? We get right to the heart of the issue to determine if the organisation has established principles and values and if these are upheld. The vast majority of organisations have some form of documented policy, but it is more important to understand what's really happening instead of what management *thinks* is happening. Are the values truly embraced? Are they still relevant? Are they known and followed (people can often parrot back what values are without believing them or embracing them)? Ask the right questions and the answers become readily apparent.

Do you have a succinct set of principles to abide by that reflect your promise (not 'catch-all' platitudes)?

Do the actions and behaviours of your people reinforce your principles?

Do you recognise and reward the right attitude and behaviour?

Do you have Performance Management systems in place that are geared around your principles and promise?

Internal Communications

Like external communications, internal communications can be divided between the formal and the informal. The informal communications in the corridor (or more likely in a bar after the annual corporate "State of the Union" address) are much more powerful than the carefully worded formal message given by the Chairman or CEO. Use these questions to understand what your employees are saying about your brand and what they really hear from the top.

Who do you need to communicate to inside the organisation and how?

Do you invest as much effort communicating to them as you do your 'other' customers?

Are senior management aligned and engaged?

How can each employee play a valuable role in embracing change?

Are you using informal channels of communication effectively?

Corporate Strategy

Corporate strategy helps with planning for the growth of your business and identifying the most important customers now and in the future. At The Brand Company, we approached corporate strategy from a customer perspective. We encouraged organisations to orient their strategy from the angle of what they want their desired customers to think and how they want them to behave.

Of course corporate strategy is much more comprehensive than this, but this is the heart of a customer-oriented and brand-centered approach. The open-ended format of questioning enables the key issues to surface and be identified, so that these can be dealt with and not lost. The structure of the questions in the questionnaire is guidelines; the format is not so prescriptive that adaptations can't be made.

What are your corporate goals and objectives?

What is your most important source of business growth?

Who are your most valuable customers (now and in the future)? How do you want them to think and behave in order to achieve your goals?

Brand

When I first meet prospects who are not clear about what our brand company can do for them, I ask them a few questions about the perception of their brand. I start from the outside of the Brand Centered Management model and work inwards. It's not designed to catch people out, or try to look smart, rather to actively illuminate for themselves important areas where there are unknowns or even deep black holes.

What is your promise to customers? (What do you stand for?)

How relevant and differentiating is it? How compelling and credible?

Are you maximising the potential of your brand?

Do you have the right number of brands in your brand family to achieve your goals?

Are the inter-relationships between brands in the family clearly defined?

How to Use the Brand Health Check

To be fair, many companies would find it difficult to answer every question above satisfactorily. Brand-building is a continuous process of improvement. By having a person think about an answer to a question, you can see quickly if this is something that is salient and important to them or not. And they themselves can internally assess if it's a good question, and if so, if they have a satisfactory answer to it. More often than not, it reveals gaps in their knowledge of their brand they'd rather not have. I try to start at the top where the decision-makers are. If the owner, CEO or MD is intrigued by the questions and wants to know answers to some of the things they don't know, there's a start-point for engagement.

So the questionnaire is like a gap analysis. It identifies the areas where greater understanding and work is needed.

I do these questionnaires one-on-one with a small cross-section of stakeholders from C-Level Officers through middle management to coalface workers, and then compare notes. It's good to have some customer feedback too as a basic reality check (is what the company thinks reflected in customer perceptions, for example?).

Often, it results in acknowledgement of the need for further Discovery research into current brand perceptions, particularly the promise to customers that relate to the DNA of their brand.

The Five Stages of Brand-Building

WHAT THIS TOOL DOES

The Five Stages of Brand-Building offers a neat way of thinking about the stages of development of a brand. At a glance you can see where your brand sits and what you need to do to raise it to the highest level of brand status.

Ingram Associates, one of our past partners at The Brand Company, identified four separate stages of brand-building; I believe there are five.

Stage 1: Unbranded
Working up from the bottom is unbranded or 'white label'. This is typically a widely used commodity that is price sensitive like rice or toilet paper, where the retailer has their own value brand in white or yellow label. Although one could argue that even commodities are branded—Tesco, Waitrose, Safeway, Target, and President's Choice—and these 'own labels' carry associations with the umbrella parent brand; the scale and ubiquity is enough to reassure consumers of quality.

Stage 2: Basic Branding
Basic branding is akin to branding a cow—the hot iron stamps a mark of ownership for identification, naming, and legal protection if anyone tries to appropriate your 'cow'. The brand equivalent is a logo, a trademark, a name or recognisable colour scheme. This aids recognition, communicates 'this is me' to users and warns competitors off. Sports teams wear opposite colours to differentiate themselves on the field in the same way.

Today it's rare to find products that aren't at least basically branded with a recognisable name and design. Often though, there is still a large degree of inconsistency in design language. Font styles and sizes vary, as do colours and schemes. Sometimes logos have been 'evolved', no doubt with good intention, by different departments or countries. At The Brand Company, we conducted design audits that gathered as many representations of the brand as possible in one place to highlight the differences of what should be a consistent look and feel. Sometimes there are practical issues with changing a design. Changing the livery on a fleet of aircraft or trucks may take years, for example. With brands like Pepsi and Coke there are multiple generations of evolved logos spanning decades, and that is something that has to be considered a part of the living heritage of a brand.

Stage 3: Brand Differentiation

The next stage is Brand Differentiation. This is where basic colour associations are developed into a visual identity with clear guidelines of 'do's and don'ts', colour palettes and visual language. Brand differentiation also begins the process of association of values or beliefs with the brand. Charters and credos are drafted to direct thought and behavior of staff. The brand is positioned within a competitive frame and efforts made to differentiate it from competitors in look and values.

The main difference between stage 3 and stage 4 is often (but not always) time. It takes time to build a recognisable brand personality. Personalities are complex and displayed over time through multiple exposure under different circumstances. I say not always, because some brands can achieve intense, multiple exposure by literally immersing their loyal users over a relatively short period of time—especially with the viral capability of social media—the digital Pokemon phenomenon is a good example.

Stage 4: Brand Personality

Stage 4 brands have well defined values, differentiating attributes, and a defining core idea or brand DNA.

Building brand personality doesn't happen by chance. Well, let me rephrase that. Over years and years personality traits become more recognisable. If you do nothing but basic branding and 'get your product out there', eventually you'll acquire attributes and personality traits. This is the default mode of many products and services where the perceived value of marketing and brand-building is lower than it might be. It is rarely a conscious decision to ignore brand-building. More often it's relegated in the face of other tasks such as searching for product improvements, manufacturing efficiency, lowering costs, managing personnel or whatever. Building brand personality by a slow process of osmosis is a legitimate approach, and post-rationalisation of a positioning or a benefit based on what your customers are telling you can be a successful way of articulating your brand promise. The problem is, it can take a very long time.

Those owners that proactively determine their brand positioning and personality can 'set their stall' early and accelerate their appeal to their defined customer base. It helps to know what you want to stand for and to articulate this. Whether it's a core controlling idea, a human truth or a brand DNA, matters less than if it is meaningful to the brand owner. The process of identifying, articulating, and delivering your promise is a conscious one. There is determined effort to develop icons that reflect core values. Desired personality traits are expressed and efforts to measure them put into place. People are held accountable to delivering against the brand promise. The notion of brand-centrism—having the brand central to everything the company does and says—is evident.

The more determined and consistent the effort, the higher the likelihood of success.

Leo Burnett, founder of the great Chicago agency of the same name that grew to one of the largest and most admired global advertising brands, was a master at iconography. Apples, black pencils, and stars were all recognisable symbols of the Leo Burnett brand, along with the green livery, found in every Leo Burnet office everywhere around the world.

Stage 5: Brand at the Company's Heart

Stage 4 is as far as most brands get. Stage 5 is Somerset Maugham's *The Razor's Edge* for brands... a long journey towards enlightenment and Nirvana.

Stage 5 brands are where the brand is at the company's heart—or brand Nirvana as I sometimes call it. The organisation is intuitively informed by the brand. If it's a service brand, the company has gone past the need to police activity because their people naturally behave a certain way. They literally live the brand.

More than likely they've not had to recruit because believers come to them seeking employment. Employees pursue delivery of service in the way the brand intends: with the zeal of missionaries. Indeed, most of them won't see themselves as employees as much as part of the family, the religion of like-minded believers.

Product brands in this space can almost achieve immortality — almost, because every brand has a lifetime and an expiry. They still take effort to maintain and are subject to unpredictable change. Famous stores would fall into this category, as would iconic hotels. If you're Harrods in London, The Raffles Hotel in Singapore, the Taj Mahal in Mumbai, or the Peninsula in Hong Kong, you've achieved a rarified status and define a category of one—your own. While it's next to impossible for a competitor to take over your space because there can only be one of you, it is possible to fade and die. Even legendary brands need to be properly maintained, just as if they were buildings. Time, weather, war, and other causes take their toll, and without constant care even the glistening turrets of the grandest castles will turn to dust. For brands that have reached stage 5, their task is perhaps the hardest of all—maintaining the status quo.

What brand has achieved stage 5 in recent years? Apple would be a good candidate. It has created a cult-like following and delivered a stream of innovative technology products that lead in design and performance. Their people do things in an Apple way reminiscent of their founder Steve Jobs. Apple's brand is rooted in battling conventional wisdom, in beating the big guy at their own game, in zigging when others zag. But that becomes increasingly difficult to do when success brings you closer to defining the establishment you stand against!

Technology is a notoriously difficult category to retain leadership in. Constantly being ahead of the curve or catching the next wave can be a challenge. There isn't a formula for success that lasts for long. I remember when Sony was at the pinnacle of admired technology companies. It owned television, it led in the black box music space, it developed portable music with the Walkman, and it was venturing into mobile telephony. One by one the corners of their castle were assaulted by competitors and market forces—LG with flat screen TVs, Apple with the iPod and iPhone, and the whole category of large amplifiers, turntables, tape decks and speakers that was rendered obsolete. Sony, like other great technology brands, failed to weather this storm.

The death of a visionary founder, Akio Morito in the case of Sony or Steve jobs in the case of Apple, is another time of danger. The conscience of what made the brand great is sometimes lost. Companies that have grown large on their success suddenly find that they are managed by committees, not led by individuals. Their fiscal obligations to deliver higher returns to shareholders—guided by logical, rational governance regulations—begin to work against the creative, emotional, irrational values that built the company. Companies can run for years on the momentum built up, but eventually the creative well of new ideas dries up. How many line extensions can you make before the cake is sliced too thin? How long will customers tolerate built-in obsolescence to keep the manufacturing wheels turning?

Stage 5 Nirvana is a wonderful goal to aspire to, but there is certainly an element of 'careful what you wish for' once you're there.

So how do you know where your brand lies on the spectrum? Think about the examples above and compare them to your company. Be truthful. The higher the stage, the more brand equity you gain, but the harder and more costly it is to achieve it. So where is it most fruitful to add value?

The chart above illustrates where the greatest return on investment is to be had in building brand value. There is value in moving from unbranded to a basic branding position, but the advances begin to grow exponentially in transforming basic branding into differentiated brand positioning and personality. This is where programmes like Brand Centered Management can have the most impact.

The 6 Rules of Brand-Building

This tool is a succinct reminder of the six inviolate rules of brand-building. It's a useful touchstone to return to if you ever find yourself lost or questioning if the whole pursuit of brand advantage is worth it.

1. Brand-builders make more money than product makers, and brand leaders make more money than brand followers.

2. Products converge, brands diverge. There is rarely space in the category for more than two or three to make a decent profit, so it is better to define a new category.

3. Brand-building usually takes time. Don't rush things. Let your customers define you based on the experience and service you provide.

4. Brand-building often requires sacrifices or trade-offs. Sometimes to have one strong brand you need to kill two or three weak ones.

5. Strong brands consistently deliver against their promises—every time, every place the customer meets the brand.

6. The rules of the category can change unexpectedly—expect innovation to disrupt your brand category at some point in time.

Why is it worth investing in brand-building? Because strong brands command higher premiums. They enjoy greater customer loyalty. They have greater potential to stretch their appeal to a wider audience. They secure higher levels of forgiveness. And they can do all of this over a longer period of time than weaker competitors. All of which adds up to increased profit.

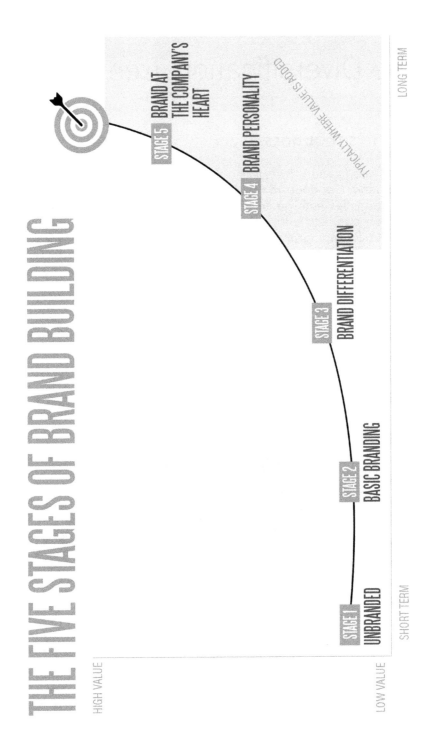

THE FIVE STAGES OF BRAND BUILDING

HIGH VALUE

LOW VALUE

SHORT TERM

LONG TERM

STAGE 1 UNBRANDED

STAGE 2 BASIC BRANDING

STAGE 3 BRAND DIFFERENTIATION

STAGE 4 BRAND PERSONALITY

STAGE 5 BRAND AT THE COMPANY'S HEART

TYPICALLY WHERE VALUE IS ADDED

The Diversification Tree

WHAT THIS TOOL DOES

The Diversification Tree is a thinking tool that helps you better understand the deep-rooted, unshakable laws about how brands and categories emerge and evolve through divergence. Much of it draws on parallels with the natural world and Darwinian principles of evolution and natural selection. If you learn these principles, self-evident in nature, you will have meaningful insight into how brands evolve in the fight for survival in their environments and against competitors.

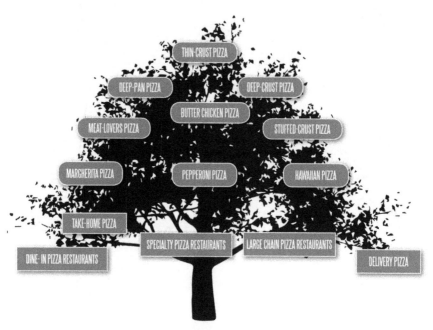

THIN-CRUST PIZZA

DEEP-PAN PIZZA

DEEP-CRUST PIZZA

BUTTER CHICKEN PIZZA

MEAT-LOVERS PIZZA

STUFFED-CRUST PIZZA

MARGHERITA PIZZA

PEPPERONI PIZZA

HAWAIIAN PIZZA

TAKE-HOME PIZZA

SPECIALTY PIZZA RESTAURANTS

LARGE CHAIN PIZZA RESTAURANTS

DINE- IN PIZZA RESTAURANTS

DELIVERY PIZZA

THE DIVERSIFICATION TREE

Brands within a category diverge like the branches on a tree. Each branch reaches out trying to capture the most sunlight available until all the gaps are filled.

The branches radiate from a central trunk—the category, be it pizzas, warships, cars, or any category you care to think of. Suddenly we don't have just plain old margherita pizza. We have dine-in pizza restaurants, take-home pizza, deep-crust pizza, square pizza, stuffed-crust pizza, meat-lovers pizza, Hawaiian pizza, deep-pan pizza, thin-crust pizza, specialty butter chicken pizza...and I could go on.

I used to listen to technology buffs talking to me about technology convergence...that we'd soon be able to control our daily lives from a touch-pad, that everything from programming the TV, to turning the lights on, to preheating the oven would be done on our smartphones. While many of these predictions have transpired, the idea at the root of them is a dangerous misperception. Convergence is the exact opposite of what happens in nature—and, as I believe, what happens with the evolution of brands and categories.

Species emerge through *divergence*, not convergence. So do brands. As Al & Laura Ries said in *The Origin of Brands*, "If you want to build a successful brand, you have to understand divergence. You have to look for opportunities to create new categories by divergence of existing categories. And then you have to become the first brand in this emerging new category."

For years, Darwin struggled to prove his theory. Apart from the religious taboo surrounding the undermining of Christian beliefs, there were no constant lines to connect species. There were still big gaps between early hominids, Neanderthal man, and modern Homo sapiens. Where is the smoking gun that proves the link?

Everyone knows Charles Darwin was the father of natural selection and the evolution of species. Who knows the co-discoverer?

Alfred Russel Wallace was a British naturalist who spent eight years on expedition to Sulawesi, then in the Dutch East Indies, now Indonesia. He studied the diversity of birds, insects and reptiles in the region, noting in particular that certain species were uniquely indigenous to the island. Through the delineation of distinct species, he identified what has since become known as the Wallace line—an invisible line that marked the divide between two continental shelves eons ago.

Wallace had figured that animals evolved over thousands of years and generations to match their environment. But he didn't make the creative leap to the concept of 'survival of the fittest' until he was struck down with malaria. Then, his own survival highlighted the brutal force of natural selection in the process of weeding out the sick and unhealthy. He wrote a nine-page letter to Darwin, his elder and respected colleague outlining his theories. Darwin, who had procrastinated in postulating the theory he had been ruminating over for more than twenty years, was 'smashed' that someone would beat him to posting his life's work.

Accounts differ, but despite the evidence of extensive written documentation Darwin produced earlier, he was gracious enough to acknowledge Wallace's discovery and the two men co-authored the first publication on the theory of natural selection. Suitably 'kicked up the backside' Darwin then rushed, with the urging and support of influential scientific friends such as Aldous Huxley, to publish his works. 'On the Origin of Species by Means of Natural Selection' was published the following year.

Although by all accounts there was mutual respect between the two men, Wallace is certainly a victim of natural selection when it comes to recognition and ownership of 'the greatest ideological revolution in the history of science,' as described by paleontologist Stephen Jay Gould.

'Get there firstest with the mostest' is a model lesson for brand leaders in emerging categories.

Mutation, Extinction and the 'Mushy Middle'

We explain diversification in natural history through genetic mutation. We explain natural selection through survival of the fittest. The same forces work with brands. Mutation is equivalent to the conscious and unconscious efforts we make to create differences in offerings. Thrown to the market they either survive and prosper or die. Similarly, brands live or die according to how well they meet the need or expectation of customers relative to competitive offerings.

A plane crash-lands in the frozen Arctic 100 miles from the nearest help, who survives? Those fit enough to hike their way across frozen tundra to reach help survive. So do those with injuries not so severe as to die from but serious enough to prevent them walking, or those too cowardly to go (or smart enough to wait inside the shell of the fuselage until rescuers find them). They are saved too. It's the 'mushy middle' that die—those who set out not fit enough to survive a long arduous journey, or smart enough or lucky enough to stay and be rescued. That's the way it is with species—and with brands.

During his famous Voyage of the Beagle, Darwin noted an

interesting variation in Galapagos turtles. Some were born with longer necks than others. Long necks gave them an advantage over others because they could reach the new leaves of plants higher off the ground. But there's a limit to which a long neck becomes an advantage. It may mean you're exposed to a greater risk of predation, or become less adapted to feed on plentiful low vegetation at your feet. Turtles with shorter necks adapted for this type of feeding are better equipped for this, with the two variants (long and short necks) both outcompeting turtles with 'normal' necks.

This explains the gaps in evolution. There is no clear link between apes and man because the two species ended up moving in divergent, opposite directions.

There are many other examples of diversification in the natural world. Has anyone noticed what happens with barnacles on the rocks by the water's edge? They move into two distinct levels: those that move down the rock to the low tide mark, and those that move up the rock to the high tide level. There are no barnacles in the middle because this is where the sea pounds the rocks most ferociously and where chances of prospering within the population are slimmest. Competition drives them further apart.

The same goes for brands. Brand leaders in large competitive categories find distinctive and opposing positions.

Coca-Cola is the establishment, the worldwide soft drink of choice. Pepsi is 'the choice of the new generation'—younger, more irreverent. Sometimes the second brand or challenger brand attempts to turn the strength of the leader against them.

Is it possible to lose share because you're too popular? Hertz was brand leader in the car rental category until Avis lived up to their promise of 'We try harder'. Seth Stevenson describes how in the early 1960s the campaign from BBDO's sister agency DDB transformed the fortune of the company. The rivalry between Hertz and Avis started in the 1940s. Warren Avis was an Air Force Officer who travelled around the country and saw an opportunity to rent cars at airports, as opposed to downtown locations, as the numbers of air passengers exploded. Within three years the share gap between leader Hertz and No. 2 Avis closed from 61–29 to 49–36. The 'We try harder' campaign ran for 50 years and helped instil a culture of customer-service orientation.

So how did it end? Well the laws we're discussing in this chapter applied. Hertz didn't sit around waiting to be overtaken. They launched their own effective 'We're No. 1 (and why they're No. 2)' re-positioning campaign. Avis never did overtake Hertz. In his 1986 autobiographical book *Take a Chance to Be First*, Avis implies Hertz moved swiftly to copy what they were doing in airports and elsewhere. This is what happens with the second law: the law of gradual improvement of the species within the category.

When it launched the Mac in 1984, Apple was the 'rebel' fighting against the establishment brand IBM. Mercedes is establishment, BMW the younger, sportier challenger. Google had Yahoo, and now the category is waiting for the next challenger to fully emerge.

Successful brands grow the category and successful large categories can host a number of brands, each defining their own territory or niche within it. Every category you imagine is subject to the law of diversification, from bread to beer to telephony. It's a dynamic, constantly evolving world and the process is accelerating.

With the internet and the information age, people have greater access to knowledge than ever before. Take internet service providers for example. The internet didn't exist until 1991, so neither did the category. Now there are multiple sectors within it: e-commerce, search engines, travel, social media, entertainment, and business to name a few. The largest player, Amazon, has revenue in excess of $100 billion. American and Chinese brands dominate the top 10, but as time goes by we'll see more new entrants from other countries.

Changes in the environment can have the same dramatic impact for brands as they do in the natural world. Online shopping has tremendous implications for high street retailers. Shopping for commodities like washing powder, toilet paper and basic grocery staples isn't sexy, so why not order it online and get it delivered? The phenomenon of customers using retail outlets as showrooms before ordering online at a lower price has created challenges for large chains. So differentiation has to come through the physical experience: with the goods and with personal interaction that offers something different from the convenience (and impersonality) of online transactions.

Over time, categories evolve into segments and sub-segments. Like branches on a tree, some die and break off while others prosper and grow stronger as they reach outwards.

Look at the diversity of snakes: from 30-foot reticulated pythons to 6-inch Brahminy blind snakes, from water species such as Anacondas and cottonmouths to desert species like rattlesnakes and sidewinders, from highly poisonous brown snakes to harmless grass snakes, they have evolved to suit their surroundings, fauna, prey, and competition.

So it goes with consumer products. Bread, yogurt, sausages, beer, apples, biscuits or cookies, chocolate, ice cream—each one has myriad varieties to suit diverse tastes and needs. The list is endless and it applies across every category.

No signs of convergence here. This is all about diversity and divergence.

In nature it happens by natural selection of the gene pool over time, by forces of environment, competition, chance, luck or happenstance—or by genetic mutation. Brands are subject to exactly the same forces. Genetic mutation in brands is equivalent to new product development and experimental product prototypes.

Why am I over-stressing the point here? Because I have such a hard time persuading clients that the laws of nature apply to brands in the same way as they do the natural world. One of the reasons for the confusion is the law of gradual improvement—something that works the opposite way to make individuals in a population look and act the same, even as they struggle to stand apart.

Strive to be Best in Category, or Develop a New Category?

So, why is it that we keep hearing about convergence? Why do things all begin to look the same after a while? Think about cars. Don't all sedans or saloon cars begin to look the same? Without the logo on the hood, it can be hard to tell the difference between a Chrysler, a Mercedes, a Toyota, a BMW, a Peugeot, a Ford. Why?

This is the law of gradual improvement of a species.

Competition between individuals over time gradually improves the species. Pick any of the cars of today and compare them with the same brands of thirty or forty years ago. They are all better, faster, lighter, safer, more luxurious, more pleasant to drive and more fuel-efficient. They have all benefited from new technology they developed or copied from others.

Four-wheel drive was once extraordinary; now it's commonplace. Automatic braking systems were once revolutionary; now they are standard equipment on most vehicles. Seat belts were once optional; now nearly all cars feature standard airbags. This is gradual improvement of the species. All makes of car have benefited from aerodynamic improvements and wind tunnel tests, and most now feature a more streamlined look. The process of survival of the fittest improves the category as a whole over time.

There are limits to this, however. Average height is used by some as a measure of the prosperity of a country. When I first took my wife and two young boys to Edinburgh, we stayed in the magnificent 15th century Bothwick castle a few miles south of the city. When we arrived, we were struck—literally and metaphorically—by the low ceilings and tiny doorways. It made me think: have we been on a gradual 'improvement of the species' in terms of increasing in height over the centuries? It made sense to me thinking about availability of food and access to calories improving over time.

Yet, the result was surprising. You'd think that there would have been a natural progression of gradually increasing height over time, but that's not the case. Until the mid-1850s, average height remained approximately the same at around 5'7" for males, with some anomalies during times of want when food was scarce. The Middle Ages, when our castle was built, was one of those periods, with an average height of 5'4". We now know that average height is closely correlated with childhood nutrition. In Britain this saw steady improvement from the mid 19th century onwards when measures were put in place to provide alms to the poor and orphanages. Still, there were dips in average height of certain populations. In Germany, the civilian population suffered greatly from food scarcity in World War I and World War II, and during this period the average height dropped. So the environment is a determining factor.

So will we keep on growing taller without limits? The answer is no. The height increase is already slowing down, suggesting nature imposes limits on selection. Being too tall puts pressure on other systems such as heart and blood pressure. A forest canopy reaches a climax community—a point beyond which there is no advantage in growing taller than competitive trees.

On 26 May 1953, Sir Edmund Hillary and Sherpa Tenzing became the first men to scale Mount Everest, the highest mountain on earth. In 2002, 53 people summited Mount Everest—in one day! In 2010 Jordan Rhodes successfully reached the summit, aged 13. The oldest person to summit was 70 years old. One man has summited Everest 20 times!

Yes, oxygen and equipment has improved dramatically. So has human capability.

After years trying to break the barrier, Sir Roger Bannister first ran the 4-minute mile in 1954. In 1957, 16 people ran a sub 4-minute mile. In 1994, Eamon Coghlin ran it at the age of 40. In 1997, Daniel Roman of Kenya ran 2 miles in under eight minutes!

So more individuals achieve higher levels of performance over time as new skills, practices and technology become more widely available. Still, we tend to only remember the first. We remember the Wright brothers, Sir Edmund Hillary, and Sir Roger Bannister, not those who came second.

The law of gradual improvement within the species or category applies to brands too. Brands form to occupy different niche positions to suit specialised needs or different environments. Brands with clear positioning and ownership of territories stand a greater chance of survival than those that are ill-defined in the mushy middle.

In the clamour for supremacy of a territory or category, brands put pressure on competitors to improve or die. As each brand steps up to the challenge, all brands improve. At the same time it becomes increasingly difficult to sustain tangible advantages for long. The differences between brands competing within the same category become marginal. We begin the full cycle towards commoditisation of categories, especially in low-involvement categories (where making the wrong choice doesn't really matter that much) such as toothpaste or bread or even hotels. When price becomes more of a determining factor than quality or value, we have moved full circle back towards commoditisation of a category.

Then what's the answer? To define or re-define a new category and own it.

When this happens, often the end benefit remains the same; it's the delivery mechanism that changes.

Capturing images to relive and enjoy past moments used to be done with photographs, and Kodak owned that territory. When the delivery mechanism changed to digital imagery, they lost it to a host of digital competitors. Storing contact names and addresses in the hard copy world of old was owned by File-o-fax, a neat personal organiser with a variety of binder covers, size and filler options. In the digital world, we now have calendars offering the enhanced benefits of convenience, storage capacity, revision, and immediacy of access.

Suddenly, all the improvement of the species or category is swept aside by the emergence of a new category that provides unbeatable advantages in delivering the same benefit. Sail gave way to steam in offering the same benefit of crossing oceans, except faster, in larger ships, with more reliable time schedules and sailing in places beyond the traditional trade wind routes. The electric light bulb swept gas lighting aside. Horseless carriages pushed horses aside. Tyres beat wooden rims. Jets beat out propeller planes, in all but a few special circumstances. And so it is with brands and whole categories of brands.

Telephony has evolved over a century, mobile telephony since 1973 (on 3 April Martin Cooper, a Motorola Executive, made the first call from a wireless handheld phone from downtown Manhattan to his rival Joel S. Engel at Bell Laboratories—must have felt good!)

The old-fashioned Bakerlite telephones of my grandmother's day (itself an evolution of the two-piece hand and ear-piece phones) has evolved into multiple forms, each carving a niche for itself driven by function and convenience. We have phone boxes (now rendered obsolete by personal cellphones), conference call devices, private network walkie-talkies, handsets, headsets and of course mobile phones. Mobile phones have seen explosive growth and diversification from the first 'brick phones' through flip-phones and Nokia-style handhelds, to the Android and iPhones now. Earpiece implants next?

Hybrids, or Pigs that Fly

Flying pigs. I'd love to see them, but it isn't happening in the real world! Why? Because there is no real benefit for pigs to fly.

Take amphibious cars as another example. Billed as 'a car that drives like boat and a boat that sails like a car,' they enjoyed brief popularity in the mid-20th century. So why don't we see people driving amphibious cars? Because they're the worst of both world combinations. The more boat-like you make the amphibious car—for example by streamlining the bow, having more powerful propellers, a proper cabin, greater depth and ballast for stability—the worse it performs as a car. And vice-versa. You can't improve one without compromising the other.

Hybrids, or forced convergences, are everywhere.

Combined football, soccer and rugby grounds are one of my bugbears. How many shared grounds between different sports actually work? Very few I'd venture. In London, West Ham United moved from their old home at Upton Park to the new London stadium built for the Olympics. The new arena is much larger and holds more fans, but it was designed for Olympic sports, not for soccer. So instead of the tight, intimate ground where the noise local supporters created was intense, they now have an Olympic sized running track between the supporters and the pitch. You need binoculars to see the play at the far end of the pitch, and despite the increased capacity the club have to put songs over the loudspeakers because the huge open bowl design spills sound out into the air.

In Vancouver, the local Whitecaps soccer team shares their BC Place ground with the CFL (Canadian Football League) BC Lions. The Canadian Football pitch is substantially longer than a soccer pitch and the markings of course are completely different, so the white line painting business is healthy when the seasons overlap. Both teams compromise by having to play on artificial turf. The soccer franchise is smaller than the football one so they have to close off the upper tiers for the soccer games to try to keep the atmosphere in. Why? Because the city council paid an astronomical sum to upgrade the facility and they didn't want the soccer team building their own (even when it was offered to be privately funded!).

The European multi-purpose fighter-bomber F-111 was a hugely expensive and predictable flop. It's easy to see how it happens: Designing a new fighter aircraft is expensive, so if we can make one do the job of two it'll be cheaper. Well, cheaper yes, but to produce a compromised machine that excels neither as a fighter nor as a bomber.

It is really hard to find hybrids that have worked. Combination washer-dryers were notoriously unreliable. It turns out that mixing water with electrical heating is not such a good idea. Two-in-one shampoo works if you're a student or a bachelor and really don't care that it's not as efficient a shampoo or as smooth a conditioner. For a while, hybrid cars were the best the market had to offer to environmentally-conscious drivers. Now, with the availability and reliability of all-battery electric cars as an option, hybrids are being rendered redundant. In all these cases, most customers tend to go one way or the other rather than opting for the hybrid.

Hybrids occasionally work when the value of convenience outweighs the perceived loss in value elsewhere. Convenience products tend to carry a premium for being convenient. Think about convenience stores: they tend to be smaller, carry fewer inventories, have lower turnover (so less fresh), are more expensive (to make up for lower turnover and smaller inventory). What they offer is just convenience. They're around the corner, or at the gas station while you're there.

Cameras in handheld phones are a convenience-based exception. It's convenient to be able to take a picture and send it from the same device without having to use a camera, download images and then send. Indeed, the mobile phone would seem to disobey the rule of convergence, bringing all kinds of applications into one simple hybrid.

But does it really? Not when the convenience exception is applied. The convenience factor smartphones provide is that they are portable. You can carry one in your pocket or handbag everywhere you go. They provide a personal transportable platform for communication, information and entertainment. The fact that you have to make compromises all along the way is overridden by the convenience of portability and the constant connection with the world that provides.

If you want to watch movies while you're on the plane though, chances are you'll use another device with a bigger screen, such as your iPad or laptop. The bigger the screen on your smartphone the more awkward it becomes to handle or carry in your pocket. If you want to take professional quality pictures you'll likely still use a digital SLR camera that gives you a greater range of options for lenses, flash lighting, aperture settings, tripod attachments, and so on. The greater space you allow for the camera, lens, and audio devices the more you compromise on aesthetics and other functions—such as using it as a phone!

So has the smartphone killed the camera business? It really depends on how you view the category. Analogue cameras ruled the domain for 65 years through gradual improvement of their species. Analogue cameras were effectively dead five years after the first digital cameras hit the shelves. By 2010 the reign of digital cameras was over; smartphones had redefined the category. So in that sense, yes, smartphones killed cameras as we knew it. The other way of looking at it is smartphones redefined our perception of what a camera is and made photography available to millions of new users. The skyrocketing sales of smartphones have carried with them a dramatic increase in portable digital cameras.

The convenience of the smartphone platform currently beats any perceived technological advantage of having a separate compact digital camera. For the vast majority of us, the quality of photos we can take on our smartphones is more than good enough, plus it's always there within hand's reach.

The convenience factor of the platform also allows it to be used as a personal device to access the internet for information, entertainment or communication. The compromise is a smaller keyboard that's not so easy to type quickly on, meaning shorter messages—which is sometimes a blessing, especially if you can use a picture to paint 1,000 words instead. But the convenience of being able to have access to the internet in the palm of your hand anywhere you go, as opposed to carrying a computer or a tablet, overrides such compromises.

At least, until the smartphone is usurped by something else.

Pruning Brand Portfolios

What happens when diversification produces too many options? Left unchecked, the process reaches its own limits. Divergence happens like limbs on a tree, each branch reaching out from the trunk to find the best place in the sun. Too many leaves from the higher branches inhibit the tree from growing stronger branches below. Pruning is necessary to keep branches (and brand portfolios) healthy.

Nature has opposing, divergent strategies for procreation of the 'selfish gene'. One is to have thousands of offspring and let them fend for themselves early on. The other is to have one or two offspring and nurture them carefully through adolescence to maturity.

In the corporate world, the former would be a commodity like coal, sand or timber (although even commodities can be branded). Strong brands, on the other hand, nearly always require a high degree of parenting in their early years and maintenance in their adult state.

In 2003, Nirmalya Kumar wrote an article in the *Harvard Business Review* titled, "Kill a brand, keep a customer," about the need for companies to rationalise their brand portfolios. He noted the surprising truth that most brands in companies with large portfolios don't make money. They follow the 80:20 rule in that 20% of their brands will typically account for 80% of their profit. He recorded:

Diageo had 35 brands in 170 countries in 1999; only eight of them delivered 70% of their profit, including Guinness, Tanqueray, and Johnnie Walker.

Nestle had 8,000 brands, 55 global, 140 regional and the rest local. The bulk of their profit came from just 200 brands or 2.5% of their portfolio.

Unilever had 1,600 brands in 1999 in 150 countries with 90% of their profit coming from just 400 of these brands. Most of the others were marginally profitable or loss making.

Of course, nothing is ever that straightforward and companies are understandably reluctant to dispose of brands that contribute revenue. Still, the rule of a few brands contributing the bulk of revenue also applies. The top 8 Diageo brands accounted for over 50% of revenue. Of Procter and Gamble's 250 brands, the top 10 accounted for more than half their sales.

Rationalisation, particularly in large organisations that have dealt with the brands for a long time, can be a painful process. History, sentimentality and territorial politics obscure objectivity. It needs to be handled sensitively and collaboratively with senior executives. Unplanned, it can pitch brother against brother in internal battles for survival. Done well, it can benefit everyone by accelerating growth and securing dominance for fewer, stronger brands that bring greater prosperity to all.

How do you tell if your portfolio of brands needs pruning?

Multi-brand strategies that have become overgrown suffer diseconomies of scale. Hidden costs of things like line extension, listing fees, distribution, advertising, packaging, management fees and so on often remain uncovered until a brand audit is conducted.

But there are quick checks too:

- Is the brand weak, declining, marginally profitable or loss making?

- Do target segments overlap with other brands in your portfolio?

- Do you have different brands in different locations for essentially the same product and target segment?

- Do internal brand managers find their biggest rivals are each other?

By 2002, three years into their five-year rationalisation programme, Unilever had reduced the number of brands in its portfolio by more than half to 750, of which the top 400 contributed 90% of profit and achieved growth rates of 5.4%, well above the average growth prior to rationalistion. Brands they deleted from their portfolio were merged into retained brands, sold, milked, or killed.

Living through such exercises can be painful. The human consequence of extracting scales of economy often means merging departments, closing divisions, mothballing factories, and losing jobs. But the goal of such rationalisation programmes is to 'prune the tree' to make it grow back stronger. It often takes a number of years, but the organisations end up stronger, more profitable, stable and growing faster than before. Ultimately, this leads to more jobs and greater stability.

The Law of Entropy

WHAT THIS TOOL DOES

As with the Diversification Tree (see page 64), this tool draws a direct comparison between the laws of nature and the laws that apply to brand-building.

Everything eventually dies, and brands are no exception. Keeping them healthy, fit and prosperous means battling the forces of entropy every day and knowing when it's better to use limited resources building new categories.

Entropy can be defined as a lack of order, randomness or unpredictability in the system. In the scientific sense, it refers to the gradual process of moving from a state of order to a state of disorder. Left unchecked, eventually everything turns to dust. Complex forms are reduced to simpler constituent parts in order to be built up again into something different. Decay is a natural process required for rebirth to happen.

Can the process be reversed? Yes, it can be delayed, deferred, even reversed through the input of energy. This is called negative entropy.

Having negative entropy is a good thing. It's like having stored up energy or extra time to stay alive and healthy, to have the ability to impose order in a state of disorder.

Think about it as fuel in your tank. The more fuel you have, the longer and further you can travel. The process of creating negative entropy is like filling your tank up, providing stored energy for future growth and survival. In humans, fuel in the tank is often equated with money in the bank—and more importantly health.

Strong brands create negative entropy. They store energy for future needs. They also provide consistency of experience in the minds of customers amidst a changing world. The relevance of that experience might change over time, and the tribe to whom the experience is most meaningful may alter in importance. But the battle to impose perceptual order in a chaotic, ever-changing world remains the same.

Given time, the forces of entropy are powerful enough to erode the strongest brand platforms. Because it happens gradually, entropy often goes unnoticed, or is ignored, until suddenly the cumulative effect is noticeable.

Entropy is an invidious enemy of the complacent. Sometimes the brand owners themselves unwittingly accelerate the process of entropy. Classic victims are 'cash cow' brands that have enjoyed decades of success, unconscious that marginal creep is eventually catching up with them. Years ago, Schweppes reduced the quinine in their tonic water by marginal amounts over a number of years. Nobody would notice just a sliver from one period to the next, they reasoned. Yet, after years of doing this, suddenly the difference was very noticeable. Confectionary manufacturers classically reduce the size of their products or substitute expensive ingredients with cheaper ones thinking customers don't notice. But over time, they do.

At The Brand Company, we spent a lot of time helping our clients counter the law of entropy, to strip back the layers of grime accumulated over time, to re-point the brickwork on the metaphorical brand house that's been eroded by weather and time.

It starts with a perceptual check and re-discovery of the core of their brand promise, provided by tools like the Brand Health Check (see page 49). The situation is analogous to going to the dentist for regular check-ups. We may not like doing it or even think it necessary, but regular check-ups mean early detection of tooth or gum decay that without early detection may require more radical remedies. Regular Brand Health Checks work in the same way to provide early detection of underlying issues. They can prevent more serious conditions emerging and keep your brand healthy and strong.

The Organisational Lifecycle

WHAT THIS TOOL DOES

Marketers are familiar with the concept of the lifecycle of brands from birth, through infancy, adolescence, adulthood to maturity, decline and death. This tool describes the phases in the lifecycle of organisations to provide a simple and quick reality check of where your organisation is positioned. The concept of organisational lifecycle is perhaps best defined by the work of Dr Ichak Adizes, Founder of the Adizes Institute in California, initially set out in 1979 and more recently in the 'Managing Corporate Lifecycles' published by the Azides Institute in 2004. Recognition of the typical challenges faced by each phase helps organisations plan appropriately.

The Organisational Lifecycle is a fast and effective strategic tool for CEOs and their leadership teams. Designed as part of a comprehensive change management programmes, it can also provide an illuminating snapshot for identifying problems and opportunities.

It is also a valuable tool for consultants to assess the nature of the client organisation they are dealing with, what challenges to expect and how to best approach them accordingly. The goal of most organisations is to achieve and then maintain prime status.

Here are the seven stages of the organisational lifecycle, originally outlined by Adizes, with general descriptors for each stage.

The Infant Organisation
- Action-oriented, opportunity-driven
- Few systems, rules or policies
- Inconsistant performance
- Vulnerability; a problem can become a crisis on short notice
- Management by crisis
- Little delegation; management is a one-man show
- Commitment of the founder is constantly tested and crucial for survival

The Go-Go Stage
- Rapid growth
- Everything is a priority
- Reactive, not proactive

- Driven by opportunities, not driving them
- Lack of consistency and focus
- Lack of skilled people; people join because they are passionate about the business or because they are friends with someone
- Organised around people, not around tasks
- Grows in a non-planned way

Adolescence
- Conflict between partners or decision makers, between the administrative and entrepreneurial types
- Temporary loss of vision
- Founder accepts organisational sovereignty
- Incentive systems reward the wrong behaviour
- Inconsistency in skills/experience among workforce
- Yo-yo delegation of authority
- Policies made, but not adhered to
- Board of directors exercises new controls over management

The Prime Organisation
- Functional systems and organisational structure
- Institutionalised vision and creativity
- Results orientation; the organisation satisfies customer needs
- Makes plans and then follows up on those plans
- People are hired for their capability
- Predictably excels in performance
- Spins off into new organisations

The Stable Organisation
- Has lower expectation for growth
- Has fewer expectations to conquer new frontiers
- Starts to focus on past achievements instead of future visions
- Suspicious of change
- Rewards those who do what they are told to do
- More interested in interpersonal relationships than risks

Aristocracy
- Money is spent on control systems, benefits and facilities
- Emphasis is on how things are done rather than what and why things are done
- There is formality in dress, address and tradition
- Individuals are concerned about the company's vitality, but as a group, the motto is "Don't make waves"
- Low internal innovation. May buy other companies to acquire new products or markets
- Cash rich—a takeover target

Bureaucracy
- Emphasis is on who caused the problem, rather than what to do about it
- There is much conflict, backstabbing and infighting
- Paranoia freezes the organisation; everyone is lying low
- Focus is on internal turf wars; the external customer is a nuisance
- Many systems, with little functional orientation
- Disassociated from its environment, and focuses mostly on itself
- No sense of control
- In order to work effectively with the organisation, customers must develop elaborate approaches to bypass or break through the system

People often ask me: Is the lifecycle a one-way journey? Over the long term, yes. But in the corporate world it is possible to rejuvenate. I've seen Stable or Aristocratic organisations move back to the Prime stage by re-focusing and innovating. Diversification into a new sector with a new brand can bring a completely new category into play, with fresh perspectives and skill requirements. Departments or divisions within large Stable organisations can act more like Infant or Go-Go organisations. More than anything, this model illuminates the cultural dissonance between the different stages to help better prepare your organisation for the challenges that lie ahead.

The Four Corners

WHAT THIS TOOL DOES

The Four Corners is a powerful tool used in workshops to illustrate different perspectives held by different generations within an organisation, where a generation is determined not by how old you are, but how long you have been in the company and the 'era' you represent.

"We select information bubbles to match our opinions, rather than basing opinions on balanced information."

President Obama said this in the wake of Hillary Clinton's surprise defeat to Donald Trump in November 2016. In it, he accurately described the problems both Democrats and Republicans have in breaking out of their bubbles to unite a divided country.

It's a recognisable phenomenon that keeps bias persisting. We like to hear our opinions echoed and appreciated. Given the choice, we migrate to environments that reinforce our beliefs and values.

Simon Sinek is one of the most widely respected brand and motivational speakers. One of his tips for success is to give yourself the best chance of success from the outset. Stack the odds in your favour if you can. He uses the example of speaking engagements to audiences that already know him and are 'onside' or positively primed from the outset. We can all relate to 'preaching to the choir'. If you flip this around, we listen to the preachers we choose. This is increasingly what is happening in a world where individuals can select from the vast array of media choices out there what they wish to consume.

When it comes to news, we make selections based on sources we believe are trustworthy, truthful and respected—or that we simply enjoy. What that means to one person may be very different to another.

For example, my online default news site is the BBC website, betraying my British heritage, but I also have in my news information-seeking portfolio the *Huffington Post*, the local *Vancouver Sun*, *The Economist*, *The Guardian*, the *New York Times*, CNN, CBC, McKinsey and many others, including occasional surprises such as Fox News. Now do I believe the BBC is the fount of all knowledge and impartiality for world news? No, I don't. I can see the commoditisation of the information as Reuters feeds every other news network. I can see the constraints shrinking budgets have had on the quality of live reporting. But, my bias or comfort zone is there. Do I think the BBC would lie to me intentionally? No, of course not. They're British, so they wouldn't dare do such a dastardly thing!

The point is, we are all drawn to bubbles that act like echo chambers to reflect our opinions and values. We tend not to go outside of those comfort bubbles into 'enemy' territory bubbles to listen to what they are telling themselves.

It's all too easy to get trapped inside your bubble and to interpret what you see and hear within it as the 'whole truth and nothing but the truth'. The danger in this scenario is that you become an isolated planet that loses touch with your position within a larger universe. It's essential for organisations and brands to understand the boundaries of their bubbles and to consciously step out of them on a considered basis to 'check the universe' from time to time.

The Four Corners is a terrific tool for doing this. I was first introduced to this technique by a very wise facilitator and friend, Vic Eduave. Vic is a sage Jesuit, worldly from life experience, intelligent, rich in knowledge, gifted with high EQ (Emotional Quotient) and wise beyond his age.

It was March 1999, and I was in the second year running the Malaysian office of Leo Burnett, along with my creative partners Yasmin Ahmed and Ali Mohammed, and Managing Director Tony Savirimuthu. It was a challenging time dealing with the effects of the first Asian economic crisis, the devaluation of the Malaysian Ringgit (that together more than halved the reporting US$ revenue of the agency virtually overnight), and a period of great political unrest with the uprisings against the ruling UMNO party and the subsequent suppression of the opposition. Holding the diverse agency together was challenge enough, let alone upholding the reputation as a dominant creative leader in the market. Oh, and we also had to earn a profit!

Despite the unfavourable economic and political situation, or more probably because of it, we took advantage of the fragmenting advertising agency world to grow in a downturn. We used depressed rental and development costs to move into a larger building that we designed ourselves. We had newcomers mixing with old-timers who'd been around for twenty years or more. We had nationalities ranging from Malay to Indian to Chinese alongside expatriates and opposing political allegiances. As the agency grew, cliques formed. Like spectres, they'd emerge at unpredictable times and disappear just as quickly. And they had a divisive effect that I wanted to eliminate.

Vic told me about the Four Corners tool, and we planned to use it on the first night of our leadership team retreat. It was held at Ye Old Smokehouse at Tanah Rata in the Cameron Highlands, a mock Tudor hostelry in the style of an English public house. It was a perfect getaway at the edge of where civilisation literally meets the jungle. We heard stories of tiger prints in the bunkers at the adjacent golf course, and we used to listen from the verandah to the booming sounds of howler monkeys across the misty forest canopy. Tales of lost travellers, jungle spirits, and wartime exploits swirled in the mist and around the open log fire at night. It was no coincidence we'd chosen this place—a three-hour drive and world away from Kuala Lumpur—to do our Four Corners storytelling exercise.

There were perhaps twenty of us, mostly senior members of the agency representing all the departments: creative, media, finance, account management, direct, public relations and design. Vic divided us into unequal groups based on the length of time we'd been at the agency. There were a couple of people who'd been part of the agency almost since its inception over twenty years ago, who had lived through being a tiny start-up to see the arrival of industry legends like Yasmin. Then there were the newcomers, people who'd been at the agency for less then two years (of which I was one), a group of two-to-five year employees, and another group of six-to-ten year veterans.

Each group took turns to speak from their corner. A spokesperson was chosen and he or she related the 'story' of Leo Burnett from their perspective for the other groups to listen to. We were all given prompts: What memorable anecdotes from your time do you recall? What created a lasting impression? What were the best and worst things you experienced? What good things have been forgotten that might be revived? What lesson would you like to pass on? What things would you like to tell the other groups?

It was a cathartic experience. People listened respectfully to each era's stories and asked questions to clarify or understand better the meaning behind what was said. People were rapt. We talked well into the small hours of the night with no agenda other than active listening to each other.

It was amazing how such different perceptions of the same agency could exist and how different the interpretations of the same events were. The insights we gained from that exercise bonded the group in a deep level of mutual respect.

What emerged was unexpected and dramatic. It became apparent that the personality and image of the agency was defined by the people who'd been there for two to five years, a period that represented a kind of 'golden age' for the company. It coincided with the recruitment of the two dominant creative forces in Malaysian advertising: Yasmin and Ali, recruited from my old agency Ogilvy & Mather. But it went well beyond these two and included the previous managing director Phil, a charismatic, talented Australian, and a band of creative and account people who had been recruited around the same time. It's no coincidence that this period also saw the greatest creative and financial success. This was the era when Leo Burnett began winning multiple accolades and awards and established the agency's reputation as a creative leader. It was identified in particular with a couple of iconic campaigns for national companies such as Petronas that resonated with the times and the need for racial harmony and national unity.

This era was perhaps the largest group represented. It was like a mini Camelot within the company. They were a group of confident, successful and respected individuals. They had by far the most positive outlook of the company. They were contented, achieving, and purposeful. Didn't everyone feel that way?

Unintentionally, the strong bonds of mutual respect within this peer group had created barriers to entry for the other groups. The notion that their perfect world was not shared by everyone was a revelation. Indeed, that all the other groups felt actively excluded from this exclusive club shocked them. They listened as the veterans from times well before them explained how the identity and fortunes of the company changed before their eyes, but that they didn't feel they'd been brought along for the journey. Success had been claimed by the golden-agers, and there was some resentment about having felt passed over. The newcomers felt equally outcast. Although they were the best and brightest from elsewhere, they didn't feel their voices were heard or respected by the golden-agers. Nothing new could be told to this group; they were the ones who'd delivered the treasure, and they were the ones who'd do it again.

I'm exaggerating a little to raise the contrast, but this was the heart of the finding. The golden-agers were genuinely distressed that others didn't share the same positive feelings they did about the success. The other groups felt it was the beginning of a breakthrough in which they could finally feel like they belonged there.

Afterward, we embarked on a plan of integration of the ages. We made a conscious effort to include all eras in important decisions. We put certain rules in place that made sure every group had some of their ideas executed. Power was devolved, if you like. And, although we couldn't force it, we put social events in the calendar to encourage mixing of the eras. We shared success and disappointments together.

When conducting the Four Corners exercise, the room, the ambience, the pre-briefing and the setting all needs careful planning. The symbolism of having one chair for the storyteller to sit in, with everyone else seated on the ground, also helps. Having the eras cluster together in their groups helps delineate boundaries and evoke memories, embellishing stories within each group. They cajole each other and elaborate on the storyteller's tales. You should also have a scribe to make sure the important anecdotes are not lost. This process captures historical memory and is incredibly valuable.

The exercise highlights the dangers of working in a bubble; a world that may function well for one group of individuals but not for others. It helps create awareness of what it looks like in other people's bubbles.

As Mark Twain said: "Don't judge others until you've walked in their skin."

Until that time, I had a particularly fractious relationship with one of my senior management team. She saw me as a transient outsider imposed on them, a dreamer with visions beyond reality and an impulsive risk-taker to the point of recklessness. (She may have had a point, but luckily this time it worked out!) I saw her as efficient but small-minded, bureaucratic and lacking imagination to the point of being an obstacle to progress. This exercise allowed us to expose and share vulnerabilities in private-public that allowed us to build a much more productive working relationship. If I'd known more then about Whole Brain Thinking (see page 96) then I would have understood and solved the problem much sooner.

We also had one individual that many of us had difficulty connecting with. There was always a defensive part of her that kept her distant. During the storytelling, she revealed that her mother had died during her birth and that she had been ostracised as a 'cursed child' by her family. She'd never told this to anyone in the agency despite having been there for over a decade. It was an emotional evening I can tell you — and a transformative one. Antipathy turned to empathy in a moment and her and our world was changed for the better forever.

The Four Corners is a powerful tool, but it needs to be handled with care. We were fortunate to have a Sensei-master in Vic to lead us through it. Use a trusted facilitator to conduct the exercise, someone who can ensure equal stage time and interpret objectively from an outsider's perspective.

There are some interesting lessons from my time leading Leo Burnett Malaysia. For more, check out the Living Your Brand tool in the Direction section on page 164.

Perspective Lenses

WHAT THIS TOOL DOES

This tool is a self-discovery tool. It helps individuals and organisations identify the echo chambers or bubbles they live within. It puts a mirror up to how your 'going in' perspective (or bias) can impact your thinking and decision-making. This section doesn't attempt to explain each method in detail; rather, it highlights examples that expose the biases that exist in each of us when we process information. The purpose is to raise awareness of the importance of knowing thyself and give you thought-starter ideas to help you develop your own set of perspective lenses.

Imagine that perspective lenses are a set of lenses in a box, like coloured filters in front of your eye, each lens you select is a thinking filter that lets you see the world in a new way. When you view things through a different lens—be it the perspective lens of an older generation, or the lens of an optimist or a thinking preference like organisational ability—it forces you to view the world from different angles.

This helps you better understand thinking biases that you and your organisation possess that might influence decisions. As Sun Tzu famously wrote in *The Art of War*, 'Know thyself as well as the enemy'. If you know your competitors well, but not yourself, you will win only half your war.

I've identified five perspective lenses here to illustrate the point (there are many more, but these are ones I found resonate most with my clients):

1. Generational Lenses
2. Organisational Culture
3. Unpredictability and Uncertainty
4. Patterns of Expectation or Paradigms
5. Thinking Preferences (MBTI / Whole Brain / Shark, Carp, Dolphin)
6. Rebel Spaceship

I've already touched on two perspective lenses. **Organisational Lifecycle** (page 78) applies the concept of life stage to organisations. **The Four Corners** (page 81) is a real life example of generational lenses at work.

Generational Lenses

Although values and interests transcend age barriers (think about 'tribes' of stamp collectors, skiers, chocolate-lovers, left-handers, guitarists, otter-lovers, or whatever) generations are influenced by shared experiences. It's no coincidence that certain age groups have been identified and given labels based on how they think and behave. Although these are massive simplifications based on generalistation, shared experiences have shaped shared attitudes and behaviours that are recognisable in certain generational bandwidths (see chart below).

World War II was a defining experience for those who lived before it, who fought in it, or were children growing up in the aftermath of it. My mother and father were both children growing up in wartime Britain. They lived through years of hardship and food rationing. They would never leave anything on their plate and abhorred any form of waste. I know this attitude towards food was shared by thousands of others that experienced the same thing. Shared experience creates empathy.

So what generational lens are you or your organisation looking through?

Boardrooms are changing, slowly, to have greater diversity, gender equality, ethnic and religious diversity and of course age. They still tend to be older, male-dominated and rational. Be mindful. A younger, female, creative, emotional world is evolving to resolve the imbalance.

Organisational Culture

The culture of an organisation can loosely be described as 'how things are done around here'. Culture is invisible but has a profound impact in how the brand is perceived and experienced. It informs employee attitudes and behavior and pervades every aspect of the brand.

It is the result of a complex interaction of history, founders, prominent people, products, services, structure, systems, beliefs, environment and habits. No two companies are the same.

Fons Trompenaars identified four types of culture, according to where they sat on dimensions of egalitarian versus hierarchical status and personality or rules driven:

- **Family Firm** is person oriented, social and hierarchical

- **Cult** is fulfillment oriented, social and egalitarian

- **Guided Missile** is project oriented, egalitarian and rules-driven

- **Eiffel Tower** is role oriented, hierarchical and rules-driven

GENERATIONAL LENS

SILENT | GREATEST
1901-24

Approx. US Population 2018 (M)

4

EVENTS
Radio
Manned Flight
Model T Ford
WW1
Titanic sinking
Russian revolution
Women's right to vote

GREATEST | GI | LUCKY
1925-42

Approx. US Population 2018 (M)

20

EVENTS
Television
Wall Street crash
Great Depression
Transatlantic flight
WW2
Atomic bomb
Radar
Contact lenses

BABY BOOMERS
1943-64

Approx. US Population 2018 (M)

75

EVENTS
End of WW2
Chinese revolution
Cold War
Woodstock
The Beatles
Highways
Nuclear Power
Supersonic flight
Photo voltaic solar panel
Contraceptive pill
Malayan emergency
Vietnam war

GEN X | LOST

1965-81

Approx. US Population 2018 (M)

70

EVENTS

Vietnam war
JFK assassination
Concorde
Man on the moon
First computers
Mobile phone
Heart transplant

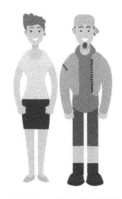

GEN Y | MILLENNIAL

1982-2000

Approx. US Population 2018 (M)

78

EVENTS

AIDS
Worldwide Web
Cloned sheep 'Dolly'
HN1 Bird Flu
Nelson Mandela freed
End of apartheid
Google founded

GEN Z

2001 -

Approx. US Population 2018 (M)

72

EVENTS

9/11 WTC attack
iPhone
Tesla
Lehman Bank collapse
Global economic crisis
IS
Facebook
Twitter

Where does your organisation fit?

The Brand Company used a questionnaire that identified current company culture using a series of statements to which respondents could agree or disagree. These included:

- There is a spirit of openness and trust.

- Meetings are always well managed and productive.

- The design and ambience of the work environment reflects the personality of the brand.

- Team-working is genuine and collaborative.

- There are few rules or procedures restricting employees from realising their full potential.

- The organisation is meritocratic. It recognises and rewards people based on performance and attitude, not length of service or other means.

- The decision-making process is effective – difficult decisions are made and implemented efficiently.

- The customer experience is delivered well at all touch points.

- The organisation is not bureaucratic or burdened by too many layers of management (those closest to the customer can usually make the key decisions).

- There is equal emphasis on solving problems and understanding feelings.

The Six Virtues of a Dream Company

I love the simplicity of these six virtues from the excellent piece, 'Creating the best workplace on earth' by Rob Goffee and Gareth Jones from the *Harvard Business Review*, May 2013.

They identify six virtues that universally would create dream companies—if companies could deliver them!

- The company stands for something meaningful

- You can be yourself

- Your strengths are magnified

- People are told what's really going on

- Daily work is rewarding

- Stupid rules don't exist

Unpredictability and Uncertainty

We all deal with unpredictability in different ways. Developed by Igor Ansoff, the Turbulence model or T-model is a means of assessing personal and corporate levels of comfort at different levels of turbulence or unpredictability. Uncertainty generates fear in some, excitement in others. The 'unpredictability and uncertainty' lens helps individuals and companies assess how they are likely to be affected by high or low levels of predictability.

I believe the level of change and the rate of unpredictability in the world is increasing. It is becoming harder to forecast future events and the consequences of decisions made now are becoming more significant.

Some people and some companies are more comfortable at low levels of turbulence. They like things predictable; the same routine today as it was yesterday and will likely be tomorrow. Others can't stand routine. They want to face new challenges every day, do different things, and be constantly stimulated.

At the sharp creative end of the advertising industry, we'd be working at T3-T4 consistently and from time to time T5 when a client review, a customer crisis, or a creative pitch was going on. It was fast-paced, high energy and often stressful in a service industry where your clients were entrusting you with their brands every day. You need to have people who thrive in that kind of environment—what I called 'white water rafting'.

TURBULENCE LEVELS	WORLD	EVENTS	VISIBILITY	PATH TO THE FUTURE	RESPONSE
1	REPETITIVE	FAMILIAR	CRYSTAL CLEAR	AN OPEN ROAD	STABLE
2	EXPANDING	PREDICTABLE	CLEAR	A GENTLE CLIMB	REACTIVE
3	CHANGING	DISCONTINUOUS	FUZZY	UNEVEN STAIRCASE	ANTICIPATORY
4	DISCONTINUOUS	PREDICTABLE AFTER	OBSCURE	A ROCK CLIMB	ENTREPRENEURIAL
5	FULL OF SURPRISES	UNPREDICTABLE	PUZZLING	'BEAM ME UP!'	CREATIVE

THE TURBULENCE MODEL

But even for those who relish it, Level 5 environments are not sustainable for long periods of time. You get exhausted trying to keep the kayak afloat and upright. Everybody needs to pull to the side to a quiet eddy of calm water to recover once in a while.

Conversely, if you're in a predictable environment for too long you stagnate. The algae forms pretty quickly on still water and before you know it there's no sunlight breaking through, little oxygen to breathe and you begin to slowly asphyxiate.

Change, ambiguity, complexity, paradox, discontinuity, uncertainty, opportunity and surprise are all sources of turbulence and unpredictability. Nearly always, the source is beyond the boundaries of control of the organisation.

The 2008 economic crisis was triggered by the North American sub-prime mortgage collapse, brilliantly demonstrated in Michael Lewis's book, *The Big Short*. In a market that had been predictable for decades, a tiny handful of individuals spotted the impending doom and bet against the market and conventional wisdom by claiming that 'too big to fail won't stop the collapse this time'. The North American economy went from T2 to T5 in the blink of an eye.

It's very difficult to make good decisions about where to go next when your ship is in the teeth of a hurricane, plummeting into deep troughs, then scaling the highest crests of storm waves and rarely being able to see the horizon or take a navigational fix. Brands with a long-term vision and a clear plan have a stable point of reference to fall back on. As has been suggested by the Singapore Institute of Management, in turbulent environments where the topography is unknown and changing before your eyes, it's more useful to have a compass—and I'd add good instincts—than a detailed road map.

Understanding your comfort level with unpredictability and uncertainty quickly allows an assessment of your own personal levels of comfort with turbulence. It can also be used as a rough guide to describe the macro-economic environment the company is operating within.

Patterns of Expectation

In my advertising days I coined the term 'breaking the pattern of expectation' to highlight ideas that grabbed attention by being 'out of step' with what was expected.

These ideas would invariably arrest people's attention. It's a basal or primitive instinct. Like a blink or a knee-jerk, it's a reflex reaction. With perception, the triggers that recognise a pattern of expectation being broken are similarly hard-wired. It's automatic. You can't stop it happening. It makes this a very powerful device. When you have it, you know you're going to grab attention (which is Rule No. 1 of advertising).

This is brilliantly exemplified by Bartle Bogle Hegarty's (BBH) advertisement for Levi's black jeans. A black sheep stands out alone in a sea of white sheep, heading in a different direction from the herd. Apart from the proverbial metaphor of black sheep being mavericks who go their own way and do their own thing (aspirational for young jean buyers then)—it also reinforced the black jeans message as opposed to 'normal' blue jeans.

It breaks the pattern of expectation—white sheep heading west, white sheep heading west, white sheep heading west, white sheep (yawn), white sheep … BLACK SHEEP! And going the other way?

That breaks the set of rules—called a paradigm—that the brain has established to impose order on the world.

Without rules there would be chaos. Things would never be learnt (you'd repeat the same mistakes over and over again). We'd never clear our memory space to allow other higher order thinking functions to be done. So rules are not bad. In nature they are highly developed tools to create competitive advantage. It helps if you get to the right answers faster and with less energy. But rules also have limits—they work well until someone or something changes the game, or the rules by which the game is played.

The set of rules establishes or defines boundaries to operate within. It says: 'think inside this box'.

The rules tell you how to behave inside the boundaries in order to be successful.

The term paradigm shift is generally attributed to Thomas Kuhn in relation to scientific revolution. Think of a paradigm as a set of rules. A paradigm tells you: there is a game, this is what the game is...and this is how to play it successfully according to the rules. Experts such as elite athletes reach the pinnacle of their sport by mastering the rules, putting the hours in and excelling at the game. The same thing happens in business and in organisations. There is a set of rules (both written and intangible, cultural rules).

Those that learn the rules and master the game succeed at the expense of those that don't. Most of us have experienced that awkward period of being the new employee, the rookie that doesn't know the rules, who has to be 'shown the ropes'...or made to learn from mistakes. Rules help organisations become automated and efficient up to a point. Too many rules have the opposite effect—they create bureaucracies.

When the rules change, all bets are off. The pattern of expectation is broken and everything changes. The old rules no longer apply and skills that mastered those old rules become obsolete overnight. Here are three examples of paradigm shifts where the rules were changed forever:

The Fosbury Flop
In 1968, Dick Fosbury won the Olympic Gold medal for high jump. He was the first man to jump backwards over the high-jump bar. Until then, the commonly used technique was the Western Roll. Fosbury broke the established set of rules—so much so that his fellow competitors attempted to have him disqualified and stripped of his medal, but the authorities could find nothing illegal about it. Whilst the increments in height of record jumps had been minimal for decades, Fosbury raised the new height by several inches in a single leap. Fifty years later and it is still the recognised technique.

Cirque du Soleil
In the 1990s, the traditional Barnum & Bailey's circus was dying. Dwindling audiences, difficulty in finding locations that would have them, the cost of transportation and accusations of cruelty to animals had everybody declaring the circus was dead. Everybody except a troupe of creative performing artists from Montreal that re-framed people's thinking.

They redefined the experience, retaining the magic of live

performances under a big top, and celebrating the incredible talent and ingenuity of human performers. Add iconic music, magical scenery, lighting and effects and tie it altogether with a mythical storyline and you have the re-birth of the circus. There is nothing like Cirque du Soleil, although it has now spawned imitators.

Swatch

Watches are expensive. You only have one and you treasure it for life, right?

Swatch shattered that paradigm with their fashionable line of almost disposable watches. They were bright, individual and cheap—affordable enough to wear several different ones according to fashion or mood.

So, why do these examples offer a perspective lens?

Well, changes in the rule tend not to get noticed until they are undeniable. There is natural resistance to change and strong resistance amongst those who have invested most in the old rules. If you know what you're looking for, you can detect changes in the rules early and take first-mover advantage.

A set of rules are like a lens on the world—a way of seeing things if you like—that some people simply cannot see, and others refuse to. Creative advertising agencies are adept at producing disruptive campaigns that 'break the rules' and establish a new way of thinking.

Even the best new ideas or rule changes can be met with resistance. In WWII, when America entered the war, Britain's Royal and Merchant navies had already been fighting the battle of the Atlantic against the German U-boats for over two years. The effectiveness of convoy escorts (re-learnt from WWI) was unquestionable, but it took hundreds of sinkings and thousands of lives before the US Navy adopted a similar strategy.

Smoking causing lung cancer is another; it took decades to beat the conscious blindness to this (see Vested interest in Inertia)—and there are still people who willfully or not, cannot or do not wish to see this relationship. They are blind to the paradigm.

Global warming and man's direct influence on impacting the environment is another one close to my heart that we're living through right now. Those that believe it to be an indisputable scientific truth find it incredulous that there are people who cannot 'see it', or even actively disagree.

Unmarried families, gay marriage, emotional intelligence, the existence of ghosts, ESP (extra sensory perception), alien life forms, racism, sexism, ageism…the list goes on of mindsets governed by sets of rules.

It's important to understand the sets of rules that you or your organisation is governed by.

Thinking Preferences

We all have thinking preferences. They operate as a lens through which we see the world. It's a filter that both processes stimuli and informs the way we behave. Given that organisations tend to mirror the way in which their CEOs and leaders behave, understanding where these biases may lie is critical.

We all have preferences for certain types of food, or clothes or colours even—so it shouldn't be too great a leap to agree we also have preferences in the way we think. We're also familiar with 'left brain (rational) and right brain (emotional)' terminology.

Psychologists have been describing these differences for decades. Many psychoanalytical models have their origins in Jungian psychology, based on the early psychoanalytical archetype theories of Carl Jung in the 1940s and 50s. Since then, advances in the understanding of brain physiology and its relation to cognitive processes has led to the development of significantly more accurate diagnostic and prescriptive tools for how we think.

Many readers will be familiar with the Myers-Briggs Type Indicator (MBTI), or with the Whole Brain Thinking developed by Ned Herrmann. The latter identifies four quadrants—organisational, analytical, conceptual and interpersonal—relating to the physiological structure of the brain; frontal, basal and left or right. His theory of brain dominance patterns determines that thinking preferences are predictable. No one thinking preference is superior to another, rather, a complete or 'whole brain' characteristic is desirable for organisations.

In the hands of skilled practitioners, these tools provide valuable perspective to individuals, teams and organisations. They expose thinking preferences strengths and weaknesses. I encourage individuals to play to their strengths and organisations to shore up their weaknesses.

For example, a large organisation I work with had a historical thinking bias that was practical/organised and relational/interpersonal, but was weaker in analytical preference and almost devoid of conceptual (creative, exploratory) thinking. Unsurprisingly, it was good at doing predictable things it had always been asked to do efficiently and in a way that didn't upset anyone. Their difficulty came when their world changed, when they were asked to be innovative in developing new beliefs and work practices—and in dealing with naysayers that were obstructing progress. Putting up the thinking preference perspective lens helped them understand why, culturally, they had found it difficult to challenge conventions and make the difficult decisions required to make positive change. In the years that followed they have successfully built a leadership team with balanced thinking preferences that has created a stronger, more balanced organisation.

Another one of my favourite perspective lenses is Carp, Shark and Dolphin, inspired by *The Strategy of the Dolphin* written by Paul Kordis and Dudley Lynch. At its most basic, the precept is you can divide the world of people and organisations into three types based on their attitude, behaviour and characteristics: Carp, Shark and Dolphin. It's an amazing, simple and powerful way of segmenting that, once known, is hard to forget.

To this I add 'psuedo-dolphins', or those carp and shark that have learnt to imitate dolphin behavior, but that are exposed under stress. Organisations need all three types to function. No one type is necessarily more intelligent or desirable than another, although each species has clearly distinguishable traits. The species aren't distributed in equal proportions.

Carp are bottom feeders. They like the security of a safe, predictable world with an abundant food supply. They prefer the security of safety in numbers to swimming alone. They can survive in relatively murky, still waters with low oxygen quite happily. Older, wiser carp evolve highly developed skills to keep themselves in the middle of the school, close to the best food source and furthest away from predators. At their best they are diligent, trustworthy, well organised, reliable and highly prized (as with Koi carp). Carp can lead long, secure, happy and productive lives this way.

Sharks are hunters. By nature, they are sleek, highly evolved and extremely efficient predators. They are territorial and solitary at heart (although they assemble and jostle in packs). When food is abundant they can be docile and approachable. When it's a little harder to find, posture and threat is often enough to get what they want. When it becomes scarce or more competitive they become more aggressive. At their best, sharks are action-oriented achievers that seek challenge and gain reward. Their natural prey is carp, but if needs must they'll turn on their own kind, the strongest and fittest surviving. Big, wise old sharks have few natural enemies and can retain an air of docility even in hard times—until another big, wise old shark happens along.

Dolphins are inventive, playful masters of their universe. They are collaborative and nurturing. Unlike the other two species that look to change the environment to suit themselves, dolphins look to create better environments in which all three species coexist harmoniously. They search beyond win-win situations for win-to-the-multiple-power solutions that improve the lives of all—and the larger environment. Because they are naturally inquisitive and creative, dolphins are most often the ones who find solutions. They use tools to help them. They are comfortable alone, in pairs or in large schools and can interchange freely between these according to need. There is one unique ability dolphins have that the other two don't. Dolphins can temporarily metamorphose to become a carp or a shark if the situation merits it, before returning to their natural dolphin state. This enables them to empathise with and benefit from the traits of the other two.

As you read the descriptions you will automatically have been thinking of people you know. Understanding the nature of the person you're dealing with—and indeed yourself—helps create more productive relationships.

What do you think the distribution of Carp, Shark and Dolphins is on average?

There are no firm answers but everyone agrees there are lots of carp, and more sharks than dolphins. The approximate ratio in any population is 60:30:10. Note that this is only a rough guide and populations vary. Many people aspire to be dolphins but just aren't—and that's okay. The world needs all types. It is possible for aspirants to adopt a more 'dolphinesque' mindset.

Rebel Spaceship

WHAT THIS TOOL DOES

The Rebel Spaceship is a strategy for tackling large, complex or sensitive projects that may have a fundamental impact on the organisation but that cannot be overtly seen to be championed — or sometimes even supported. This is a tool wise leaders can use more frequently than they do to challenge conventions and discover new solutions. Often these are necessarily covert operations.

"Search in all your parks in all your cities. There are no statues of committees!"
—David Ogilvy

Change rarely—I'd go as far as saying never—happens by committee. There are simply too many checks and balances to make the radical, irrational leaps of faith that tend to be required to break out of existing paradigms. This is one of many reasons why large organisations struggle to change even in the face of obvious need to do so.

Change occurs at the periphery. It's at the periphery where the explorers and pioneers are found and where risk and experimentation is highest.

So how do they change? How can they hedge their bets against their current path if there's concern they may be on the wrong path?

Rebel Spaceship is a highly effective tool that helps encourage this kind of thinking.

Rebel Spaceships are small teams of creative-thinking explorers. The word 'rebel' suggests opposition to existing government or authority, but that isn't necessarily so. As with Han Solo, Luke Skywalker, and the Millennium Falcon in *Star Wars*, rebel spaceships tend to operate far away from the gravitational pull of the mother ship. It may be operating MI6-style, secretly, so that there is plausible deniability from the leaders if things go wrong. Or they may simply be working independently.

Either way the rebels are operating at the periphery, where change occurs. If things go right and discoveries or revelations are made that strengthen the despatcher's position, then central command take ownership of the good news. So what's new in politics!

It takes a special type of leader to captain a Rebel Spaceship. They need to accept the odds are often against them succeeding, that they are flying in dangerous territory, and that they're unlikely to get the credit they deserve even if they're successful. Sounds like a thankless task. But these individuals tend be driven by their own belief-set and moral compass. They're highly intelligent, maverick, and independent. They enjoy a measure of disruption and calculated risk. They may have issues with authority because they challenge conventional wisdom. They tend to be 'outsiders' who have the skill to operate at high levels inside organisations. They attract loyal followers (whether they like it or not). While the financial rewards can be very high, their real reward is the self-satisfaction of knowing they have shaken the world on its axis for a brief moment, perhaps even changing it forever in some way. Very few will know it was them. They don't seek the spotlight. They are Fantastic Mr Fox.

These animals are rare and elusive. They're good at disguise. But their effect is unmistakable. My first boss at Ogilvy London, Les Naylor, was then and still is one such rare creature.

The crews of Rebel Spaceships are small, perhaps only four or five people. Each of them plays a specialist role and is expert in their field. They share beliefs but have diverse skill sets and backgrounds. They combine to create a whole brain.

Commanders and crew are the good kind of rebels — Robin Hoods if you like. They fight for causes they believe in at the risk of being misunderstood and persecuted.

Rebel Spaceships are also commissioned to scout ahead, to explore the dark unknown space (see Johari's Window on page 46). What they find can shape the direction of the brand for years to come.

I've used the Rebel Spaceship approach to good effect for a number of clients and for different purposes. A private school I consult to was interested in whether it should continue to offer boarding or not. This was a divisive question. Older alumni felt strongly it was an essential part of the school whilst others felt it was largely irrelevant to them, even a drain on resources. The large difference in numbers of day students and boarders made any democratic debate nonsense. A small Rebel Spaceship team was charged with 'going out there' to objectively assess the category and the implications for the school. They came back with facts, insights and a recommendation that it was an important component of building a world school that should be nurtured and developed.

Part 2: Definition

Definition helps you define your brand and position it to own a territory in the mind of your customers.

The primary Definition Tool is Brand DNA, an integral part of the Brand Centered Management process which we will explore in depth in this chapter. The philosophy and practice of Brand Centered Management applies across categories, cultures and geography. It moves with time because, like its genetic counterpart, your Brand DNA is a living thing constantly impacting and being impacted by the environment it lives in.

Brand DNAs are forged in fire. Like many creative processes the most effective results come only after intense heat and pressure. The equivalent to compressing diamonds from coal is our Brand DNA development workshop. Time pressure is part of the process.

Use the tools in this section to define who you are as a company, and what you offer to your customers.

Brand DNA

WHAT THIS TOOL DOES

Brand DNA, like its genetic counterpart, is a unique template for replicating consistent experiences. And delivery of consistent desired experiences is what makes great brands great. This tool describes what the components of a Brand DNA are, how you obtain them, and how they can be used to inform strategy and action.

Your DNA is your brand's distinctive positioning in the minds of your customers. It acts as a guiding light for all you DO and all you SAY in order to create the desired perceptions for your brand.

At the heart of a Brand DNA is the promise you make to your customers. This promise cements the relationship between the organisation and its customers, employees and business strategy. Delivering this promise consistently through everything the brand says and does is the foundation for building strong brands.

In developing a DNA for clients, The Brand Company would work closely with the client leadership team to articulate a relevant, compelling, differentiating, and credible promise to their customers. From there, Brand DNA comprises the following parts: the role the brand plays in your stakeholders' lives (why it exists in a meaningful way for them), the promise or expectation of experience it delivers to them, the benefits they derive from delivering against the promise, and the spirit or personality that stands your brand apart.

It sounds complicated, and it takes a great deal of discovery and preparation work to craft a watertight DNA, but it is simplified by completing these five short prompts.

- We are...(we exist to...)
- We believe...
- We will...
- In order to...
- By being...

This may not seem much, but simplicity is part of the beauty. These were forged after years of experimentation and fine-tuning. We were looking to find a concise but exhaustive formula for capturing the essence of a brand. It has to be inclusive enough to capture the unique complexity of the brand, yet crisp and memorable.

We are...
What role does the brand play in customers' lives? What is it you really do for them? This goes beyond the literal interpretation of the business category or function. For example, a client of ours who saw their role as a mobile service provider was defined as relationship-builder, bringing people together.

We believe...
Why does the brand exist? What is its raison d'être. As Simon Sinek says, people don't buy what you do; they buy *why* you do it. It's easy to sell to customers who believe in what you believe in. You don't have to try hard to be something you're not either. If you stay true to your beliefs, you'll attract like-minded followers.

The catch? The strongest beliefs can be polarizing. For a brand to be strongly affiliated with a core group of loyal users often means it must *actively exclude* other groups, something many brand owners are reluctant to do.

We will...
What is the clear, compelling promise being committed to for your customers?

In order to...
What is the benefit of delivering against your promise? Is it tangible, measurable? How will it make you feel?

By being...
Identify the three or four adjectives that most accurately describe how you deliver your promise. Often, brands deliver similar product experiences. There's little to discriminate between performance characteristics for example. The difference is often in *how* the experience is delivered. It's tempting to have a long list of adjectives. These give the appearance of multiple attributes that imply strength and diversity, something to tick everyone's box. We encourage the opposite: try to commit to three truly meaningful descriptors that together you deliver better than anyone else, and effortlessly.

Below are four examples of Brand DNAs: a telecommunications company, an insurance company, a hotel group, and a school. They are just four of many that I have helped to craft over the years that demonstrate both the universality of the Brand DNA tool and its resiliency over time. The same template creates unique genetic blueprints for every customer to build differentiating and compelling brand experiences over the long term.

Please be mindful that these look simple and concise, as they're supposed to, but the process of reducing them to these critical essentials is a disciplined one requiring many hours of work and collaborative creative processes to craft.

SmarToneVodafone

One of the earliest Brand DNAs my business partner James Stuart and I developed for a large telecom client in Hong Kong called SmarTone. They were faced with an extremely competitive marketplace in which six or seven companies were vying for the same set of customers. The government had hinted that the number of licenses granted to telecom companies could be limited to three or four; so it was vital to be one of the top three players.

Their platform was technology-based, and this was the basis of their proposition when we came to the problem. Our Discovery process uncovered that their technology was indeed marginally superior, but that it did not translate into a tangibly superior performance benefit, such as clearer calls or greater coverage. Moreover, even if it did, these benefits were attributed to the phone hardware (then Nokia) rather than the service provider.

> SmarTone was correct in claiming their 'widget' was superior to competitors, but it was difficult for them to accept that customers didn't really care about it. As the Brand Driver model will show later (see page 128), their superior technology benefit fell into the category of 'fool's gold'—something that may be true, but that carries little value to the customer.

When we began conducting our Brand Centered Management process, SmarTone was the number three Hong Kong mobile service provider, but they were in danger of slipping to number four. The company was seen as ill-defined and vaguely geared toward middle-aged Chinese businessmen. It was positioned on a technology platform of clarity and coverage, which was not differentiating nor owned by the brand. It was becoming fragmented with brands aimed at teens, distracting effort and energy away from a weakening core brand.

The Discovery and Definition process revealed several illuminating insights. Perhaps the most important was a recognition that the role they were playing in their customers' lives was a *human one*—building relationships between people, information, and entertainment—as opposed to a technological one. This led to a realisation that the desired values for the brand were feminine ones—not the masculine positioning they'd been adopting.

Our process also identified an opportunity. The benefit most valued by their customers—that of communication building relationships (whether business or personal)—was up for grabs. SmarTone also had high ratings for customer service, but these had been overshadowed by assertions of technical superiority in the past. So their claim to an emotional platform of relationship builders would be plausible if they could deliver against it consistently. They committed to an intensive and continuous customer-oriented service programme in order to deliver their desired promise before claiming it. Properly, they invested in doing the 'DO' before saying the 'SAY'.

They transformed themselves from a superior technology provider into relationship builders—quite a fundamental shift and one for which the courage of their leadership should be admired.

Of course there's a lot more to it than that, but this Brand DNA drove a fundamental change in all aspects of the SmarTone brand, from its identity and advertising (the typical first steps) to the behaviours and actions of its people, a new product offering, and an overhaul of the retail experience —going as far as a complete re-design of sales staff uniforms.

All of these adjustments were designed to deliver their core promise: To bring their customers closer to the people, the information and the entertainment they sought. To express this in a short tagline, we chose 'Get Closer'.

Over the course of two years, SmarTone reversed the decline and rose to the No. 2 spot. Net profit increased by 350% a year after the re-branding. They were nominated in Asia's top 20 brands and led the Hong Kong retail management association's service rankings.

In the analysts' report of the turnaround, Credit Suisse attributed effective brand management as one the three key reasons for SmarTone's success, a success that ultimately culminated in their partnership with Vodafone.

Shangri-La

We won the Shangri-La business by a lucky chance. They were expanding their network of outstanding 5-star hotels into North America and felt that expat brand strategists (as we were then) would have a better understanding of the market. If they'd known that our Brand Centered Management process would eventually lead them full circle back to their core Asian heritage and roots, perhaps they wouldn't have hired us! Fortunately for us (and them too, I like to think), they did.

I've been involved in more competitive pitches for business than I can remember. They've included every type of brand in a broad spectrum of categories. What I've always found to be axiomatic is the measures that pitching agencies would take to position themselves as 'category experts'—and for clients to encourage them to be so.

I can understand why. If you're in hotels, or airlines, or feminine hygiene, or property development, or fast food, or diamonds or whatever, it's comforting to work with people who 'speak your language'. Indeed most categories have developed their own language with acronyms and coded meanings that only insiders would understand. (Investment banking takes the biscuit on this one!)

For sure, it helps to endear oneself to a prospective client, and there is unquestionably comfort in familiarity. There is also value in better understanding the dynamics of a category and demonstrating to a prospect the effort you're prepared to make to make it a continuous learning curve.

My belief, though, has always been this: **You're not hiring us to be experts in your field. You're hiring us because we are experts in *our* field.**

Comfort in the category can lead to complacency or blindness to the changes going on in the outside world that impact your brand.

Innovation is much more likely to come from divergent thinking than convergent. Breakthrough ideas in categories typically come from outsiders. These are typically specialists in other fields that find themselves transported into a completely different category and transpose learnings from one category to another to create breakthrough ideas. This kind of cross-fertilisation can be seeded by specialist companies that can bring a breadth of cross-category experience to bear quickly on a problem.

Sometimes the breakthroughs are in innocent novices, young Turks who have not learnt the ropes yet and who stumble by accident or design on solutions. Because they don't know the rules, or haven't been programmed by the culture, they have no preconceived notions or assumptions. Established employees have already learned what management will and won't accept, what gets reinforced and what doesn't. I can't tell you how many times I've heard, 'We've tried that before and it didn't work'. Chances are they're right, but then again that might have been years ago. Times may have changed, and what failed then would work now. In a strange way, naivety can be an asset when it comes to innovation.

Owned by a prominent Asian family with diversified interests in property development, beverages and newspapers, the Shangri-La was their jewel in the crown. The Shangri-La group of hotels is synonymous with Asian elegance, style, and outstanding service. With flagship hotels in Singapore, Hong Kong, Bangkok, Beijing, and elsewhere in Asia, they were considering spreading the brand west into North America.

When they came to us, they had a very straightforward question: With so many excellent 5-star hotels offering superb facilities and service, how would Shangri-La stand apart? Should they become more Westernised in décor and demeanour to cater to this new market?

Our Discovery process quickly revealed that the essence of the brand lay in its Asian-ness, particularly the sensitive, feminine, caring aspects. Parts of the experience were symbolic — spacious reception areas with ornate chandeliers, the silks and cheongsam skirts of the waitresses, stunning Asian art, and graceful Asian hospitality.

Only one other hotel could credibly claim to provide a similar level of Asian hospitality — the flagship Peninsula Hotel in Hong Kong — but they had no plans to bring that style westward.

Looking at their brand critically, we realised that they might be uniquely positioned to bring an Asian hospitality experience to the West. The secret was in the name. Shangri-La is truly unique and evocative. Inspired by the fictional place in James Hilton's 1933 novel *Lost Horizon*, set in a utopian lamasery in a fictional country modeled on Tibet, the name Shangri-La evokes a tranquil idyll retreat, a lost imaginary world where time stands still. It is a restorative place for reflection, introspection, and nurturing. It has a Buddhist feel. It is a peaceful haven for restoring the soul. The name that evokes imagery no other hotel could own. We dug deeper into the heritage and the book to unlock the secret for the service offering, and then honed in on a forward-looking promise to keep the brand relevant in the future.

The DNA we developed for Shangri-La helped them visualise the promise and articulate the desired personality of the brand in a relevant and memorable way. It also gave a hint of the living nature of a DNA—something that evolves over a period of time, requiring honing and refinement to boil the essence down to only the essential elements that define the brand.

Brands like Shangri-La have a broad appeal to different types of customers. There is a big difference between business and leisure customers, for example. Searching for a happy middle ground can often result in broad catch-alls that satisfy neither group: you end up describing lowest common denominators instead of highest.

Some of the descriptors we used may have seemed too precise, but we tried to do everything we could to 'keep the edges sharp'. Fuzzy imagery and blurred edges create grey patches of nothingness in the brain that are soon forgotten because they don't imprint. We tried hard to create colourful, distinctive imagery and sharp relief. The more impossible it is to forget a positive image, the better it is.

Sometimes one part of a DNA resonates more than any other and becomes the hook or handle that people most associate it with. In the case of Shangri La this was the personality or spirit of the brand. Working with the client team to craft their DNA, the image that most resonated was 'An Asian Audrey Hepburn'.

The Shangri La was only one of the hotel brands owned by the group and part of the task that emerged was to define the brand architecture for the family of brands. The Brand DNA had to be broad enough to perform a parental task for the family of brands yet distinctive enough to differentiate it from competitors. It also had to be deliverable. Natural hosts delivering time-honoured Asian values in an enchanting, graceful, feminine way was the heart of the Shangri La brand experience, and continues to be.

AIA

The Brand DNA we developed for AIA demonstrates the contrast in brands. Where Shangri La was feminine, nurturing and graceful, AIA was all about masculinity, protectiveness and the notion of applied strength. At that time, their greatest asset was their visibility, size and financial strength in a category where all of those values provide reassurance for customers concerned if the life insurance policies they take out today will be honoured many years later.

At the time, AIA was Asia's largest life insurance company with billions of dollars in sales, so this wasn't a small company we were dealing with. As a leading provider of life insurance in Asia, AIA already had a high brand saliency and presence in the market. Anybody interested in life insurance knew AIA, and it was most likely the first brand that came to mind.

A common dilemma for consultants is being told by clients that you're only telling them what they already know. That's often true; it's rare that any consultant would know more about a client's

business than they do themselves. Why pretend otherwise?
The notion of strength for such a financially strong company might sound like the ultimate common sense 'no-brainer' to an outsider, but believe me, hindsight is a wonderful thing.

The issue is what they know is often buried under a million other things they also know. For AIA, 'strength' was there, but hidden away, obscured by hundreds of other promises and expressions.

I see the brand consultant's role as 'clearing the fog' – providing clarity, context and focus to enable our clients to make their own decisions.

It's a long journey to establish consistency in a huge, diversified organisation – you get there partly by design and partly by osmosis.

The Brand DNA becomes the beacon to direct everything the company DOES and SAYS.

So it started with the huge advantage of category leadership, but it also faced challenges. Under-insurance was both a problem and an opportunity. The emerging middle class in China perceived the value of insurance as lower priority, and the competition was intense.

The challenge with life insurance is selling a product which the purchasers never really want to use and won't be around to evaluate whether the promise was fulfilled. It's a topic most people would rather not have to think about, so most put it off until they become parents with responsibilities for their children that goes beyond their own lifetimes.

A couple of things struck us in the internal interviews in the Discovery process. One was the pride with which AIA executives treated their product and service. 'AIA never takes the trust of its customers for granted', we heard many times. We also discovered the multiple advantages that size and financial strength provided AIA's customers in terms of reassurance for return on investment in an unpredictable world. The ultimate benefit to AIA customers was the applied strength the company could bring to bear through their products.

From this promise of applied strength came the tagline: "Our strength is your strength."

The strength platform originated in Asia for AIA later became the central positioning platform for the AIG Group in the region. It's interesting to see how the benefit of the DNA has remained in their current positioning as 'your partner for life helping you and your loved ones to live longer, healthier and better lives'. I like the new expression even more than the original. It shows the evolution to the end benefit. The financial strength, applied to both corporate and personal, was always the means to an end to deliver the benefit of peace of mind and the ability to live life to the full.

St George's School

St George's School is a private boarding and day school for boys located in Vancouver, BC. It prides itself in being at the forefront in understanding and educating boys. If St George's were a retail store it would be 'Boys 'R Us!'

It goes way beyond academic and athletic records (although these are stellar). The school is a community of stakeholders with the boys at the heart of it. Shared values, character building and individuality are central themes along the journey to build fine young men, one boy at a time. Although it leads the rankings in almost every dimension, it doesn't rely on these for support. Rather, it challenges itself to find new relevant and currently immeasurable measures to achieve. It is constantly improving, with creative innovations in curriculum and learning environment.

Without a doubt, St. George's is a privileged community with high academic standards and selective entrance standards, but this is by no means a guarantee of success. The challenges of a diversified, engaged stakeholder community are formidable. There are differing views on educational philosophy and approach between different sets of parents, alumni, junior school, senior school and the faculty. And that's before the boy's opinions!

These challenges are all magnified by the educational revolution happening all over the world. With the advent of the information age spawned by the Internet, knowledge is literally at your fingertips. Information is accessible to more people in sufficient quantity to satisfy even insatiable appetites. The most revered educational establishments have had to consider how they are impacted. MOOCs (or Massive Open Online Courses) challenge the multi-billion dollar educational bricks and mortar business with access to courses online at a fraction of the cost and in the convenience of your hometown and home.

There's an increasing need to navigate the right path between the business of education and the business of businesses. In a multi-cultural environment, what does the right mix of religious and cultural diversity look like? What choices for sports or extra-curricular activities are optimal? Is it better to offer a wide range to satisfy all tastes, or to be stronger in a limited number? How many intelligences are there? Are the current assessment measures adequate for assessing multiple intelligences? These are just a few of the myriad questions facing schools today.

I was fortunate enough to be invited to help the school at the beginning of a long-term strategic planning project. I worked with the Chairman of the Board, the Headmaster and his leadership team to develop the long-term vision, mission and values for the school in the form of its Brand DNA, using our Brand Centered Management process.

Headmaster Dr Tom Matthews described how the Brand DNA was the genesis of the strategic plan in the school magazine *The Dragon*:

"This Strategic Plan represents the culmination of more than three years of hard work and extensive research and consultation. What began in 2008 as an exercise in branding soon morphed into a more ambitious strategic planning process. Defining the essence of St George's through a DNA statement, the participants identified a number of Pillars, which then became the focus for additional collaboration involving all stakeholder groups..."

This was the original St George's Brand DNA:

WE... build fine young men

WE WILL... develop happy, confident, well-rounded individuals inspired to fulfill their potential

IN ORDER TO... create men who shape positive futures for themselves, their families, and the global community

BY BEING... Canada's World School for Boys practicing twenty-first century renaissance principles without fear or favour

It was expressed in Mission and Vision terminology below:

MISSION: We educate and inspire boys to become fine young men shaping positive futures for themselves, their families and the global community.

VISION: Canada's World School for Boys

When it comes to crafting a DNA, what you call it is less important than how effective it is at inspiring and informing action. Although the key aspects of the DNA remain consistent, the way in which it is interpreted and represented varies. People come to express it in ways that are most meaningful to them. The Brand DNA was translated into the strategic plan that initially comprised four pillars (see The Four-Pillared Parthenon on page 153). These have been refined and expanded on during the ensuing years as each self-descriptive pillar was translated into detailed action plans: Project Endowment, Project Renaissance, Project Boarding, and Project Engage.

Project Endowment has been effectively hived off into its own division within advancement, but the focus on the need to raise substantial capital has enabled the plan to be realised. The endowment pot has increased tenfold since the inception of the plan. The plan also gave fund-raising a priority profile with a goal and an unashamed permission to 'go forth' to seek investment. It had a vision behind it that gave purpose to the ask, beyond building buildings. This was something more. It was about building a different value system and way of thinking. Building character in the boys, a belief in being able to provide an endowment fund that gave more opportunities for deserving boys with the capability but not the money to attend the school. The ultimate goal is to have at least 50% of the boys funded through endowment.

Project Boarding gave attention to a critical area of the school. Boarding brings the world to the school, opening borders and minds to different value systems, experiences, religions, and ways of thinking. Boarding was integral to the school; it's how it started out. But it was in decline, partly since the interests of boarders and those who only attend by day are at odds with each other. The strategic pillars drew attention to the need to support the boarding programmes and find ways to integrate it with the rest of the student body. Boarding has thrived since then, with a new head of boarding, a dedicated weekend curriculum, and expanded intake. Many of the students now want to partake in the boarders weekend activities.

The Renaissance, or innovative curriculum, pillar was always going to be the most demanding, though. It became the 'catchall' pillar for describing a new, more open approach to educating boys that took into consideration the scientific advancements in knowledge of brain physiology and development (and how it differs from girls). It also takes learning from common-sense experience of decades of teaching boys. For example, we've known for ages that boys are more kinesthetic. They fidget and need to move around more and more often than girls, so giving them environments where they're allowed to do this freely helps with classroom attentiveness. A whole discipline was put in place to codify the knowledge about how boys learn and the consequences for educating them.

Finally, Project Engage is an ongoing communication programme to and for the community. It seeks to highlight the work being done behind the scenes and grow the potential student body. As a result of this outreach, St George's received a glowing endorsement from CAIS (Canadian Accredited Independent Schools) for the full embodiment of vision and translation into action. But more than awards or endorsements you can see the benefits of having a solid strategic plan emanating from a well-crafted brand DNA. The school is thriving and continues to strengthen its position as one of the most admired and progressive schools in Canada, appealing to students from across the globe.

> I always take pleasure in revisiting an organisation years after a brand-building project and seeing the effects of the seeds that were sown. The Boys of Character pillar at St George's is one small example of a seed that produced a multi-coloured flower that blooms throughout the year. Character was translated into six values that the boys themselves defined as most reflecting the desired character of a St George's boy: Empathy, Resilience, Humility, Respect, Integrity and Respect.
>
> When my then Grade 5 son proudly announced out of the blue that he'd been nominated by one of his peers for the 'man of character' award, I knew this initiative had seeped through to the grassroots level and resonated where it mattered most, with the boys.

It would be doing an injustice to the tremendous work the leadership team, faculty and the whole St George's community has put into developing the strategy and bringing it to life to suggest that this simple four pillar strategy was the answer. It wasn't.

What it was, though, was the starting point of change. Eight years into the execution of the strategy, it has evolved into a much more complex and detailed plan.

The Brand DNA Development Workshop

I have customers come to me asking to jump straight to the Brand DNA. Why can't we do that now, it's only a few words?

Well, it happens that Brand DNAs are often best forged in the heat of a DNA development workshop that is conducted in a day. A lot of preparation work should be done ahead of time, though, to make everything work on that day.

I have seen companies try to cram their Brand DNA discussion into a rushed three-hour workshop session with a group of people who've only just met for the first time. The end result wasn't bad, and most people left feeling as if they'd achieved something and been listened to. The problem is that if you rush to build without fully understanding the issues and the opportunities, or without building on solid, level, deep foundations, you end up building a house of straw on shifting sands.

What we say to our clients is invest in the building materials— proper planning, quality building materials and a sound foundation— then build a house of brick. Something that will withstand the test of time and the inevitable harsh conditions it will have to endure. Spend some time with the Discovery tools in Part 1 of this book, and make sure you have a good handle on your company's strengths, weaknesses, and goals before you approach Brand DNA.

Once you are ready, there are three factors that are critical to a successful Brand DNA Development session: the right number and mix of participants, the right preparation with rich, well prepared stimulus material, and the right environment.

The Right People
The ideal number of participants is between 8 to 16. I've done sessions with as few as six people and as many as 60, but the ideal number is around 12. This gives enough richness of diversity but is small enough to have deep involvement from every individual with everyone's voices heard. It allows the group to be divided many ways into teams of two, three, four or six people. When forming teams I try to match complementary skill sets so you get the debate within the groups rather than between them. I find this results in more constructive discussion of difficult choices and better resolution of differences. Small groups of three or four tend to try to 'get along' while acknowledging differences. Even if they have to agree to differ, there tends to be greater respect in smaller groups and less 'ganging-up'. Teams tend to unite to defend their choices and that creates healthy debate when ideas are shared.

Who should attend? Everyone who participates should have the long-term interest of the brand at heart. They must want the brand to succeed and prosper.

They should have the courage to speak their minds and fight for what they believe to be the truth. Surprisingly, they do not have to be senior experienced authorities in their brand or even in their category (remember that innovative change is often brought by experts from other categories applying insight from 'other worlds'). I like to get a mix of junior, middle and senior management, a good gender mix, and some external or outside representation. It helps of course to have the problem owner or leader and their key team members there because attendees are the most likely to own what they've authored.

There are many ways of extending ownership and a feeling of contribution in cascading the process through the organisation to refine the Brand DNA beyond the workshop. The BCM process is designed to cascade responsibility and ownership throughout the organisation.

In most instances this will be a senior group with a sprinkling of the best and brightest young members and one or two invited outsiders. I have facilitated workshops where a senior competitor attended and contributed to crafting a terrific Brand DNA. There was perceived value for both parties in this cooperation with the recipients getting the benefit of a competitive perspective and the competitor being given an insight into a process that enriched him. Of course, these occasions require mutual respect and the ability to make the decision to attend (or, rather, to be able to overcome standard norms that would prevent competitors even walking into the lobby of 'the enemy').

I believe competition is healthy and engendering a degree of rivalry can accelerate advancements within categories. I also believe some of the measures to protect secrets, ideas, and intellectual property are futile and ignore the laws of human nature. Do I think it's wrong to steal other people's ideas? Of course it is. How difficult is it to prove that someone else didn't just come up with the same idea, though? Very! Integrity is a perception. Where the truth lies is dependent on multiple perspectives, not necessarily what actually happened. One human truth is that history is written by the victors, so the best way of protecting your ideas is to execute them successfully and own them through perception.

Anyone familiar with the 'Pandemonium' model of perception will relate to the fact that it's not always the first to market that becomes the perceived owner of ideas. It's more likely to be the one that gets to the top of that particular hill first and shouts loudest and longest.

There needs to be the right amount of friction within the group. By that, I don't mean fisticuffs. I mean a healthy difference of opinion—enough to grasp nettles and dig into the marrow of meaty differences in a respectful and constructive way. You need sharp flints to create sparks. A group of like-minded head-nodders rarely generate anything edgy or revolutionary.

More important than being revolutionary—more often it's simply positive evolution we're looking for—is avoiding the trap of groupthink. Groupthink is when everyone goes away feeling they've done a good job, but really they've not got beneath the surface of the real issues or searched for innovation that will make a real difference. Complacency can creep into some sessions where agreement comes too easily. Unanimity is rare in these sessions and consensus implies compromise, so sometimes people have to leave with a feeling of 'close but not quite there'. And that is often a very good result.

You don't want one or two participants dominating the workshop either. This is especially difficult if the leader is a dominant type that likes to speak first and have the followers follow. I always brief the leader to hold back their comments until the end of a discussion. Casting votes, either verbally or physically, can direct others to follow whether intended or not. We want everyone's voice to be heard and everyone's vote to be equal.

I've only once had to ask a senior client member *not* to attend a Brand DNA development workshop. I do a certain amount of organisational culture assessment in the Discovery process that gives me a decent sense of how a particular client organisation is going to behave in a creative strategic workshop.

This individual was highly successful in his role as General Manager and had terrific attributes for the role including discipline, order and organisation. He was also a bit of a tyrant and intimidated many of his staff. I foresaw a situation in which the majority of attendees would be uncomfortable opening up and guarded in their responses. From my experience with him, I doubted he could play the silent game without leading the group, so I politely suggested we hold the session without him. To his credit he agreed and the end result was something he could be proud of.

Attendees are discussed with the client leadership team and carefully selected to create a balance of youth and experience, wisdom and what I call smart naivety. Smart naivety often comes with newcomers to an organisation. They may be young 'greenhorns' or experienced players who have recently joined the organisation and are not yet familiarised (or influenced/tamed) by the rules. They are typically the ones who ask the naive questions that old hands don't bother to ask any more because they know the answer will be 'no'. Or they could bring fresh insight from another category, or a grasp of technology or something new to the group.

People often tell me they're not good in group sessions because they're not extroverted. We look for a balance of extroverts and introverts. Introverts tend to be good active listeners and good at summing up situations with a few well-spoken words.

The Right Preparation

Essential to success is the preparation of the right stimulus material for the workshop. Central to this is the Discovery Report. This should be thorough, insightful and already 'signed off' or approved by the team leader. The Brand DNA development workshop is not the place to reveal big surprises to the leadership team or to embark on lengthy discussion about contentious points. The Discovery Report, often in condensed format, is there to bring everyone up to speed quickly and to get everyone on the same page.

What it should do is provide clarity on some points in relation to the brand. It should also be able to highlight the main challenges and opportunities for the brand moving forward. Getting respondents to better empathise with how different stakeholder groups perceive the brand is also extremely valuable in stretching the thought process.

There are several other stimulus tools and tricks to 'get those little grey cells working' as Hercule Poirot would say. These are not just interesting mind games but are made directly relevant to the brand.

Depending on the client and the discovery findings we tailor-make two or three thought-starters that begin the process of creative thinking.

Opposites

Opposites is a quick fire 'first thought that comes into your mind' complete-in-60-seconds task that cleverly identifies Top of Mind (TOM) perceptions about the brand. Here's an example of a template:

What are you? (Don't think too hard about it.)

Adults	Children
Global	Local
Family	Individual
Inclusive	Exclusive
Liberal	Conservative
Risk Taker	Risk Avoider
Masculine	Feminine
Boring	Fun
Young	Old
Spontaneous	Cautious
Extrovert	Introvert
Formal	Informal

It doesn't have to be a precise science; the group can very quickly begin to see through the mist, some things more clearly than others.

Portraits

Another useful stimulus tool is using a selection of images or still portraits, often taken from past and current marketing material for the brand such as brochures, advertisements, leaflets, pictures, people and so on.

Then it's a simple picture sorting exercise: rank the images according to those that are 'most' and 'least' your brand. We try to use images that have already been associated with the brand in some way because it means they've already been through some sort of selection filter. Even then, you'll find many are deemed by their own people as 'not us'.

Visual images are good for prompting rich discussion and evoking memories that might otherwise be forgotten or missed. This is a useful way of bringing historical aspects of the brand into the discussion to assess their relevance without spending too much time looking to the past rather than looking forward.

Stand Against

This is a way of getting to what the brand stands for by starting with the easier approach of what the brand stands against.

Imagine your brand is protesting. What would the protest banner or placard it was holding say? For a fashion company, it might be:

- 'Down with bad taste'

- 'Good style for everyone'

- 'Down with grey suits!'

- 'Shoes for President!'

These are simple but effective ways of setting the tone for a creative development session while adding useful input.

Development Workshop Logistics

The third element essential to the success of a Brand DNA development workshop is the right environment. Experience has taught me to *always* do a recce to ensure the environment is conducive to a creative session.

Having enough space to accommodate the size of the group,

with enough room to move around and shift into breakout groups, is essential. Better still to have different spaces outside the main session room for teams to hold breakouts. I try to make it a rule not to hold these important DNA development sessions in a new or unfamiliar venue that hasn't been 'checked out'. Occasionally that's impossible—for example, when the group is overseas for an event. In those cases, take every measure possible to get visual references of rooms and facilities and ask what potential problems there may be. I have had images of rooms look perfect—good space, natural light and so on—only to find on arrival it's looking over a busy rail line with trains roaring past every few minutes!

Often clients ask to hold the session in their offices, both for convenience and to save money. Good reasons, and sometimes this is perfectly fine, but I prefer these meetings to be off-site if possible. It gives an added sense of importance and neutralises territory.

A typical Brand DNA Development Workshop Agenda
A typical agenda for a brand DNA workshop might look something like this real example:

Brand DNA Development Workshop, Friday 6 July

12.30	Assemble and sandwich lunch
1.00	Introduction: Purpose of Workshop What makes great brands great? Criteria for building strong brands
1.30	Discovery Report Highlights
2.00	Brand Exploration Exercises: two creative exercises to express the brand
2.30	Alternative Positioning Routes: presentation and appraisal
3.00	Coffee / Tea Break
3.10	Brand DNA Development: Promise & Benefit
4.00	Brand DNA Development: Brand Spirit expression exercises
5.00	Brand DNA refinement: Role exercise (if required)
5.30	Summary, next steps
5.45	Wrap

As with every formal meeting it helps to have an agenda with a schedule for the day, morning or afternoon. The Brand DNA Development workshops often gather several senior executives together and it's hard to get into their diaries to lock in a time that works for everybody. It needs to be scheduled well in advance. With large organisations, sometimes this can be as much as 6 to 9 months in advance. Others may only need a few weeks. Either way the time needs to be maximised. Done properly these are invigorating, stimulating sessions that are also mentally exhausting. Planning the efficient use of time is essential to cover the ground that needs to be covered while keeping things moving.

That said, these are not rigid run-by-the-clock affairs. As all good facilitators know, there needs to be flexibility. If the group is on a roll in generating productive creative solutions, let it run. Conversely if you're meeting resistance or low energy, break off and regroup. Experience allows the practised Brand DNA development workshop facilitator to know what can be achieved in the time available, when to intervene to hurry things along and when to step back and let things run free.

Some parts of the Brand DNA are easier to produce than others. Most find it easy to generate a long list of adjectives to describe the spirit or culture of the organisation, for example. Condensing these to the three or four that are most meaningful may be harder to do in the time; it's okay to have a slightly longer shortlist that can be boiled down after the session.

Capturing the role or purpose of the brand may be more difficult. People find it difficult to be singular. Brands and organisations are complex, multi-faceted organisms with many benefits and meanings they argue, with some justification. A large part of the Brand DNA process is to disaggregate these into their separate singular attributes. It's a bit like unravelling a complex knot to reveal the two or three strands that really hold it all together.

There are a few tricks to help with the process. One of them is to ban the use of 'and'. So you can't bolt-on thoughts, they have to be posted in singular thought-packets. The benefit of this is that it allows comparison within and between teams. With multiple teams, each generating singular thoughts that they prioritise it's easy to share and compare. With, say, four teams each prioritising three singular thoughts, the important 'ands' that one team may have sacrificed will likely be represented in another team's output. As a combined group output they are captured and become important thoughts in their own right rather than add-ons.

Brand Blueprints and Brand Books

WHAT THIS TOOL DOES

Every brand needs a blueprint—a documented plan of what it intends to be in the future. It's amazing how basic this is and yet how few brand-builders do it well. The Brand DNA (page 102) is my preferred brand blueprint, but it is not the only useful method. In the same way that Brand Centered Management™ is an inclusive, strategic model-agnostic approach, so can Brand Blueprints accommodate other useful tools. Vision, Mission, and Value (VMV) statements are widely used and this section touches on the benefits of these, as well as pointing out some of the deficiencies of them.

If a property developer asked their building constructers to start building without an architect's blueprint we'd think they were foolish. What kind of building would they construct? Who is it for? What function does it perform? What's it going to look like? How tall, long, wide? What's going to make it stand out from every other building? What materials are you going to use? What's going to make people want to live or work there? What kind of ambience and experience are you trying to create?

It seems ridiculous to suggest a builder would start building without having a clear plan of what they were going to construct, yet that's what thousands of *brand*-builders do every year. They start building their brand without a well thought-through design or plan.

It's a common problem. Brand-builders are in a rush to see something physical they can touch...a logo, an advertising campaign, a shop interior or a product prototype. Few take a measured step back to develop a proper strategic blueprint for their brand before 'diving in'.

A well-crafted blueprint for the brand—based on a Brand DNA analysis—provides strategic clarity and focus. It gives a clearer picture in the mind of the constructors of exactly what they are being asked to build.

Despite all the marketing literature, all the seminars and all the evidence in the market place, it's still a challenge to persuade clients to invest sensibly in the intangible area of brand strategy. But this is precisely what delivers the tangibles. It helps with 'right first time' delivery, faster with fewer mistakes.

Companies waste millions of dollars rushing to execute a flawed strategy—or a half-baked one—when a little experienced planning could have prevented the problem.

As one of my favourite quotes aptly puts it:

"If you don't know where you are going, all paths take you there".

I should caution anyone who thinks they've got a strategy for their brand and there's no need to read from this point onward, that this is probably the single biggest reason why brands don't have good blueprints—their owners think 'we've done all that'—'ticked that box'. They also forget that they don't own their brands; their customers do. Brands are what customers think they are; not what brand owners tell them. They're in a constant state of flux and in need of regular maintenance to ensure relevancy.

But if I ask brand owners if they have a blueprint, it's surprising how many blank looks I get. What do I mean? Yes, we have a marketing plan and a communications plan. Is that what you mean?

Well, not really. You see, a Brand Blueprint is much more than a plan for how you're going to allocate an annual budget. It's a strategic plan for how you are going to construct your brand over the long term. What the core pillars or constructs are that will hold the brand up and stand the test of time. What the benefits of the brand are and what the desired experience or out-take is for brand-users. How it will stand itself apart from other brands. What bits of the brand are sacrosanct and what can be experimented with?

It's less about the building materials and precise detail or dimensions and more about the desired experience; how you want users to feel about the brand and therefore why you think building it this way, to serve this purpose, using these materials and looking something like this, will work.

Vision, Mission, and Values

There are different definitions for VMV statements and I've selected the ones I like best below:

Vision

A word picture of your company in the future. The willed future, expressed in words that is:

- Leader-initiated
- Inspiring
- Aspirational

- Complete and concise
- Tangible (and recognisable when you've got there)

A vision is always, tantalizingly, a finger-tip out of reach.

Mission
The purpose for your organisation, or your 'raison d'être'. What you wake up for every morning (with a passion) to do for your customers.

Values
What you believe in and stand for.

The pros of having these statements comes from the exercise of going through the shared process of thinking about the desired future in a customer-oriented way. It is liberating to let go of the constraints of today's reality to think about creating a better future. It is useful to have a set of values against which performance can be measured. Good VMV statements can be invaluable tools for organisations to help them set and achieve 'stretch' goals.

The cons of these instruments are that too often they become box-ticking exercises, delegated to the marketing department or a handful of individuals. The organisation is not involved or engaged in the process. The process can be rushed and superficial resulting in a set of bland platitudes that could apply to any organisation (try it with your own statements if you don't believe me). Once the exercise has been completed, the box ticked, it goes straight from the website to the shelf to gather dust.

Brand Books

There isn't any one template to create the perfect blueprint. Every organisation will have something different about the way they construct their blueprint. The important thing is that they *have* one.

Brand Books are useful in this respect. The concept of having a book that captures the essence of what the brand is, stands for and where it's going is easy for customers to grasp. It can often be combined with 'Look Book' visual identity guidelines that describe how the brand should be represented graphically.

I encourage my clients to produce physical Brand Books that can be picked up and read. They are terrific lobby coffee-table reading and of course can then be represented in digital and social media formats.

They work best in two parts; the strategic 'thinking' part that explains the positioning of the brand and the Brand DNA, and the 'doing' part that expresses that positioning in tangible design-related forms such a visual language, logomarks, written language, brand properties and icons.

These books require thought and skill, but they don't need to be long or expensive to produce. Self-publishing is accessible and affordable.

Here is a skeleton structure of a Brand Book you may find useful:

BRAND

1. Introduction
A succinct summary of who you are, what you believe and why – your elevator pitch in a sentence or two

2. History
A short summary of how the brand started, your roots, traditions and characteristics

3. Brand DNA
Description of your Brand DNA, itself a succinct summary of positioning, promise and culture

4. Vision, Mission, Values
A sentence or two for each in this recognised VMV format, if it adds without replication

5. Positioning
A short description of who the brand is for and why, if required

6. Our Customers
A description in simple terms of who your target audience is, often described as an individual. Often requires descriptions of main customer segments, archetypes and their differences

7. Our Voice
The tone and manner of the brand. How it speaks to your target customers

8. Where Customers Meet our Brand
A description of the touch points where the customer or stakeholder is most likely to experience the brand

9. Reach / Media
A short summary of the media—traditional, social and other—typically used by the brand to connect with your customers

10. Our Community
A description of your core community – what binds the core brand loyalists

11. Products and Services
A brief description of the main products and services offered

12. Packaging
The what and why of your brand packaging

13. Our Future
Your hopes and aspirations for the brand in a nutshell

Visual Identity
This section is a design guide targeted towards marketers, graphic designers and creatives who are working with the brand. It serves both as a helpful instruction manual as well as policing guide to ensure consistent representation of the brand.

It may be part of a Brand Book or a standalone 'Look Book' guide in its own right. For large international brands with multiple franchisees and outlets, these guidelines can run into hundreds of pages. For most, a concise, neatly illustrated guide of 15 to 30 pages is adequate.

1. Our logo

2. Logo States/Arrangements

3. File Types

4. Logo Do's and Dont's

5. Logo Padding and Minimum Size

6. Brand Colour Palette + Usage

7. Typography

8. Typesetting

9. Illustration

10. Supporting Elements

11. Photography

12. Legibility / Special Cases

13. Using our Logo with Images

Make the Right Promise

WHAT THIS TOOL DOES

This tool identifies the four criteria of successful promises: Relevant, Differentiating, Compelling, Credible. If your promises are all four of these, chances are you are going to build a strong brand. Without one or two your boat is not going to hold water.

At The Brand Company, we deliberated for long hours over beers on the roof of the Foreign Correspondents Club in Hong Kong about a single, perplexing question: What was it about the promises made by the strong brands that stood them apart?

We came up with four characteristics that applied across the board.

Relevant

Relevance is essential. If the promise is meaningless or irrelevant to the target it is pointless to excel at it.

Your product or service must carry meaningful value to its customers. It sounds so blindingly obvious that it should go without saying, but all too often it's forgotten.

Relevance is something that needs to be constantly checked. What was relevant yesterday can quickly become irrelevant tomorrow. Sometimes the transition from once relevant to now irrelevant is slow and managed. Sail gave way to steam gradually as the cost and time taken to transition 'inventory' that still worked was slow and expensive. At other times it's immediate. The atomic bomb changed the relevance of conventional weaponry in an instant.

So relevance is the starting point.

Differentiating

Does your promise differentiate you from your competitors? Unless you're promising something different (and superior) to them, how do you expect your performance to differ from theirs?

The need to stand apart and be noticed is the other side of the relevance coin—the two must always go hand in hand.

"See the naked lady—buy my matches" as the phrase goes, describes how attention-grabbing without relevance simply doesn't work. In fact it is likely to irritate and diminish the appeal.

So the promise has to offer something different to customers.

Compelling

Is the promise you're making compelling? Does it engage the customer, arouse interest, appeal to their senses?

"You can't bore people into buying your product," as David Ogilvy said, "you can only interest them into it."

You can be relevant and differentiating without being compelling. And that's okay if you accept that you won't be of interest to every target customer—but you must be compelling to your desired target audience: the brand loyalists who will comprise the bulk of your profitable business.

So compelling is another essential criterion.

Credible

Finally, we concluded all the greatest brand promises were credible. Did you do what you said you would do? Without credibility, the three other criteria are meaningless.

Delivering against your promise is the key reason why strong brands grow strong. It is the foundation of trust. It is built up over multiple repetitions of successful experiences that reinforce the perception of honesty and trustworthiness that merits a customer's loyalty.

Remember these four criteria every time you think about the promise your brand is making to your customers. Fall short on any one and you lose the balance and stability of a solid brand platform to build on. Deliver against them and you will enjoy great success.

Brand Driver Matrix

WHAT THIS TOOL DOES

This is based on a McKinsey model that traces back to Herzberg's psychological two-factor theory. It helps identify what attributes of a brand actively drive preference based on relevance and differentiation.

Frederick Herzberg identified two factors in his hygiene-motivator theory of job satisfaction. He proposed that job satisfaction and job dissatisfaction were separate entities and determined by two different sets of factors, both of which had to be managed to create a productive, happy workplace. Hygiene factors are things that, no matter how much you improve, can only get you to a base level of satisfaction. If you ignore them or get them wrong however, they can have a significant negative impact.

Money is, perhaps surprisingly, a hygiene factor. People relate what they're paid to what they deserve—they rarely believe they're worth less than they're paid. Somehow, even the most outrageous bonuses paid to some are justified on the grounds of 'having earned it'. Other hygiene factors are things like work environment—'so what if you've upgraded the toilets, they were disgusting before...so what if you've provided a creche, put in a gym, given us all individual work space and refurbished the lobby—have you seen what the people at Apple get—free buffet at their own restaurant!' You get the idea. A safe, pleasant work environment with proper compensation is the minimum price of entry for employees.

Motivators on the other hand, are factors that can positively motivate employees and lead to greater job satisfaction. This includes personal development, growth or professional development, reward and recognition, intrinsic interest in the work (passion), achievement and responsibility.

So rather than think of satisfaction as one continuum, Herzberg proposed they were two separate factors, both of which had to be managed independently.

I encourage clients to think of the two-factor theory when they think of building their brands. What factors that you are currently promoting as motivators are actually hygiene factors? I think of hygiene factors as only ever being able to get you to base zero... you can only go negative with hygiene factors, as these are base expectations of the customer. Still, it's a lot better to be zero than a large minus number. If you fail to maintain your hygiene factors at or above the category norm you will lose competitive advantage.

Thinking about price as a hygiene factor—something that can only get you to zero, never above it—has interesting implications for brands. I was schooled in the old-school discipline of SOQNOP—Sell on Quality, not on Price. For fighting or value brands it may play a more significant role in positioning relative to competitors and establishing a low entry point mark for the category, but it often comes at the cost of lower perception of quality. There is truth in the statement that we don't value what we don't pay for.

When I worked on Shell, we went to great lengths to dissuade them from entering promotional wars with their competitors. Selling on price, or on promotions for 'widgits' is selling for other reasons than your core brand. Promotions are easily neutralised by competitors, but once a promotional war breaks out they are difficult to stop. The oil companies stuck to an agreement between themselves for many years before a new Chairman of one of them was tempted to launch a retail promotion—it was the first £1 million prize giveaway. It took them several years before 'peace talks' stopped the promotions war. By then, the cost of running promotions had escalated to astronomical proportions, the main winners being the manufacturers of cheap drinking glasses that by then filled every kitchen cupboard in Britain!

Working with McDonald's in Asia, promotional widgets had become such an integral part of their strategy that there was a danger of them losing sight of their core business. When higher profits can be made retailing cheap plastic toys than selling hamburgers there's a real danger the fundamental nature of your business model changes.

Before the promotions companies call foul, promotions can play a valuable role to stimulate interest, create fun and encourage trial in the short term. Strategic promotions can even add value to the brand (the 'Put a tiger in your tank' that Esso ran in the 70s giving furry tiger tails away with petrol purchase was a good reinforcement of the perception of having more powerful fuel and a direct association with their tiger symbol).

Ultimately, one way or another, the cost of promotions gets passed on to consumers.

When a competitor launches a successful promotion, it's very difficult to sit back and watch market share erode. Even if promotions tend to appeal first to the fickle 'brand switchers' who are less likely to be loyal to any brand and therefore low lifetime value acquisitions—it's still difficult to watch numbers go down and do nothing.

My advice on promotions has always been to avoid getting into them if you can. If you must, use them as a defensive means to neutralise an opponent swiftly and permanently, in order to get back to differentiating your brand on a more solid platform. Think about it. With everything we've just been saying about differentiating on emotional platforms, motivating factors, delivering tangible experiences...what do promotions do? They tend to give distracting reasons *other than the core benefit of the brand*, which are temporary and relatively easy to counter.

As with employee satisfaction, brand satisfaction and preference is driven by motivators. How does the brand make me feel?

The Brand Driver Matrix helps assess which brand attributes are the most relevant to your desired target group and which are the most differentiating.

BRAND DRIVER MATRIX

HIGH

HYGIENE
Attributes that are important to consumers but are provided by all competitors at a similar level.

DRIVERS
Attributes that are both important to consumers and highly differentiated from those of the competition.

RELEVANT

IRRELEVANT
Attributes that are neither relevant or differentiating to consumers

FOOLS GOLD
Attributes that are distinctive to the brand, but not meaningful to consumers.

LOW

DIFFERENTIATED

HIGH

130

Attributes that are neither relevant to customers nor differentiating are clearly not valid. Those that are both relevant and differentiating are the most desirable.

The matrix is useful for highlighting where clients are investing too much in building the 'hygiene factors'—those benefits that are relevant to customers but no different from what your competitors are offering. Another pitfall is the 'fool's gold' quadrant of pushing things that are different but are not meaningful to customers.

This last quadrant is a common trap for brands; it's difficult to resist pursuing something you know is different from competitors and the belief that 'consumers just need to get used to it' (which is sometimes the case) when in fact they're providing something that doesn't mean that much to them.

Practical Segmentation

WHAT THIS TOOL DOES

This tool is a concept for applying the principles of customer segmentation in a practical way that is easy to assimilate and understand. It also enables users to short-cut expensive quantitative data analysis saving time and money. In this tool, I use examples developed by David Black, founder of Blackbox, Singapore.

One of the problems we frequently encounter with customer segmentation programmes—if they exist at all—is that they are often scientific in their findings with complex statistical modeling to define clusters, but impractical to implement. Often they are usage or behaviour-driven because this is easier to measure, but critically short on the 'rich differentiators' of attitude and motivations.

I encourage our customers to narrow their target customers into different **interest groups**. What is it that interests a particular group of people about your particular category and what is the underlying motivation behind that interest?

Not everybody buys a product or service for the same reason. If you're in the hotel trade, some customers are primarily interested in the conference facilities you have to offer. Others are interested in the food and beverage. Others like the competitiveness of your room-rates, or the leisure facilities you offer, and so on. And of course, the same people can be interested in different things at different times: the most convenient accommodation close to the office today and the most relaxing resort for a holiday break tomorrow.

Once an interest group has been identified, the scale of importance of the group in terms of numbers and $ potential can be calculated. Interest groups can then be categorised and prioritised.

The important point here is that a small amount of qualitative research up front to identify the 'rich meaning'—what feelings, beliefs and attitudes motivate different interest groups to behave how they do—can save thousands of dollars in expensive quantitative analysis later.

Typically, segmentation studies we encounter are based on factor or cluster analyses of existing quantitative data, which is normally lower-order usage and selected attitudes rather than open-ended. For example, it's common to have sales data on each type of goods over time, often you'll have price data and location too—but there's nothing about the 'why' customers purchase.

Typical segmentation constructs are divided into three categories that 'drive' the segmentation: Functional, Behavioural and Motivational.

Functional drivers are things like $ spend and $ profit contribution, usage frequency and loyalty (tenure).

Behavioural drivers are factors like lifestage and lifestyle. And motivational drivers are the 'rich insights' such as perceptions, attitude and beliefs—the reasons why people in that interest group behave the way they do and have the functional purchase habits they have.

Most often, segmentation studies begin and end with the functional data. Tracking studies or Omnibus surveys tend to concentrate on functional aspects because these are easier to 'count'. Sometimes behavioural information is thrown into the mix. Remember, it's often the things you can't count that count the most.

What practical segmentation does is work from the rich data of motivational insight early in the process, marry it with data on customer value, then work backwards to quantify a hypothesis.

As the segmentation process chart below shows, it begins with defining what customer value means to the brand or organisation, then identifying working segments by value and loyalty (i.e. lifetime value).

The Pareto Principle is a useful rule of thumb—the assumption that 20% of your users will account for 80% of your profit. (My experience suggests the concept is valid but it's closer to 30:70...i.e. 30% of customers account for 70% of profit). Recognising this allows you to concentrate on properly identifying that 20%. For our Hong Kong telecom client we identified one high value segment that was astronomically profitable: travelling C-Officers with gatekeeper secretaries. At that time, roaming charges were very high and these customers would run up hefty bills from overseas visits. We suspected they didn't even look at their monthly bills as these were automatically paid by their secretaries or administrative staff. As you can imagine, the value of one of these customers was several multiples more than the average and a dedicated special team was assigned to handle them.

Qualitative research early through interviews, buddy-groups, or focus groups helps identify the motivations of these working segments. Combining insights from customer value data and customer motivation

THE SEGMENTATION PROCESS

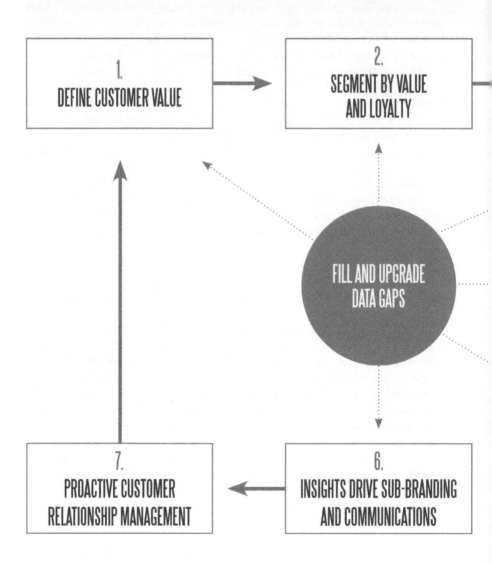

1.
DEFINE CUSTOMER VALUE

2.
SEGMENT BY VALUE
AND LOYALTY

FILL AND UPGRADE
DATA GAPS

7.
PROACTIVE CUSTOMER
RELATIONSHIP MANAGEMENT

6.
INSIGHTS DRIVE SUB-BRANDING
AND COMMUNICATIONS

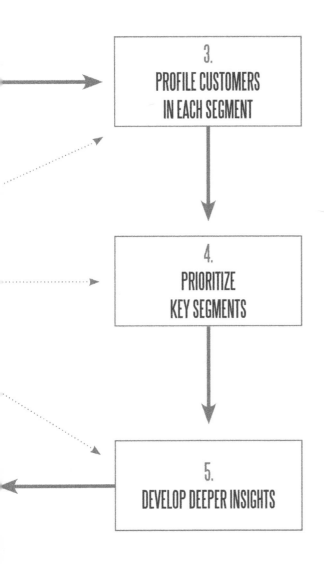

3.
PROFILE CUSTOMERS
IN EACH SEGMENT

4.
PRIORITIZE
KEY SEGMENTS

5.
DEVELOP DEEPER INSIGHTS

data allows one to hypothesise the number of interest groups based on underlying motivations and estimated lifetime value. Further quantitative analysis can then test the hypothesis and determine the number and size of interest groups.

I have seen statistical tools such as factor or cluster analysis come back with 13, 14 or 15 segments—too many to practically be able to market to.

It can be helpful to impose a limit on the number of segments to say five, up to a maximum of seven, in order to keep it practical to execute.

Once customers in each value segment have been motivationally profiled, the segments can be refined and prioritised. Further insights can be obtained that drive brand strategy and communications.

Don't dismiss the low value segments. Some of them are low value now but will transition to high value over time. You might find that a low value segment is quite large and that there are ways of handling them more efficiently that can raise profitability.

Good segmentation early in the Brand Centered Management process has many benefits. It focuses marketing effort and resources and can help companies develop discrete strategies for approaching each segment. It helps create tailor-made product and service offerings and can inform brand strategy in terms of sub-brand development and brand architecture. Do you have the right number and type of brands to match the needs of your valued customer interest groups? Does one brand adequately cover them?

Design and packaging offerings can be modified to suit the specific needs of different interest groups.

And customer loyalty and retention strategy can be determined by forecasting the lifetime value of each segment.

I've seen good segmentation studies literally transform organisations. Internal restructuring of customer teams to match the special needs of identified interest groups for example, as one large general customer service group becomes three or four specialised units each catering to the specific need of a different segment.

The end result for our customer took the nine identified segments and boiled them down to three, based largely on motivational and behavioural characteristics: business, social and family. This made it easier to manage mass media and to bundle services and promotions around each broad interest group.

Brand Family Architecture

WHAT THIS TOOL DOES

This tool explains how brand families are defined according to the inter-relationships between family members. It describes how brand family architecture can be analysed by type in existing organisations. It provides a platform for creating or refining a portfolio of brands.

The family is a related group of brands within an organisation, be it corporate, range, product or service. The architecture of the family demonstrates the positioning of each brand in the family and the relationships between them.

A single brand name is focused. It is easier to remember than multiple names and easier to control. Several brand names may be more individualised and suit more tastes, but are harder and more costly to manage. A brand family can provide the best of both worlds: a single, integrated, mutually reinforcing system of brands.

There are three broad architecture types:

- Monolithic—Those that have a close bond to the parent through a single shared name

- Endorsed—Those that have an association to the parent (from strong to loose bonds)

- Independent—Those that are distant from the parent

Monolothic Brand Family Architecture

Examples of monolithic brand families are Shell, Disney and Virgin. The parent or corporate name is singular and strongly associated with all the offerings (e.g. Shell UK, Shell Chemical, Shell Bitumen, Shell Aviation etc.). Purpose and personality are similar across the offerings. The target group is homogenous, with similar attitudes toward the category. The corporate brand plays a powerful role in endorsing the range of product or service brands as they share many similar characteristics. Every time the Shell or Disney brand name is reinforced, it reinforces every product brand carrying the name.

Mutual reinforcement is an asset and having a single, shared brand name helps 'deposit brand equity in the same bank account'. The risk is that, if disaster strikes, every member suffers. If the corporate brand gets sick, everyone catches a cold. When the Exxon Valdez oil spill occurred, there were protests outside Esso stations all over the world.

Endorsed Brand Family Architecture

Endorsed architectures allow companies to vary the level of association with the 'mother brand' according to need. They allow for a greater degree of autonomy and independence for divisions or products that have a distinct purpose and personality.

An example of a closely endorsed brand family is Armani. Giorgio Armani, Emporio Armani and Armani Exchange provide a range of designer offerings from exclusive to mainstream. The number of brand family members can change according to need (Armani Collezione and Armani jeans were recently removed from the portfolio).

TimeWarner, the media and entertainment giant, also has an endorsed brand family, but at a lower level. HBO, Turner and Warner Bros. are divisions of TimeWarner but also behemoths in their own right, with distinctive identities.

Microsoft is an endorsed brand family that sits somewhere in the middle. It has a strong parent brand name association with brand family members, but with each of those members also having strong individual identities: Microsoft Windows, Microsoft Office, Microsoft Xbox, Microsoft Surface—each work with the parent name or without.

Independent Brand Family Architecture

With independent brand families the association between the parent or corporate brand and subsidiary or product brands is diffuse. It may be that only investors or the financial community are even aware of an association. For example, Philip Morris and Kraft were once both owned by the Altria Group. Philip Morris was rebranded Altria is an attempt to distance Kraft (and Philip Morris) from the negative association of tobacco. Kraft was spun off to Altria shareholders in 2007 to further distance itself.

WPP group owns 'independent' agency groups such as J. Walter Thompson, Ogilvy and Grey amongst many others. These sister companies regularly compete against each other so it helps to keep independent identities within the large WPP family.

Understanding the nature of brand family architecture and the role brands play within corporate, range, product or service brands is an important part of any brand strategy development project.

What type of family is it? How many family members are there?

How are they related? What does each family member do and why? Who does each family member appeal to?

The overriding principle of brand family architecture is to have the *least* number of brands that will:

- Attract and maintain relationships with your key customers and stakeholders

- Distinguish your product ranges, products and services

- Avoid confusion between one distinct offering and another

- Ensure no brand is stretched beyond the limits of where it is credible

There are several factors that determine the type of architecture including the number and types of customer groups being served, the breadth of the product offering, the benefits provided, the existing strength or heritage of brands in the family, resources available and future market expansion.

Defining a New Category

WHAT THIS TOOL DOES

This tool is a reminder of the value of consciously trying to create and define a new category, then taking ownership of the category by branding it.

We covered diversification earlier in the book. When setting out to move your brand in a new direction, it is important to ask yourself: Are you looking at a marginal improvement of the species, or defining a new species?

According to recent BrandZ rankings, Google has taken top spot as the world's most valuable brand alongside four other technology giants: Apple, Microsoft, Amazon and Facebook. Ten years ago Apple, Amazon and Facebook weren't even in the top 10. World-leading brands such as Coca-Cola, Toyota, Shell, GE and others continue to strengthen and grow but slip down the rankings, overtaken by the explosive growth of new categories such as integrated technology. Time waits for no one. A strategy of leadership with continuous marginal improvement only lasts until someone changes the game.

There are two different approaches to creating new categories.

One is to proactively look for the gap between the branches and exploit it. Perhaps an old branch has died or been broken off in a storm, and suddenly there's an opportunity to fill a gap that wasn't there before. Sometimes, the gap is very small and hard to see until a new branch has broken through into the sunlight.

The second is to let things diversify naturally, but have excellent mechanisms for early recognition of emerging new categories that can then be developed, acquired, or countered with a challenger brand.

Either way, there needs to be conscious intent to make developing new categories a priority. Even with a culture of creativity and innovation, and even with huge resource capacity, it is extremely difficult to develop new categories.

A line extension is not a new category. Filling ever-decreasing gaps between product offerings is not creating new categories (an iPad mini is still an iPad). Planned obsolescence is not creating a new category either.

So how do you know when you've created a new species or when a new species has emerged?

It's difficult, because it often takes time for new categories or paradigms to be come apparent. Dividing lines are blurred. Scientists define same species as being able to interbreed to produce fertile offspring. It's a stretch, but it's a way of delineating categories.

When the differences between two things outweigh the similarities, they begin following different paths. They move further away from each other in a divergent way. As with a change in rules of the game, new categories are easier to spot after the event, which isn't much help for innovators, even those with a head start.

If it follows that leaders are in the front of the queue when it comes to creating or catching the next wave, then Sony should have owned portable music and flat screen TVs. Kodak should have owned digital imaging. Facebook should have created Instagram or Snapchat.

It doesn't work that way.

The law of diversification and the law of gradual improvement are at odds with each other within the same organisation. Do you put all your resources into improving what you've got, or looking for something different?

Brand Loyalty Diamond

WHAT THIS TOOL DOES

The Brand Loyalty Diamond is a reminder that not all customers are created equal, or should be treated the same. It leads towards the development of different strategies for dealing with each type.

The term 'brand loyalist' is widely used as a broad descriptor for brand users, but there are different types of user based on their level of affinity with the brand. We've established that it's likely that approximately 30% of your brand users will account for 70% of your profit, and it is important to identify those users.

What is also true is that there will be a group of 'anti-customers,' for want of a better term. These may be disgruntled past users, or advocates of a competitive brand. The stronger the brand, the stronger the emotional affinity, so it shouldn't be surprising that loyalists of competitive brands will often be antagonists to your brand. With long-established duopolies, these rivalries can become intense. In the 188-year history of the Oxford and Cambridge boat race, there have only been three incidents of rowers switching teams.

The pattern of usage follows a bell-curve or diamond pattern.

EVANGELISTS

ACTIVE ADVOCATES

PASSIVE LOYALISTS

USERS

PASSIVE NON-USERS

ACTIVE AVOIDERS

ANTAGONISTS

EVANGELISTS

ACTIVE ADVOCATES

LOYALISTS

USERS

BRAND LOYALTY DIAMOND

PASSIVE NON-USERS

ACTIVE AVOIDERS

ANTAGONISTS

Evangelists are people who will promote your brand with the zeal of missionaries. They are pro-active believers that translate that belief into action in order to convert others.

Active advocates are loyalists who will spontaneously promote your brand. The values of the brand are internalised and attuned.

Passive loyalists are still loyalists. Their purchase habits or consumption may not differ greatly from active advocates and evangelists. The difference is they don't spontaneously promote the brand to others; they are passive in that respect.

Then you have users that may become loyal users or slip to passive non-use, depending on their experience.

Active avoiders stay clear of your brand. They'll only purchase or consume when there is no other alternative.

Antagonists are active disrupters. They will 'do your brand down' if given the opportunity. This may be the result of a past negative experience or active advocacy of a competitive brand.

As raised in Practical Segmentation (see page 132), when using the Brand Loyalty Diamond, care must be taken to separate attitude from usage. You might meet an octogenarian evangelist for The Balvenie single malt whose consumption is less than an average user.

The philosophy of building on strengths applies to brands as well as people. Although it is tempting to try to convert non-users, it is easier to gain a return on investment from existing loyal users. The goal is to create an unbalanced 'top heavy' diamond with a disproportionate number of active loyalists compared to non-users and avoiders.

Occasionally it is necessary to address the negative noise from antagonists. The first task is to protect your loyal users by communicating to them and reinforcing the positive attributes that align them to your brand. If absolutely necessary, as a last resort, correcting any misperceptions that might have been propagated may be needed.

I say as a last resort, because 'qui s'excuse, s'accuse' applies. You may inadvertently generate awareness of negativity that wasn't there before. As comedian Marty Feldman quipped, no one wants to hear their captain say from the cockpit, "Ladies and gentleman, the left wing is NOT on fire! I repeat, the left wing is NOT on fire!".

"If you don't know where you're going, any road will take you there."
George Harrison

Direction is the part of the process that sets the course for the organisation to build the brand. Like a compass setting it sets a path towards a desired place to be in the future. The journey may take course corrections along the way, but what the first stage Direction process does is the equivalent of saying, "We're heading Northwest". By doing so, it's implicitly saying, "We're going in the opposite direction of Southeast". It's also saying, "We've chosen not to follow other directions we might have taken".

Direction tools are strategic planning tools that help you determine where you are going. They help you make choices. No tool will ever make the decisions for you, but they can help you make those decisions by illuminating the path ahead and navigating the journey.

Britain's 'Iron Lady' Prime Minister Margaret Thatcher was famed for her insistence: "This Lady's not for turning". The determination of a leader to relentlessly pursue a belief or vision is essential to give followers the courage and confidence to follow a path, especially when the outcome is unknown. Determination to follow a path should not be confused with blind obstinance— strong leaders know when to be flexible and occasionally divert from the path in order to regain it later.

With brand development the outcome is almost always unknown, heading into an uncertain and unpredictable future. There is a difference between the immovability in seeking a vision and the need to move or adjust to achieve it. The French have a mountaineering term, decalage, to describe a rocky overhang that you have to go backwards, under or around in order to go up. Sometimes this is necessary in brand-building too. Wise leaders know when to make camp, rest up and if necessary take a course correction in order to stay on the long-term path.

Strategic direction is narrowing your choice of actions to two or three priorities that will help you achieve your vision.

The primary Direction tool is the Strategic Ladder (see page 147). If you're looking for a template to develop a customer and brand-centric strategic plan, start there.

The familiar tools here are goal-setting objectives. Perhaps more interesting are the tools that set the context for decision-making, such as Models for Change (see page 158).

The Strategic Ladder

WHAT THIS TOOL DOES

The Strategic Ladder is a 7-step template to create a customer-oriented and brand-centered strategy for your business. If you took only one model from this section that helped you ask the right questions about the choices you need to make, this would be it.

This self-explanatory model combines goal setting within a customer and brand-oriented questionnaire. In seven simple steps you can cover all the most important territory a strategic plan needs to cover.

It is powerful and straightforward. There is no hiding. The Strategic Ladder is short, but getting to succinct, sharp answers is difficult. It requires all the depth of insight and hard work that every great strategic plan demands.

1. What are our key growth goals (or commercial objectives)?
a.   Revenue and profitability
b.   Brand share / brand share growth
c.   Category (new category?)
d.   Geography
e.   SMART

2. Who are our most valuable customers? (Now and in the future)
Practical Segmentation:
a. Hard: $ spend / usage / demographics or life stage
b. Soft: psychographics or lifestyle / attitude / motivations / ... answering the 'Why?'

3. How do these customers need to behave to achieve our goals?
a. What do we want them to Know, Feel, Believe?
b. What do we want them to physically do? (e.g. buy / try / buy more frequently / trade up / refer others / buy exclusively)

4. How is the brand currently perceived by stakeholders?
a. Strengths and weaknesses
b. Competitive threats and opportunities
c. What perceptual changes are required?

5. What singular promise does our brand make? (In order for stakeholders to perceive the brand and behave in the way we want)
a. What unique experience do we create for our valued customers?
b. Is it sufficiently credible, relevant, differentiating and compelling?

6. Do we deliver that promise consistently in everything we DO? What must we DO differently to deliver our promise?
a. Our products and services?
b. Our people?
c. Our processes?

7. Do we deliver that promise consistently in everything we SAY? What and how must we SAY it in order to reinforce our promise?
a. Our external communications?
b. Our internal communications?
c. Our design identity?

The Four-Pillared Parthenon

WHAT THIS TOOL DOES

The Four-Pillared Parthenon is a visual metaphor for a strategic plan with a foundation — a purpose or reason why the brand exists and on which all brand activity is founded. The four core pillars each represent a major project or action initiative, and a roof, which is the over-arching communication that spans the four pillars. This simple construct helps people visualise what is essentially an intangible structure for the brand.

The Discovery process will have thrown up dozens of meaningful questions for the brand to answer as well as challenges and opportunities. The Brand DNA helps define the desired future state of the brand, what it stands for and why. So how do we start implementing what we've learned?

A useful image to think about is a four-pillared Parthenon. The four pillars stand on a stone foundation or base and have a roof structure overhead.

Why three or four pillars? Stools have either three or four legs for a reason — that's the minimum number of legs that can provide a stable platform to carry weight. Three is arguably more efficient, four is more stable. With either, though, the loss of even one leg can be fatally destabilising.

Once your Brand DNA is defined, the question is how do you bring it to life?

It's a question you should never stop asking and attempting to answer in better ways. But you also need to make a start. Like most things in life, having a good start is hugely advantageous. Even the most complex of plans start from a solid base that needn't be complicated.

For St George's School, now approaching a second decade since the strategic planning process was implemented, it started with a four-pillar action plan honed from two Brand DNA workshops. Their Brand DNA included their vision: to become Canada's world school for boys. The four pillars they identified were:

- Raise capital to fund endowment and development of projects

- Focus on expertise in the education of boys, developing 'renaissance' (new age) teaching philosophy and practices

- Preserve and strengthen boarding to build global mindedness and diversity

- Engage stakeholders through a professional strategic communications programme

Since these pillars were first set, the St. George's plan has evolved significantly, as discussed in Brand DNA (see page 102). Strategic plans are living, changing things that need to be interrogated and refined on a regular basis. But it really helps to have a plan that everyone knows and understands from the outset.

Now of course, I've over-simplified how the plan manifests itself. Over time, each pillar spawns separate support pillars or action plans and a divide and conquer rule applies to implementation, with departments and individuals taking responsibility for delivering their part of the plan.

So how do we arrive at the four priority pillars when there are so many choices to make? Consider the four-pillar example we did for the men's haircare company, BluMann, on the next page. It led to the development of the tagline 'On your hair, in your soul'.

It's surprising how fast a well-briefed, experienced cross section of stakeholders can develop a strategy once they know what it is they stand for, what purpose they exist to fulfill, and where they want to go. The ideas, plans and actions to get them there are plentiful. The challenge is to get them all out on the table and prioritise them against a set of criteria.

There are countless creative ways to get ideas for action out of people's minds and onto paper. I like to take the straightforward route and ask a direct question and get respondents to give direct answers. This is done quietly and individually at first, then shared. Idea exchange is then often stimulus enough to promote a second wave of idea generation building on thoughts presented by the group.

THE FOUR-PILLARED PARTHENON

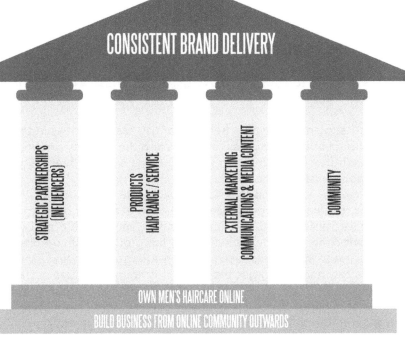

Example of the Four-Pillared Parthenon for BluMann

The Impact-Urgency Matrix

WHAT THIS TOOL DOES

This is a simple tool for a group to quickly prioritise a number of tasks against a vision or goal.

This self-explanatory matrix helps prioritise tasks or ideas in terms of their impact in achieving desired goals and the urgency required. You can substitute other criterion on the x-axis such as feasibility (cost and resource requirement).

Below is an example of an Impact-Urgency Matrix first round exercise. Several numbered ideas have been evaluated by a group and categorised according to their impact and urgency. This is done by listing and numbering each idea, then having the group shout coordinates to the facilitator who 'posts' each idea on a large grid below. It takes a group a few minutes to get the hang of it, then each idea is classified very quickly and 'posted'. This way a log list of ideas can be sorted in a matter of minutes. Highest impact and highest urgency would be a 9–9, lowest a 1–1. A 9–5 would be high impact, medium urgency.

It must be made clear that everything cannot be classified as important. The tool is designed to tease apart the ideas so they can be more easily prioritised. Participants quickly see a map of where ideas are positioned relative to one another and can correct throughout the process. For example, they might assess that developing teachers is higher priority than upgrading classrooms and reverse the positions. Clustering also happens at this point—several ideas might be related to each other and can be clustered in a group. It may still require a second round to tease apart the top quadrant ideas (illustrated in yellow below).

It is tempting to focus entirely on the top right section (Do Now). The reality is that many of the most powerful ideas lie in the section below (Impactful but slightly less urgent). This is because many 'urgent' classifications may be due to deadlines or other pressures that raise the perceived importance but that are not actually as impactful as some of the less urgent ideas in the quadrant below (the Do Next box).

Once a long list has been narrowed down, greater attention can be paid to the top 6–10 ideas. These can each be given more attention, including a second round of Impact-Urgency if required.

IMPACT URGENCY MATRIX

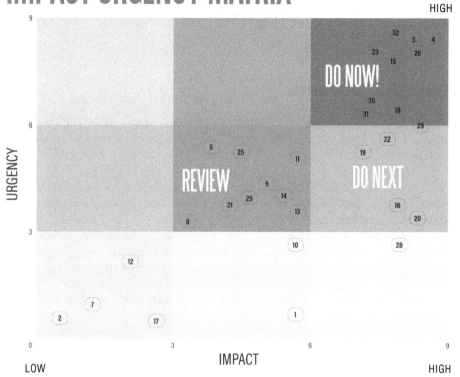

Models for Change

WHAT THIS TOOL DOES

This tool offers three different models for understanding and managing change, with perspective on how change happens in the real world.

According to a 2008 McKinsey Quarterly Survey of 3,199 executives from around the world, *95% of them had undergone 'significant change' within the last five years.*

Significant change meant major good to great initiatives, rationalisation to reduce costs, restructuring, an acquisition or merger, a divestment, turning around a crisis situation such as a product failure or competitive incursion, expanding geographically or preparing for a privatisation. Only 5% claimed they hadn't experienced significant change within a five-year period.

Change is something all of us experience in our personal and business lives. Few of us actually take a step back and think about how we might understand and manage the process better.

Ron Cacioppe's Change Model

Of the hundreds of strategy and change management models, Ron Cacioppe's model is my go-to model that my clients find easy to understand and use. It defines the steps required for change and is a useful diagnostic tool for identifying reasons why change may not be happening successfully.

I was first introduced to it during an Ogilvy Strategic masterclass by Ian Strachan in the early 1990s, and it's stuck with me since. In those days, the big agency groups invested heavily in training and Ogilvy & Mather, with the legacy of founder David Ogilvy, was seen to be the University of Advertising. It had full time training 'professors' and Ian was one of the best.

I like the model because my clients like it. It is both a diagnostic and prescriptive tool in one.

The illustration on the next page is the simplified version. It was later extended to include three more factors: 'model the way' (or walk the talk), 'reinforce and solidify change' and 'evaluate and improve'. Without modeling the way or leading by example, there is scepticism and mistrust. Without reinforcing and solidifying change there's a risk of falling back into the old ways (think about the military establishing beachheads, recognising and rewarding victories, and protecting new territory gained). And without an evaluation there is no feedback to modify direction and improve.

Pressure for change is what we call the burning platform. Although change is a constant it's human nature to resist change. Once you've invested effort in mastering the rules you don't want them to change because it takes time and effort to adjust. Our default mode is more commonly wired to conserve energy, including thinking energy, rather than to proactively explore or innovate. This is especially true if you have interests to protect in doing things the way you've always done them.

Now, there will be some young explorers out there who feel the opposite. There are different thinking preferences (see page 196), different circumstances, and different life stages that affect the desire and capacity to change.

Pressure for change can come from external or internal forces. Market dynamics such as competitive inclusion, changing consumer habits, geographical relocation, or political policy changes are external forces. Internal pressure can come from the top down or the bottom up within organisations.

Without the stimulus of a need to change or the 'pain' of the problem that needs to go away, the tendency is to maintain the status quo. Even in the face of approaching disruptive change, habit, disbelief and complacency hinder attempts to change. With a burning platform, you have to move off or you die.

Charles Handy's image of the boiling frog is a terrific metaphor for what happens when the heat is turned up only gradually on organisations. If you put a frog in a pan of water and very slowly raise the temperature a degree at a time, it slowly boils to death. If you drop it into boiling water, it hops out immediately.

So where are you going to go?

That's where the change strategy discussion begins and the need for direction arises. If there is no image of the future place you are trying to reach, how will you know when you've arrived?

Successful change agents create powerful visions of a future state, currently out of reach, that are aspirational but attainable. They bring believers together in a coalition of the willing and set achievable first steps. Every long journey begins with the first step, as the Chinese saying goes.

Direction for change is expressed in different forms, often a vision or mission statement, or as in this book, a Brand DNA that describes a future desired state. I liken this stage to identifying

| PRESSURE FOR CHANGE | + | DIRECTION FOR CHANGE | + | CAPACITY FOR CHANGE | + | ACTIONABLE FIRST STEPS | = | CHANGE |

CHANGE MODEL

PRESSURE FOR CHANGE + DIRECTION FOR CHANGE + CAPACITY FOR CHANGE + ACTIONABLE FIRST STEPS = BOTTOM OF THE BOX

PRESSURE FOR CHANGE + DIRECTION FOR CHANGE + CAPACITY FOR CHANGE + ACTIONABLE FIRST STEPS = FAST START THAT FIZZLES

PRESSURE FOR CHANGE + DIRECTION FOR CHANGE + CAPACITY FOR CHANGE + ACTIONABLE FIRST STEPS = ANXIETY, FRUSTRATION

PRESSURE FOR CHANGE + DIRECTION FOR CHANGE + CAPACITY FOR CHANGE + ACTIONABLE FIRST STEPS = FALSE START HAPHAZARD EFFORTS

points on a compass. When you set out you may not know the precise coordinates to a single degree, but you should know the general direction in which you are heading.

Capacity for change is equivalent to asking: Do you have the tools to do the job? Whether it is financial resources, personnel, or technical capability; if you don't have the capacity for change it will result in anxiety and frustration. One of my Vancouver clients was a recycling company, quite a visionary, one owned by a husband and wife team. They had dreams of expanding and revolutionising the collection system to enable simultaneous multi-stream waste processing. This required new equipment and a new site. They were restricted by capacity for change until they acquired a new site and built a state-of-the-art facility. Which they did.

Capacity for change is a big bucket. Skill sets, structure and systems all need to be in place. Recognition and reward of new desired attitudes and behaviours are vital.

Actionable first steps are, surprisingly, often the forgotten step. The pressure is there, you've got the direction, and the capacity isn't an issue, but you don't know how to get started. The reality is there are multiple first steps. Sometimes it's better to just get started and course correct later. Writers are encouraged to just write, then edit later.

Divide and conquer is the rule here...brainstorm to generate action ideas then assess them according to impact and urgency. Note it's not always the most urgent tasks that are the most important. Sometimes the urgent ones are necessary distractions, but distractions nonetheless. I encourage my clients to empower their people and to execute multiple tactics through division of labour. Examples of multiple tactics could be establishing KPIs with recognition and reward incentives, skills training, mobilising senior executives to model desired mindset and behaviour, finding ways to give frontline staff ownership of change, communicating an emotive change story, or establishing accountability for progress.

John Kotter's 8 Steps Change Model
John Kotter's 8 Steps model below is one of the most respected, and it mirrors much of Cacioppe's change model.

1. Create urgency
2. Form a powerful coalition
3. Create a vision for change
4. Communicate the vision
5. Remove obstacles

6. Create short-term wins

7. Build on the change

8. Anchor the changes in corporate culture

Steps 1-3 are creating the climate for change. Steps 4-6 are engaging and enabling the organisation. Steps 7 and 8 are implementing and sustaining change. He also addresses resistance to change and how to deal with it that we'll touch on later (see Overcoming VIII on page 214).

The weakness of both these models is not the models themselves, but the context within which change occurs. It assumes that change is a planned, almost linear process designed and led by senior management. I've found that not to be the case in real life.

We tend to think of change as a controlled process that occurs in stages and that can be foreseen and managed in a planned way, like a caterpillar changing into a pupa that transforms into a chrysalis and then emerges triumphantly as a beautiful butterfly.

In reality, organisational change rarely happens like that. Change is more likely to arrive unannounced and uninvited. It's an unexpected attack from underneath from unseen dark waters—and it's often fatal. A Great White Shark attack on a hapless seal is a brutal depiction of predation in the real world, but brands live by this "law of the jungle" too.

Often it's categories that become obsolete and the brand leaders in those categories that suffer. I've already referred to Kodak and Nokia in this context, but it's got to be tough being a London cabbie. For a century or more 'doing the knowledge' of learning the streets of London was the passport and entrance barrier to the job—securing respect and employment for those that have put in the time. Then, almost overnight, we have mobile phones with GPS apps in our hands. Suddenly everyone can track the quickest routes, and avoid traffic congestion too! Street maps in the glove compartment? More like in the museum.

Now Uber is taking over the taxi's market, offering door to door service, using personal vehicles and centralised systems at lower rates than traditional cabs. The whole infrastructure built up to protect the taxi system—licensing, training, regulation—is flipped on its back by a disruptive new entrant. Only the most stubborn political protection is saving licensed cabs from the Uber model, and eventually those towers will fall too as the cost of preventing the inevitable becomes too high.

The cycle of birth, growth, stability, decline, death and re-birth is constant. The challenge for brands is to sustain the periods of growth and stability—deferring death if you like—for as long as possible by reversing the entropic process.

When unexpected change happens it's often not a pleasant surprise.

The Kübler-Ross Change Curve

Elisabeth Kübler-Ross, the prominent Swiss-American psychiatrist, identified the five stages of grief from studying terminally ill patients. The relevance of her stages model is such that it has been modified many times and applied to other personal situations, such as children dealing with the divorce of their parents, or to adults losing their jobs.

Her five stages are:

Denial—refusal to accept a diagnosis

Anger—frustration and angst

Bargaining—attempts to avoid the source of grief, reforming lifestyle to negotiate more time, or a change of behaviour

Depression—despair at the recognition of mortality, helplessness

Acceptance—embracing the situation

There are parallels too for businesses and brands experiencing change:

Denial—"They aren't really going to go through with it"

Anger—"What a waste of time and money. How much do those stupid consultants cost?"

Bargaining—"If they want me to do that then fine, but I won't have time to do my normal duties" or "If they make me do that I'll resign"

Depression—"This really is happening and there's nothing I can do about it"

Acceptance—"Well this is how it is, but things aren't so bad"

Moving on—"Actually this new set up is better than the old and I can see how I can make this work for me"

The last part of 'moving on' is an important addition for the business and brand change application. For those people with fewer vested interests in preserving the old world (i.e. the young, newcomers, the senior drivers of change and those energised by change) this is an exciting process.

I also like to think of the curve line as a line of hope. Hope takes a downward turn at first, reaching its nadir in depression, but over time, with acceptance, it rises and then energises activity as hope returns and increases.

As with people, not all brands or businesses experience all five stages. Sometimes they skip one or two, but more often they get stuck in one or two stages that they circle around in before moving on.

This world accepts that change is all around us and coming to you soon! It encourages early understanding and recognition of change, embracing it rather than resisting it, and enjoying the ride. That is easier for some than others as already explained.

For brands, change does not mean death (although failure to change may). Change can prolong life, reinvigorate and stimulate renewal or growth.

What is the single most important factor in a change management programme? I believe it is the commitment of the leader to change and the mindset he or she instils in the workforce as a consequence. Behavioural change is essential of course, but it stems from a change in beliefs or attitude.

Look to find the two or three vital behavioural changes that inform all change. For example, everyone knows you need to consume fewer calories than you burn, but it's no good talking about it if you don't eat less and exercise more.

Want to know what the three vital behaviours for successful weight loss are? They are eating breakfast, weighing yourself every day, and exercising at home.

Transformational Change

There are different levels of change.

The base level is little or no change at all—nothing much different really happens on a day-to-day basis. This might be an acquisition or divestment of assets at a corporate headquarters level, for example, that has little or no impact at a local branch office level.

Then there is incremental change that occurs without the need to dramatically change mindsets. This might be a way of operating more efficiently, adopting new practices, learning new skills or perhaps a structural change that doesn't radically change people's attitudes, although it may modify behaviour.

Then there is transformational change. This requires adopting a completely different set of beliefs—a fundamental cultural change— from conservative to progressive, from hierarchical to egalitarian, from domestic to global, from myopic to far-seeing.

The 2008 McKinsey Quarterly survey on transformational change suggests the following five criteria are required to achieve truly transformational change:

- A clear and significant stretch goal (the most important factor by some margin)

- Visible, involved CEO or leader championing change

- Early engagement of staff (...all stakeholders)

- Emphasis on communicating the need in a positive way... balanced with clear challenges or problems to overcome

- A combination of tactics to keep stakeholders engaged and involved...multiple activities

To this I'd add:

- Perseverance, or what we used to call 'stick-to-it-iveness'

Change happens when people see the point of it and get behind it. They become proactive agents of change rather than obstacles to it. Sometimes that means going through one or more of the denial, anger, bargaining, and depression stages before acceptance.

You're ahead of the game if they can answer yes to the questions: Will it be worth it? Can I do it?

Storytelling is a powerful means of helping people understand why change is worthwhile. I've found it's always easier to tell a CEO about a problem experienced by someone else in a different category. They can relate without feeling defensive or needing to explain why their own problem exists.

We all have problems; what we're here to do is help you solve them. You just need the right tool for the right job.

SMART BHAGs

WHAT THIS TOOL DOES

SMART BHAGs are a reminder of well-known, easy to remember goal-setting tools. BHAGs in particular is a good exercise for organisations that normally struggle to stretch their thinking beyond annual 'refreshers'.

Smart stands for:

Specific

Measurable

Actionable

Relevant

Time-Bound

SMART goals and objectives are hard to wriggle out of. They are also easier for leaders to be held accountable to. They are a counter to 'hockey-stick' growth projections that are not likely to be realistic.

"But don't they stifle creative, big picture thinking?" I often hear from workshop audiences. Not necessarily. I find they should be used in tandem with BHAGs to counter that tendency all the same.

BHAGs are good for longer-term future envisioning. SMART objectives are good for the more near-term actionable first steps.

BHAGs

BHAGs are Big Hairy Audacious Goals.

They present a huge daunting challenge equivalent to climbing Mt. Everest. They are clear and compelling and can be a catalyst for team spirit. There is a clear finish line. It may take five to 10 years or more to achieve, and may require thinking beyond current capabilities.

BHAGs have a success potential of only 50-70% and require extraordinary effort. Here are some examples:

- 1890s: "Become the Harvard of the West" —Stanford University

- 1950s: "Become the company most known for changing the worldwide quality image of Japanese products" —Sony

- 1960s: "Put a man on the moon and bring him back" —JFK

- 1970s: "Crush Adidas" —Nike

- 1990s: "Become a US$125 billion company by the year 2000" —WalMart

- 2000s: "For people (the world) to stay connected with friends and family, discover what's going on in the world and to share and express what matters to them" —Facebook

Clearly, there was no guarantee that any of these goals would be achieved. But when they were, they changed their organisations forever.

Living Your Brand

WHAT THIS TOOL DOES

This tool is a reminder that your place—both the physical and emotional (cultural) aspects of your workplace—have a tremendous impact on your brand. For reasons I will never understand, it is often not given the priority or investment it deserves. It is an opportunity to celebrate your brand values. Likewise, organisations are only people. If your people don't believe in your brand, if they don't 'walk the talk', how do you expect anyone else to?

Living Your Brand Through Place

The physical environment of the workplace says a lot about the organisation. So does the culture, or 'how you do things around here'. The two are closely related.

It still surprises me how dull and uninspiring our work environments often are despite how much of our lives are spent there. Uninspiring offices with partitioned open-space areas, each desk reflecting the maximum degree of personalisation allowed by the culture. Even supposedly creative organisations can struggle with this. We've moved to more flexi-hours and working from home (or coffee shops!), which helps. But it still leaves vast areas of opportunity for improvement in the tall buildings many head to each morning.

Money is nearly always given as the reason why more isn't done to improve the physical aspects of work places. "We'll never recover the sunk costs. Besides, we're only tenants and the owners won't let us." Well yes, these are legitimate reasons for inaction, but they can nearly always be overcome with imagination and effort.

I've always advocated for investment in more interesting, creative work environments. They invariably pay for themselves in more engaged, alert and productive workforces that work harder, longer and more happily.

Advertising is always the first industry to suffer in an economic downturn and the first to recover when the good times return. (Champagne sales are a similar indicator.) It's a knee-jerk reaction to cut costs from easy-to-access budgets that are difficult to account for direct sales. Despite countless studies that suggest a downturn is the best time to maintain or increase spending (higher value, less competitive clutter) this phenomenon persists.

With currency devaluation and client budget cutbacks happening simultaneously and almost overnight in Malaysia in 1997, the industry experienced an almost 100% decline in reporting revenue in a month. It simply fell off a cliff. With prescient foresight, I arrived to manage Leo Burnett's Malaysia office the week the economic crisis hit!

Other agencies responded to the crisis by slashing staff and cutting back; a few highly respected international companies even withdrew from the market. We decided that the best way to weather the storm was to zig when everyone else was zagging. We were one of the larger agencies in the market, and we felt the best way to sustain ourselves was to reinforce our stability to our clients, our people, and others around us.

We made one round of cuts quickly. We cut back management salaries and froze the rest, with the exception of the lowest paid for whom it meant the most. Then we sent the signal out load and clear to our staff, clients and the industry that we were going to grow in this downturn. No more cuts—here today, here tomorrow.

We took advantage of an expiring lease on our office and the record low rentals to move into a larger office space downtown. We designed and built a spectacular environment that exuded creativity and optimism. We hired a young creative architect and designed an amazing office space on a relatively low budget. It celebrated all the Leo Burnett icons, so above the escalator that brought people into the office we had gold stars hanging from the ceiling. The company motto was 'Reach for the Stars' (...and you won't come up with a handful of mud was the full saying from Leo).

We recognised that although it's a team effort, our milking cows were the creative people who conceived the ideas. We gave them their own prime area, with elevated wooden walkways and platforms.

We had an open plan reflecting our flat structure, but with a few offices for private conversations. Every department was separated and distinguished by the use of colour and materials on floors and walls so that as you passed through the agency you transitioned seamlessly from one 'land' to another. We had four different meeting rooms: one was a standard one with table and chairs, another was an elevated 'boxing ring' with open walls, one was a standing-up-only area for short meetings and one was a sunken-floor room, like a Japanese restaurant, where clients had to take off their shoes and meet in an intimate, informal environment.

(About the last room: whenever we were in trouble with a client, or in imminent danger of losing an account or piece of business, we'd take them into this room. The thinking was that nobody would fire you without their shoes on. As it turned out, nobody did!)

Of course, we had a terrific product too and we maintained our high standards of delivery. But our new home sent out a clear signal of hope and optimism in a time of darkness.

We even had a full-size snooker table in the entrance lobby!

Living Your Brand Through People

PepsiCo CEO Indra Nooyi identified 5 Cs of success:

Competence/Courage/Confidence/Compass (morals)/Coaching

What more do you need when looking for the right type of leader and identifying desired characteristics in emerging leaders?

What I like most is the acknowledgement of leaders being coaches. I was once admonished by my (very senior) boss for describing part of my role as being an inspiring coach for my subordinates. He thought I should be focusing on earning more revenue. Somehow, he missed the point that it was more effective to do that through multiple empowered people, not just one.

Influencers

In any population there are influencers. These are not necessarily the smartest, or the first to pick up on new ideas. Those are the pioneers. Pioneers are often maverick, oddball, or geeky. Influencers bridge the gap between the pioneers and the mass of early adopters. They are popular, smart, and tend to be gregarious. Often they are sociable connectors who have large contact lists that they stay in touch with. With the endorsement of influencers, brands can go through an explosive growth that accelerates them past Malcolm Gladwell's 'Tipping Point'.

There is no sure way of describing who these individuals are in a company or society, and yet they are recognizable. Identifying and converting influencers in your organisation is the first step. Winning them over is not always easy as they are mostly free-spirited independent thinkers who will resist overt attempts to persuade them. If the belief system is aligned though, then they are like an individual army.

Teamwork at the Top

Three 'Obvious Adams' from McKinsey that aren't so obvious to leadership teams it would seem.

Get the right people on the leadership team, and get the wrong ones off it.

It's the second part of that sentence that most have difficulty with. I spend the most time with leaders finding constructive ways of fixing 'wrong types'. Much can be done to re-orient, re-train, re-energise and reintegrate before the last resort of remove.

The leadership team should focus on the things that only the leadership team can do. If any of the things that the top team is spending time on could be done be anyone else, they shouldn't be doing it. What things can only they do? Things like setting and approving a vision, deciding corporate strategy, confirming new directions, changing policies and establishing cultural norms.

In my experience too many board teams use their time together to catch up on status and review financials. It's information exchange that could and should be done before the meeting. The real purpose of leadership teams, I believe, should be to discuss strategy, share ideas, and make choices in the context of insight.

Think about flipping the focus: Make people the cornerstone of your company, supported by strategy and vision.

'Deeds not words'

Delivery requires partnerships. This section focuses on tools that can help create productive working relationships with other companies, communities, consultants, and specialists.

Brand owners must concentrate on the things they can control. Well, to be clear, no brand owner can exert total control over their brand no matter how diligent. The law of chaos and Murphy's Law apply: if something can go wrong, it will. No matter how carefully safety protocols are adhered to, extraordinary circumstances may lead to accidents. Or, as the Americans say, 'shit happens'. Product quality is affected by a bad batch of raw material, a competitor highlights a weakness, a system fails, a change in customer preferences occurs. Any one of a million circumstances can affect perceptions of your brand, sometimes in an instant.

That is the world of managing brand perceptions. You'll go crazy if you try to pre-empt every possibility that might occur. What you can do productively is increase the strength of your brand, or build up its store of negative entropy by delivering against the six areas of the 'Delivery Doughnut' (see page 171).

Delivery is not all done in-house. In fact, with outsourcing all the rage to reduce fixed operating costs, delivery is mostly done through contracted third parties. Product manufacturing is often franchised out, albeit to exacting quality standards (think McDonald's or Starbucks). External communications can be subdivided into traditional advertising, public relations, sponsorship, social media, trade marketing, event marketing, and so on. HR departments may be large, small, or non-existent when it comes to delivering the 'people' component of the brand promise.

Strategy is choice—how the organisation

chooses to allocate limited resource to achieve its aims, most often expressed in the shape of a strategic plan. Delivery is where the flower opens up and the whole process can expand dramatically, mindful of doing the DO before saying the SAY.

The Delivery tools in this section help execute the strategic plan developed in the previous three sections. They help you deliver the deliverables. Some are ways in which you think, others are more direct methods. All are geared towards action—making the visions, goals, and dreams for your brand come to life.

The Delivery Doughnut

The Delivery Doughnut is one of the most widely referenced tools by my customers. It's easy to hold the image in the mind and it's an elegant reminder of what needs to be done to 'deliver' the Brand DNA (see page 102) to stakeholders.

Everything the brand DOES and SAYS is represented by the six segments in order to effect perceptions. The top half reflects what the brand DOES through its products, services, people and processes. The bottom half represents what the brand SAYS through external communications, internal communications and design. The outer ring of the doughnut is customer perceptions of what the brand is. This may or may not reflect the reality of the brand.

Customer perceptions are the sum of all their associations with and experiences of the brand. Since it is nearly impossible for two different people to experience the same brand in exactly the same way, and no single person can interact with every aspect of a brand, these perceptions are necessarily subjective. And yet, so many of us end up feeling the same way about brands, despite our differing experience. How do brand loyalists share so many positive perceptions of their favoured brand?

They do it because the brands are delivering consistent experiences, often in different times in different places. Consistent experiences and, consequently, consistent word of mouth reinforce similar perceptions.

Inside the doughnut, there are three DO actions representing the things the organisation does to deliver against the promise of the brand: products and services, people, and processes. Then there are three SAY areas: internal communications, external communications, and design.

Let's look at each element of the doughnut and how it relates to the brand.

PRODUCTS & SERVICES

These are the primary drivers of stakeholder experiences that create perceptions. This segment of the BCM doughnut covers:

- Market research and analysis
- Product and service definition
- Product portfolio or brand family architectures (how many products in the range or family)
- Product and service innovation
- Customer segmentation strategies
- Customer loyalty and retention strategies

PEOPLE AND ORGANISATION DEVELOPMENT

This is the principles, actions, and behaviours of an organisation's workforce that deliver the experience, including:

- Principles (values)
- Organisation structure
- Organisation culture
- Performance management
- Recruitment & orientation
- Training & development
- Leadership development & succession planning
- Compensation strategy
- HR information system

PROCESSES

This describes the systems, structures, and processes that enable or hinder effective behaviours and actions. A BCM process would look at:

- Customer complaints & needs analysis
- Process and systems audits
- Product information systems

- Customer complaints management
- 'Priority Customer' support programmes
- Governance
- Formal and informal meetings

EXTERNAL COMMUNICATIONS

These are the means by which the brand is communicated externally to customers and other stakeholders. Areas reviewed within the BCM process include:

- Historical advertising and communications
- Brand communications strategies
- Resource planning
- Budget planning
- Performance measurement
- Agency selection and management

DESIGN

The visual articulation of everything the brand stands for, including:

- Corporate identity (logos, trademarks, colour palette)
- Packaging
- Retail design
- Interior design (ambience)

INTERNAL COMMUNICATION

This is the process of internal engagement with the brand. It covers every way in which the brand communicates with and guides employees. It includes:

- Staff information systems audits & planning
- Internal communications strategies
- Formal and informal communication channels
- Communications effectiveness
- Staff appraisals and recognition

The Brand Company later added a third dimension to the BCM Doughnut in order to graphically represent the corporate strategy and goals that direct action and behaviour, and the systems and structures employed by organisations.

At the center of the doughnut, informing everything else, is the Brand DNA. The Brand DNA is the golden thread of the Brand Centered Management process that runs through every aspect of the business, linking internal corporate strategy and staff behaviour with external customer perceptions in the outside world.

We negotiate corporate goals in tandem with identifying the most valuable customer segments or interest groups that the company wants to target. The two go hand-in-hand and each informs the other. Despite the customer-oriented philosophy that is an integral part of good marketing, I have found customer segmentation is not as well practiced as it is understood.

Do Before Say

WHAT THIS TOOL DOES

This tool is an important reminder that doing is more powerful than saying.

What works better for you: The loud, flamboyant claim of a spokesperson promising satisfaction 'or your money back', or the quiet, unsolicited endorsement of a satisfied customer?

For most, it would be the latter.

One of my favourite commercials produced at my old firm Ogilvy & Mather (now Ogilvy), and arguably one of the best corporate commercials of all time was for Shell. It opened on bucolic Welsh countryside with rolling meadows, birds tweeting in the hedgerows, shots of foxes, owls, farmers with their sheep... an undisturbed peace across a pastoral landscape. An announcer spoke over this saying:

"If we told you that a certain oil company wanted to push a pipeline through this lovely Welsh valley...a pipeline that would stretch for 78 miles across the countryside...that would cut a swathe 30 yards wide, that would mean cutting down seven feet into the earth, sending bulldozers into the Snowdonia National Park...you would probably, quite rightly, be very alarmed. You might with good reason form a protest group, ask for a special enquiry, write in the strongest terms to your MP.

You needn't worry. This is the valley after, not before, Shell laid its pipeline.

Shell had consulted the local people and when work finished we restored the valley as you can see to its natural beauty. Can we develop the industry we need without destroying our countryside?

You can be sure of Shell."

The message was incredibly powerful. Not only did it empathise with the concern people feel about preserving the countryside, it demonstrated they were as good as their word in restoring it to its natural beauty. This was a message about a promise already kept, not one that still needed to be met.

And that's the point of DO before SAY.

One ounce of action is worth ten tons of talk. Deeds not words.

The Delivery Doughnut (see page 171) puts the DO segments on top for a reason. Your products and services, your people, and the systems and structures that enable you to deliver your promise—these are tangible actions that you should do first. Once done, then you can talk about them, not before.

Why do property developers have show flats? Because they know it's more effective to have customers walk through 'the real thing' than look at architects' concepts. Even today's virtual reality technology is no substitute for real reality.

This often creates a dilemma for marketers. How do you generate excitement ahead of the launch of a new product? How do you create momentum before the day so you can 'hit the ground running'? How do you inform people about what is planned in the future? Well, all of this is still possible if you don't over-promise. The risk is, so many people are tempted to make promises at the podium today that they cannot fulfill in reality tomorrow.

Far better, once you have achieved something meaningful, then you can talk about it. The more times you live up to your promises, the stronger the reputation and trust you'll build up over time.

The agency didn't always get it right either. Knowing that people mostly think all petrol is the same, despite the additives and formulas, Shell looked for a service proposition on which to differentiate themselves. They put an extensive customer service training programme in place and we made an advertisement for them promising visitors would be greeted with a smile and a windscreen wash. Well, that was true...but only for about a third of the network of stations. What we'd misunderstood was that ownership of retail station franchises had passed from the original parents to the second or third generation who were much less engaged in the business. So despite the training programme, they didn't really follow through on delivery. Customers expecting a smile and a windscreen wash were instead met with a disinterested pump attendant, or none at all. The more the advertisement ran, the greater the level of disconnect between the promise and the experience. That campaign was pulled much quicker than planned.

Emotional Differentiation

WHAT THIS TOOL DOES

Emotional Differentiation isn't so much a tool as a philosophy. It reminds people that the true power of brands lies in the heart rather than the head.

Mark Wnek, who was Creative Director at Ogilvy & Mather on the famous Guinness 'Pure Genius' campaign, used to say, 'Why continue to search for answers in the diminishing, crowded world of rational differentiation instead of exploring the wide open domain of emotional differentiation?'

There's a dilemma with the insight that emotional differentiation has to offer: some people will not see it and not relate to it. The irony is it's these same people that stand to benefit most from accepting it.

When I'm talking about this tool, I try to do it in a group so that people can hear what others really think. It's quite a private revelation so it works better with smaller groups who are comfortable with each other.

I ask them this question: "Tell me honestly, for the big decisions in your life—who you decided to marry, where you decided to live, where you decided to work—were these decisions that you made with your heart or your head?"

Now, we may not like to admit it to ourselves, or to others, but the vast majority will confirm these big, life-altering decisions are made with the heart, not the head. We don't get out a list of pros and cons and rate our potential spouses on a quantitative 7-point rating system before comparing them with competitors, do we? (please say no!) Even the hardest left-brain rational thinkers don't do this.

What we do though is 'post-purchase rationalisation'. So once a purchase has been made — forgive the crude analogy with finding a spouse — we find multiple, rational reasons to back that choice up. He's dependable, has a good job, will be a good provider, is kind to animals, and so on. At the same time we play down or ignore other reasons that don't reinforce the choice we've made—the charisma bypass, lack of imagination and low sociability skills, for example.

When you ask someone why they bought a Mercedes, they rarely tell you that it was because the prestigious marque reinforced their feeling of having achieved a certain status in life. They are much more likely to give you a rational justification such as the quality craftsmanship, the German-engineered quality assurance, the heritage of leadership for over a century, the performance. Perhaps they got a great deal on it, too.

Why is an admission of being led by emotion or irrationality viewed as a weakness by so many? I don't know, but it surely is. We're getting a little better at it as a society, but there's a long way to go. Perhaps it's because the perception of being smarter requires cognitive processes that we admire—logical, rational Vulcan-like values. Conversely, conceding that these processes were overridden by a 'primitive brain' is seen as just that—primitive.

Again, I feel differently. I think those basal instincts are intelligences that we've developed over millennia and play just as significant a role in our behaviour as the cerebral brain. I believe that the 'sixth sense', if it does exist, is more closely linked with tapping into this hard-wired instinct than with the higher-function frontal lobes. Have you ever had that sense walking into a place that something is just not right, it's not safe, you just don't want to be there? You can't put your finger on why, but the feeling is powerful and undeniably there. That feeling is just as valid as a more reasoned assessment.

The reverse feelings of warmth, comfort, security, happiness can also be instinctive and extremely powerful attributes for a brand that can harness them. Imagine how powerful a brand could be if it evoked these types of emotions. How a brand makes you feel is more important than what it does.

Sometimes during presentations I will show a photo of a winding mountain road with a solitary man riding a motorcycle in the distance. When I ask the group what brand this photo represents, nine times out of ten they will respond 'Harley Davidson'.

I ask them: Why Harley Davidson? Can you see the logo on the fuel tank? Is there something distinctive about those wing mirrors? No, of course they can't tell from the rational stimulus being given to them. What they are responding to are the emotional cues. It's the freedom of the open road. It's 'Route 66', USA, California even. It's the feeling of independence and, for a brief time, a sense of empowerment and control over your own destiny that so many middle aged North American males yearn to feel again. This is an association that women read just as well as men. After all, they're the ones allowing them out at the weekend!

What Harley Davidson has done so well is to associate itself with a powerful emotion: freedom. Brand advocates literally tattoo the brand name on their shoulders. The affinity with what the brand represents to them means so much. You don't see that with brands of toothpaste.

It's true that certain categories are more emotionally meaningful than others. Cars and motorcycles are expensive items that say something about their owners. They are literally 'clothes for driving in'. Not everyone cares about fashion or how they look, but most people do care about how they are perceived by others.

Emotional differentiation isn't just a whim; it brings very tangible benefits. The old example of GEO Prism and Toyota Corolla is still one of the best because it's a rare controlled experiment where an identical product is sold under two different brand names.

Both cars were manufactured in a joint venture between 1990 and 1994. They are virtually identical twins. So what happened with sales?

GM sold 80,000 Geo Prisms at $10,700 each. Toyota sold 200,000 Corollas at $11,000 each.

Some will argue that there were other factors influencing sales such as efficiency of the sales force, convenience and appearance of the showrooms, advertising, and so on. There is some validity to that, but it doesn't detract from the main point, though. Consumers 'perceived' Toyota to be superior to GM. They attached a higher value to the brand name.

There was a significant advantage to the Toyota brand equity due in large part to the emotional attachment people had for Toyota. Toyota was the largest carmaker in the world with a reputation for reliability and value. This gave Toyota a tangible advantage over GM in terms of customer behaviour. Not only did they sell more than twice as many vehicles, they sold them at a premium over the GM model.

This is not to dismiss the importance of rational benefits. If your brand has tangible advantages over competitors that are meaningful to customers, then use them. These rational differences tend to be short-lived in the crowded competitive categories of today.

Brand-building is both an art and a science. Both rational and emotional. The rational side addresses tangible needs such as how a product performs and how much it costs. The emotional side addresses intangible needs like how a product makes you feel and what it says about you.

So, always be mindful when positioning your brand to search for the wide open space of emotional differentiation. Find a place in your customers' hearts, keep your promises to them, and you will find there's a place in their wallets for you, too.

I owe my start in advertising to an emotional appeal. Having found my calling after visiting a small agency while at University in Edinburgh, I realised I was going to have to do something special to get into advertising. The handful of graduate trainee places in the big agencies almost always went to Oxbridge graduates. After a year of post-graduate studies in advertising and having sent 200 applications out with little success, I managed to get an interview at McCann Erickson. When I got home I sent them a small soft toy tiger that my girlfriend at the time had given me. He had a note around his neck saying, 'My name is Typewriter—If you want to put a real tiger in your think tank, call my master' (playing on the classic McCann's campaign for Esso 'Put a tiger in your tank'). It was a bit gimmicky, but fortunately for me it appealed to the hearts of the secretarial group who opened the package and insisted their boss call the owner.

EEEEE!

WHAT THIS TOOL DOES

EEEEE! is one of the simplest memory tools of all but also one of the most important to remember. It was written for advertising messages but applies to all paid-for marketing communications. It is a simple reminder to ensure your message justifies the intrusion.

ENGAGE, ENRICH, ENTERTAIN, EDUCATE, ENLIGHTEN
(INFORM but it doesn't begin with an E!),

Advertisements are mostly unwelcome interruptions. They break into programmes people are enjoying. They come in between printed pages or columns people are reading. They are unsolicited pop-ups on a computer or phone screens. They bookend movies or are barriers you have to pass through before getting to the information you want.

Every advertisement must *justify the intrusion* it makes.

Rule No. 1 in advertising is to get noticed. Rule No. 2 is to be relevant. To be engaging, your communication has to be both distinctive and relevant. Engagement is attracting and holding the attention of your audience. Too often communicators use tricks to catch the attention that aren't integral or relevant to the message. They're just distractions, and distractions tend to be annoying. Over time, viewers build up defense mechanisms to prevent them from being distracted. We instantly click shut unwanted pop-up advertisements or fast forward through commercials on DVR.

Consumers are so bombarded with unsolicited selling messages, these defensive barriers are becoming more and more impenetrable. Marketers employ stealth tactics to 'get under the radar', but this is no easy task.

Engaging ads appeal to the intelligence of the recipient. They don't insult the reader's intelligence; they aspire to it. As David Ogilvy once wrote, "The reader isn't a moron. She's your wife!"

"Too many ads that try not to go over the reader's head end up beneath his notice" is one of Leo Burnett's pearls that echoes the sentiment.

Enriching communications add something to the recipient, even if it's only in a small way. It's either interesting, informative, or educational, or best, all three. If it's none of these, but it's amusing or entertaining, that might be sufficient to justify the intrusion too. As Freud pointed out, humour disarms criticism.

It's no surprise so many commercials adopt a humorous approach. They're subconsciously attempting to disarm criticism, to endear themselves before inserting a selling proposition of some sort. Sugarcoating the pill has been around ever since sugar was invented, and it can still work.

Educational communications—telling people something they don't know—is a way of enrichment, if it's done correctly. Adults don't like to be told they don't know things, so the educational approach has to be subtle. Inferred learning by association through storytelling, for example, avoids the fingerpointing of ignorance and lets smart people work out for themselves the moral of the story. Getting someone to want to take the pill themselves is a lot more effective than trying to force it down their throat.

Enlightenment is a level above education. It is a revelation. Like discovering something you had dreamed of actually exists. It's rare, but when it happens it can have a devastating impact. Most often it would be a category-defining new technology, like introducing a television or a fridge before anybody had one. Once seen it cannot be 'unseen', and the world is not the same.

Occasionally, enlightenment comes in the true sense of the word and facilitates a perceptual change in the mind without the need of a new technology or product. 'Seeing the light' isn't restricted to religious conversion. A new way of thinking or believing only takes a fraction of a second to occur, and brilliant communications can be the trigger. Saatchi & Saatchi's 1970 iconic advertisement of a pregnant man asked: "Would you be more careful if it was you that got pregnant?"

Focus on the Take-out

WHAT THIS TOOL DOES

Focus on the Take-out is a reminder for all brand communications that it's not what you put in, it's what customers take out that's important.

After 25 years of dealing with clients who are constantly trying to shoe-horn more information into their communications, this tool deserves its own chapter!

When it comes to communication messages for your brand, 'less is more' is a good general rule. I used the tennis balls image earlier. Throw three or four at the same time, and the catcher will likely drop them all. Throw one hard, and they can catch it one-handed. The same goes with messages. One crisp, concise message is difficult to miss and difficult to misinterpret.

I used to spend hours with clients who'd insist on going through multiple copy revisions, mostly trying to put more stuff in, not take it out. Producing 30-second commercials is a good discipline for rationing words. You don't have many before it sounds compressed or rushed.

I remind clients that they should be less concerned about what they put into their messages and focus more on what the receivers *take out* from them. What one says is not the same as what another hears. What someone means by what they say is not the same as what others interpret that meaning to be. How often is something we say misheard, misinterpreted, or misunderstood?

Sometimes it's difficult to see another interpretation once you've been primed or locked-into to one. Audiences are also predisposed to receive messages. They have their own filters, bias or preferences. A liberal and a conservative may have very different takes on the same message.

Ambiguity is not desirable in brand communications, unless intrigue and reward in deciphering is part of your brand promise!

Experienced copywriters tell their younger team members to boil the message down. Reduce it to the core, where the omission or addition of a single word could not improve it. Singular, focused messages are most effective. Many blunt blows on the head from a boxing glove can still fail to break the skin. A sharp, focused arrowhead can pierce the skull.

Experimentation is a useful tactic. When interpretation is unpredictable, it's a good idea to look at more than one right answer. Direct marketers know this and are skilled at trying different messages to see what delivers the best result. Alternative headlines on the same body copy can deliver significantly different response rates.

So, don't be obsessed by what you put in your messages. Concentrate on what your desired customers are taking out of them. Is it what you want them to take out? If not, what do you need to change to make it so?

Generating, Evaluating, and Nurturing Ideas

WHAT THIS TOOL DOES

Ideas are the catalysts for change. This tool suggests methods for generating, evaluating, and nurturing ideas, taking from my own experience in advertising and from creativity experts like my friend Wayne Lotherington and cult figures like Edward de Bono.

Why is it that some people always seem to have good ideas while others are bereft?

Some can be explained by thinking preference types, but we can all be more creative thinkers and idea-generators if we learn to develop more creative habits. As Edward de Bono observes, most people would like to be more creative. Creativity is the key requirement for achievement and certainly for new ideas. Without it there is no innovation, only repetition and routine.

Many people don't see themselves as creative people or capable of being creative, but it is a skill that can be acquired.

What can we learn from what creative types and entrepreneurs do?

Creative people tend to have the following habits, they:

- Challenge conventional wisdom
- Break patterns of expectation
- Produce multiple solutions
- Ask better questions
- Aren't constrained by established rules
- Move around obstacles
- Link unrelated thoughts
- Think in different, multi-sensory mediums
- Suspend disbelief
- Brainstorm effectively with others

Entrepreneurs:

- Are persistent
- Believe fiercely in their ideas
- Are adventurous
- Experiment
- Treat failures as necessary steps to success
- Develop creative environments, creative cultures
- Marry frontal right brain conceptual thinking with frontal left brain business and financial acumen
- Treat success as reward, not money

An easy exercise many of us will have tried before is this (if not, try it yourself without looking if not): List as many uses for a brick as you can in one minute.

The typical response, without having been primed by the thoughts above, will list things like:

Build a house / build a wall / support a car / throw it through a window...

The creative responses will not be constrained by the conventional uses of bricks, although they will likely include these as well, they will go beyond these to include things like:

Strike a match on / kill ants / sharpen an axe / create a brick tortoise / cook a chicken / grind into dust and use as sand / make a mouse bed / put in your underpants / square football / art display ... and so on.

The point of the exercise is not how sensible the ideas are, but simply *how many* uses you can think of. Those constrained by conventions will struggle to find 10 or more different uses. Those thinking outside the box can often list 40 or more — even if most of them are nonsense.

'That's not fair!' I hear all the time after I've done this exercise. What's not fair about it? I didn't say they had to be sensible, or even good, or even in English. All I was looking for was how many ideas you could come up with in a minute.

The rational thinkers object to this concept, but the more creative types accept and even embrace it. Our world tends to criticise bad ideas more easily than it rewards good ideas.

What does creativity or being creative mean?

It's no coincidence that creative people are often prolific. They have lots of ideas, even if they don't like them all. de Bono describes creativity as *"bringing something into being that was not there before"*.

The great Australian creative agency Campaign Palace says:

"Truly creative people and companies have the imagination to see beyond the present reality and invent new, different and better ways of doing things".

Wayne Lotherington, a good friend and ex-colleague of mine at Leo Burnett, describes creative thinking as: *"The behaviour we use when we generate new ideas... creativity itself is the act of connecting or merging ideas which have not been connected before. New ideas are formed by connecting current ones within our minds."*

The first idea is something we already know, the issue at hand, the problem, current situation or brief. The second idea is also something we know but completely unrelated to the first idea. The third idea is what emerges as a result of colliding the first and the second.

Examples might be a ballpoint pen and deodorant, resulting in roll-on deodorant. Or a surfboard and sailing dinghy, resulting in a windsurfing board. Horse drawn carriage and an engine...you get the idea.

Separate Idea Generation from Idea Evaluation

Fertility is an asset when it comes to idea generation. A neat trick to increase idea fertility is to separate the generation of ideas from the evaluation of ideas.

It is human nature to critique thoughts or ideas as soon as they're born, and this can bring the process to a grinding halt as opinions are exchanged as to the relative merit of each idea or thought. Let the ideas flow, and save the critiques for later.

Suspending disbelief and encouraging the free-flow of idea exchange keeps the creative pipeline open and flowing. It's OK to allow clarification or build off someone else's idea, but it is not OK to shoot down ideas at this stage. It's incredible how many ideas that would have been killed at birth as 'stupid' or 'unrealistic' go on to inspire real solutions.

Once the flow of ideas is exhausted (and there are many ways of squeezing more thoughts out of the collective grey matter than most groups imagine they're capable of) only then do you begin the process of evaluation.

Overcoming Obstacles to Creativity

Getting started is often a problem. Writers are encouraged to just write, anything at first, just to get the creative juices flowing. Athletes warm up before the game, and your brain needs to warm up too.

If you hit a block, take a rest and return refreshed. Or try any one of a myriad of idea generation and lateral thinking tools, including the following creative thought-starters:

- Word association: What's the first thing that comes to mind when I say...?

- Type association: If you were a fish, what kind would you be? ...a car? ...a bird? ...a food item??

- Object association: how would a spoon relate to the issue? ...a guitar? ...a hairbrush?

- Take three adjectives from a group-generated list, and have your neighbour write a short story using these adjectives

- Write an epitaph for your product or service

- What would get you fired?

- What do you stand against?

- Write a newspaper headline featuring your brand in five years' time

- Write a movie logline

- Go outside, bring back an object, then describe how it relates to solving the problem

(If you want more ideas, Edward de Bono's *How to Have Creative Ideas* lists 62 different exercises to develop your creative habits. Wayne Lotherington has a wealth of creative methods too in *How Creative People Connect*. Check out methods such as Eyes of Experts, Relevant Combinations, Random Words, the 3 Is, Extremes, and more.)

Once you've started, it's common to encounter obstacles that prevent progress. Too many give up on their own inherent creativity too early and too easily. Have faith in yourself and your ability to open up your creative mind. It's liberating and fun!

We developed quite a reputation for rocking the boat at Ogilvy & Mather Philippines under the creative leadership of David

Guerrero with support and guidance from worldwide Creative Director Neil French. David and I inherited a small agency of 50 or so people, with one client accounting for 75% of the revenue. We agreed that the market was naturally creative, but the entire advertising industry had never received an international award, ever. And people were more into copying than originality. It all said to us that we needed to have confidence in our own ability. Raise your sights and 'come to the edge', as Saatchi's famous saying goes.

We agreed that building our creative reputation was paramount to our success. Creative, award-winning advertising is directly correlated with greater awareness, engagement, and sales, so we would single-mindedly focus on becoming the most creative agency in the country. We would do this by judging ourselves against international creative standards, not just the local awards.

One of our first ads was a simple print ad for Pepsi-Cola. It had just three lines running from top to bottom:

Say no to dope...
Say no shabu...
Say no to Coke*
...and in small print in brackets at the bottom (*a public service message from the Pepsi-Cola Company).

Well, this tiny little ad caused an enormous commotion at Coca-Cola. Coke had a >75% dominant share of the Asian market at that time. How dare Pepsi take an underhand swipe at them? But the public saw the joke and Pepsi began to gain share.

Recognising and Nurturing Creative Ideas

It's difficult to recognise big ideas when they're created because big ideas often start off as small ideas.

Think of them as seedlings. They start as small green shoots. It's hard to tell if they'll grow to be a weed or a mighty oak. They are still small, delicate, easily crushed underfoot. They need nurturing and protecting. They need the right environment; fertile soil, nutrients, sunshine, water and temperature all have to be right for them to grow. Later they'll need fertiliser and perhaps pesticides to ward off disease. It will need to be pruned and cared for to grow strong and healthy.

How many seeds land on barren ground, or don't get watered, or get eaten by the birds? When a seedling gets crushed, few people mourn it. It wasn't developed enough to be recognised for what it was, so nobody misses it. We don't know what we never had the chance to know. It's a lost opportunity.

It's the same with ideas. They need the right environment to survive, develop, and flourish.

Creative companies have receptive environments to protect and incubate ideas. But even then they can't keep them all, and only the rarest few turn out to be mighty oaks. So how do they identify those ideas with promise early on?

At Ogilvy, Leo Burnett and BBDO, we were often generating work under the intense pressure of disappearing deadlines, alcohol, and fear of failure. We had a good rule: No decision made at three o'clock in the morning is a good decision. Sleep on it and review it then. For creative ideas that seemed wonderful (as many do when you're dog-tired and wanting to see the answer) we called it the 'stinky fish test'. It looks great and smells sweet now, but let's put it aside and see what it looks and smells like the next day. If it looked and smelled like rotten fish then, it probably was rotten! And if not, it may be a keeper!

That sounds like a flippant test, but I can't tell you how much time and effort is wasted 'polishing turds', as Neil French so eloquently describes it. The more effort the polisher puts into polishing it, the more reluctant they are to discard, what in the end, is still a turd.

Great ideas tend to generate energy and excitement around them. They have a buzz. They have a knack of surviving attempts to crush or kill them. They keep reappearing, popping up at strange times and in odd places. They begin to polarise people into positive and negative camps. This polarisation increases over time as does the antipathy between the opposing camps. Polarisation is the first sign of something truly different that could be revolutionary. Truly different ideas tend to break the established order or rules and are thus strongly resisted by those with a vested interest in protecting the way things are.

Polarisation against big ideas can occur even within the most creative of creative communities. At Leo Burnett, the worldwide creative council met annually to self-appraise the pool of best creative work prior to award show submissions. I was privileged to be one of the rare 'suits' to be invited to attend one of these worldwide judging panels at HQ in Chicago. It was a rigorous process with a panel of judges scoring each advertisement electronically against a set of criteria. The consistency of scoring was extremely high with the exception of one or two pieces that polarised the group. One such advertisement was a print ad for a well-known gay wine bar with a close-up visual of a corkscrew trying to open the bottom of the bottle instead of the top. (You get the picture!) Well this polarised the group. Half scored it very low and 'in bad taste', breaking acceptable boundaries. The other half scored it extremely high and felt it pushed boundaries that needed to be pushed to break new ground. We must have debated that one ad for a whole morning (demonstrating how seriously a great creative agency treats its creative product regardless of which side of the fence one sat on). Eventually, the ad was passed. It went on to win major international awards.

A few tips for those running agencies, design houses or other creative businesses. I had a terrific relationship with my partner in Manila, David Guerrero. He ran the creative side, I ran the client and business side. We were committed to raising creative standards despite the skepticism of some clients in the value of doing so.

How did we do this?

Well, we had an ongoing educational programme that made the case for creative solutions as the key to profitability, and we invited junior client members to join our agency classes. The senior client members naturally wanted to know what their staff was learning, and information would filter upwards that way. We'd covertly educate when we sold ads too. We'd celebrate victories with our clients and give them the ownership of the idea they deserved. Slowly, we built up a shared belief in the value of creativity. It didn't work everywhere or with every client, but the message began to seep through and our reputation grew.

David and I had a client classification triangle, with three sections. At the top of the triangle were clients that championed, even demanded, award-winning work. Agency people clamoured to work on these businesses because they were professionally rewarding. This 'top triangle' segment of clients were perhaps no more than 15% of our portfolio of clients. We aimed to double the size of this segment.

The largest section occupied the middle ground of the triangle. These were clients that didn't necessarily champion creativity, but neither did they resist it. They were open to suggestion. We committed to do everything we could to move these customers up the creativity triangle, but we wouldn't die in a ditch for battles that couldn't be won. We would reward work that 'pushed the creative peanut' for the middle-ground clients. There was nothing more uplifting than having one of these clients taste what creativity and creative recognition felt like — and more importantly see the results in their sales. These were perhaps 60% of our client portfolio.

Then there was the remainder; the 25% of clients at the base of the triangle. These were creative 'no hopers', either non-believers, resistant to new ideas, or wedded to rigid executional formulas or 'pattern' copy from elsewhere. Unless they were profitable (and therefore effectively subsidising the creative work produced for other clients) or had the potential to change, we would move these clients out of the agency and replace them with others that were better matched.

Naturally, every creative team wanted to work on the clients that gave them opportunities to show their creativity and be recognised for it. This system allowed us to distribute clients fairly between teams and reward them with the better prospects based on their success. An ad agency is not a democracy, it's a meritocracy. My philosophy on generating great creative work and managing top creative talent was this; if you have thoroughbred racehorses in your stable you've got to let them run. The best jockeys earned the right to ride the best horses every day. That's how we won the big races.

Playing the Joker

Creative people were often frustrated by our internal creative review processes that filtered out concepts they felt were capable of doing well before they were even presented to the client. There are great ideas out there that are never seeing the light of day, they'd claim.

So David and I conceived the "Playing the Joker' rule. Once every quarter we'd allow the Creative Director to select an ad of their choice, that may have been rejected internally or externally, and 'Play the Joker'. That meant the Account Management team weren't allowed to question it. As long as it was legal, decent and truthful, we would do our utmost to sell it, no questions asked.

This made the creative team think really hard about what ads they felt deserved a second chance. It had the double benefit of self-prioritisation, reducing the pressure on the selling team to push every ad. And it focused everyone on one ad or campaign that merited it. We didn't always succeed, but the team recognition and effort strengthened the bond between creators and sellers.

Selling Ideas

WHAT THIS TOOL DOES

This tool shares a philosophy and a few tips for selling ideas from decades of experience selling ideas to just about every type of client you can imagine in the advertising and consulting worlds.

Believe in what you're selling and it's easy. If you have doubts, your clients will sense it like dogs sense fear in a person.

Regardless of what you're selling, the best sales people have tremendous faith in the product or service they're selling. In the advertising world, we were often selling ideas or concepts that had to be visualised. Selling an intangible concept to non-conceptualisers is about as difficult as it gets.

If it was a TV commercial, you didn't have the hundreds of thousands, even millions, of pounds it may cost to shoot a big commercial just to sell it. We'd do mock-ups, storyboards, and occasionally teaser videos, but it still left enormous gaps open to interpretation. Scenery, casting, scripting, delivery, chemistry, comic timing and that 'pixie dust' element of magic that's required for everything to come together — none of that exists. And the picture one person paints in their mind is never identical to another's.

Not all of us are natural conceptualisers. What some can conceive, others will struggle with. We had to convert these conceptual sales into a language that our clients could relate to. Buyers can instinctively sense your level of belief. Passion and sincerity stem from that belief. Time spent back at the ranch getting the product as right as possible before trying to sell it is never time wasted.

Put an Egg in the Mix

Giving ownership of the process to your client early on improves your chances of making a sale.

Cake mix brands such as Betty Crocker learned this early on. They could produce a formula for their ready-mix cake products that didn't require putting a raw egg in the mix, but they discovered that the act of adding an egg to the mix is the bit that makes housewives feel they've done the work. It's the critical act that bestows ownership of the process, making it feel more like their cake.

We would find meaningful ways for our clients to 'add the egg' into the creative product. Perhaps it's a scene, or change of copy line, or a location. It could be one of a million things that gave a real sense of ownership to the client. With that internal ownership, the process of selling the idea up the client ladder became easier with someone pushing from the inside too. Some clients like Pepsi were highly creative, and we'd go as far as involving them in creative concept or tissue sessions. It produced outstanding collaborative results, and we ended up with more than one worldwide campaign that way.

Nailed It!

Another way we strengthened the mutual respect and effectiveness between the creative department and the other departments was through a simple act of gratitude. A person would come into the agency one morning to find a huge plastic nail on their desk with a 'thank you' on it from the creative team. This was random and could be earned for minor or major efforts that helped sell great ads.

Of all the rewards we had, this was the most coveted. Having a creative team recognise your contribution lifted young account executives into the clouds. A $2 plastic nail was far more powerful than any monetary reward.

My colleague and CEO at BioCube, David Tait, is an ex- Goldman Sachs investment banker. He knows a thing or two about selling. One of his favourite sayings is: 'Sales begin at "No"'. Discovering the opportunity and having the persistence to find solutions is what it's all about.

When I was running BBDO Asia Pacific, I happened to notice an ad concept for FedEx lying cast aside in a pile of concept boards. It was brilliant in its simplicity. At the time, FedEx competed in a duopoly with DHL and they were constantly challenging each other for supremacy. This was an outdoor ad with no headline, no body copy, just a visual of a DHL box inside a FedEx box. The ad succinctly communicated that when you really have to ship it, FedEx is the one. The best poster ads 'say it without words'— the visuals do all the talking. They also make the viewer work a little at it before they get the reward of understanding it. This ad did all of that.

'We couldn't sell it to the client', explained the Creative Director Khun Suthisak.

I took the ad back with me to Hong Kong and I met with the Regional Head of FedEx. I said to him: 'I'm not trying to pull the wool over your eyes. I want to run this ad not just because I think it's a great ad and it will endear your users to the brand, but because I think it has a great chance of winning a major award.' I value awards because award-winning ads are proven to be more effective at grabbing attention and selling. They are also valued by my creative people and I like to keep them motivated and rewarded. When I see great work done by my offices, I want to give it every chance to run, to show to my people that the quality of the creative product we produce is important.

Well, credit to this fantastic client, he not only sanctioned it, he offered to cover the costs of producing and running it.

The happy consequence was the top honour at arguably the most prestigious of all award shows — the Cannes Gold Lion.

Three Strikes and You're Out

We were persistent in selling ideas that merited it, but there were limits to how far we could push clients. We had mechanisms that improved our success ratios and prevented us from wasting too much energy 'flogging dead horses'.

One of the curses of agencies is the client that requests interminable revisions to a concept. It goes to and fro from the agency to the creative department on an endless string of changes until it is unrecognisable from the first concept presented. This syndrome is particularly prevalent in large client organisations where approval processes are funneled upwards through several layers of management.

Les Naylor used to have an image of a skeleton of an art director, covered in cobwebs bent over his desk with the headline: 'The last revision!'

The 'three strikes and you're out' rule resolves this issue. We'd give clients fair notice that we would entertain three rounds of revisions; if they came back for a fourth, we'd take the idea away.

Now of course we'd use sensible discretion to ensure clients didn't lose face, but this would either kill or cure pretty quickly. It controlled enormously wasteful time and resource pursuing dead-ends.

When we had big campaign ideas that we felt were strong and we couldn't sell, the notion that someone else would like it was often a reality check to a buyer. Neil French used the metaphor of selling a Rolls Royce: "You've taken it for a spin around the block, and you didn't like it. Now it's on the forecourt for another buyer. We have people who'd like to buy it. Are you asking me to keep it on the forecourt and not sell it?"

It was never positioned as a threat. We wouldn't ever say it if it wasn't true or if we weren't prepared to act on it. Empty threats are unproductive to say the least.

> The reality is many good ideas stay good ideas for a very long time, waiting to find the right client, environment and timing. Every good creative has a cupboard full of ideas that have never seen the light of day for one reason or another. Sometimes, it's better to keep an idea in the cupboard for a better opportunity than waste it or compromise it for less than it's worth.

Focus on the Customer's Customer

Have you ever struggled to get past personalities when trying to sell something to them? You try to couch the selling message in their language. You use words and phrases they want to hear. Mirroring techniques to reflect back what you know they'll respond positively to. You might be lucky and hit the right note, catch the right mood, but you can't guarantee that.

What is more certain is that if your idea solves a key problem for your customer's customer, it is very hard to argue against. We would spend time and money challenging ourselves to understand our client's customers better than they did. If we came up with insights and problems or needs we could resolve, these were invariably of interest to our clients. Then we used the 'language of our customer's customers' in our advertisement and selling message.

Elevator Pitch, Silver Bullets, or Movie Logline

We've all heard of the elevator pirch before, but we rarely have it ready when it's needed.

Top guns tend to like it short and snappy. You've just spent two hours trying to sell a new campaign to the marketing group. You're on the way out of the building when the chairman steps into the elevator. It's just you and her, and you've got 30 seconds maximum to get your message across and persuade her to go with it. After a while your elevator pitch becomes so rehearsed and practised you can roll it off your tongue instantly and naturally.

Some people prefer the idea of silver bullets—three or four bullet points that trigger the memory and then allows you to express them verbally. Below are the silver-bullets for a fantastic young entrepreneurial company I'm working with called BluMaan. They design, produce and distribute premium men's haircare products and market them through online channels they create and own:

- Confidence-building community
- Believe great hair can transform the world
- Meraki (a Greek word meaning done with heart and passion)
- Online business

These silver bullets might trigger a stream of consciousness like:

'The confidence-building community is a reminder of the ultimate benefit of our product...our hair care products style hair to make men look good and feel good...when you feel good you have more confidence in yourself and being more confident in yourself improves your chances of achieving goals in life that you want to achieve. That's why we believe great hair can transform the world, one great hair look at a time. We approach our business with a Meraki philosophy; it's a Greek word that means things that are done with a heartfelt passion. Great hair is a passion for us and we put it into every product we produce. We are in constant dialogue with hair addicts like us who are always looking into new and interesting products. We are the dominant men's haircare brand online with over 1.5 million dedicated subscribers to our YouTube channel'.

Movie loglines are similar. Give me the plot in a sentence. These are a fun exercise in workshops, and they create plenty of empathy for copywriters afterwards.

One of the best known examples quoted in the screenwriter Blake Snyder's book *Save the Cat* was for a movie about rampaging grizzly bears, the logline pitch was 'Jaws with paws'.

The Camel Caravan

WHAT THIS TOOL DOES

The Camel Caravan is a useful visual metaphor for coalitions of the willing. It demonstrates how essential it is to embrace change and bring it to fruition. It's also a helpful analogy to manage pioneers and laggards—those that run ahead or lag behind change programmes.

The Camel Caravan is the favourite tool of one of my favourite clients, Greg Devenish, the ex-Principal of St. George's Junior School in Canada. It captured perfectly for him the challenges he was facing trying to implement change in his organisation.

My small brand consulting company conducted a Discovery Report as part of a BCM process and went further with a cultural assessment of the school, including an assessment of the entire leadership team. It was easy to understand why the school had been such a pleasant place to work in, but the team struggled to embrace new concepts in teaching and learning. They had also avoided the difficult business of firing persistent non-performers.

We found a bias towards relationship orientation and administrative organisation (as in 'a place for everything and everything in its place'). The majority of teachers in the school were exceptional, but as with most organisations, there are always one or two bad apples. With the cultural default mode being a desire to placate and 'get along' with everyone, these one or two antagonists found themselves almost immune to criticism, protected by a culture of caring and a multi-layered administrative system. It doesn't take many antagonists to disrupt a change programme.

To those who don't believe the cliché about a couple of rotten apples spoiling the barrel, I say think of adding a teaspoon of dogs dirt to a gallon of ice cream. You're not going to touch a drop, are you? Sorry, the image is a little disgusting, but the point is made. It only takes a little to ruin a lot.

The Camel Caravan is a metaphor for the adoption of change illustrated in the bell curve below. The majority of the faculty was embracing the change programme and actively involved in implementing change. Some were extremely positive and keen to lead the way. Others were not excited or positive about change, but not necessarily resistant if persuaded otherwise.

Then there was the handful of braying old camels at the back. These camels whisper at first, then bray loudly as the caravan starts moving.

They say to those who will listen to them, "Hey, why are you following them? They don't know where they're going! These leaders are clueless. They say they're taking you to an oasis but they've never been there before or seen it for themselves…it doesn't exist…it's just a mirage. Stay here, we're fine here. Let those guys wander off into the middle of nowhere; we'll laugh at them when they come back exhausted and dying of thirst."

What happens? After investing a disproportionate amount of resource empathising, explaining and encouraging prior to embarking on the journey, the braying old camels at the back don't budge. The gap between the last camel and them grows larger. The other camels talk amongst themselves…'we have to go back for them, we can't just leave them there'… they turn their heads back to where they've just left. A couple of camels who can talk with them are sent back to persuade them to come. This circling back to bring the malcontents up with the rest of the caravan happens two or three times, slowing the progress of the entire troop.

Sound familiar? In the real world this process can go on for years, sometimes decades. You can't move forward if you're constantly circling backwards.

Braying camels need to be identified and dealt with swiftly. In the private sector, this is often easier than in some of the larger public sector bureaucracies. The opportunity and incentive to 'get on the bus' must be fairly given—and importantly, witnessed by the influencers in the organisation. Those resistant to change may hold legitimate concerns that need to be heard and heeded. Sometimes this act alone is enough to mobilise resistors—and a converted sceptic is a powerful means to encourage others.

But once that's been done, if the intransigence remains, they need to be cut from the train swiftly and irrevocably.

The Principal in this story had the courage to cut the braying camels loose. He was amazed at the impact it had. After years of trying to encourage change with positive reinforcement, severing ties with the troublemakers gave a tremendous boost to the rest of the faculty.

Knowing the top reason why good people leave organisations, it was not a surprise to me.

What is that reason?

A lack of consequence for non-compliance in meeting minimum standards or expectations. If your best people see the organisation tolerating, or going out of their way to pacify persistent troublemakers and underperformers, they understandably lose the motivation to perform better themselves

You can't sail the ship when it's dragging an anchor. Cut away the drag on the ship, and it rights itself almost instantly.

> The best run ships scrape the barnacles off their hulls every year to keep them moving smoothly through the water. Scraping barnacles was the sentiment behind one of the sections I had to present to my corporate bosses in my annual plans. I had to identify the bottom 5% of performers and recommend who should be moved out of the organisation.

Good people have no fear of cutting away deadwood. They fear the opposite: getting strangled in the overgrowth through lack of pruning.

A word of caution about over-eagerness. It's tempting to let the keen supporters run ahead of the rest of the train. It's a risky business. Many pioneer camels get lost looking for the oasis. Some don't make it back, or they can lead the whole caravan off course.

When you set off on a long journey into unknown territory, it's best to leave with a coalition of the willing; people who've 'signed up' for it, at least as best as they can know.

The Silent Majority

With all the focus on the laggards and the pioneers, it's easy to forget the significant silent majority. This is where the bulk of employees and customers are in any change scenario. They are the mass that are more often than not willing to go with the flow, neither the innovators, early adopters or laggards.

'The squeaky wheel gets the oil' is unfortunately all too true. Management gets pulled in two opposite directions by the extremes of the bell curve. Think about politics. The far right and the far left get the bulk of the media coverage; the majority of silent moderates aren't as newsworthy it would seem.

Don't make this mistake. A small amount of effort in this area can reap large dividends, accelerating the adoption of change by moving the whole bell curve through faster. The same goes with recognition and reward. Don't forget the main population of adequate performers in the middle. They are doing their bit and finding the right moments to celebrate them can be extremely rewarding for both the individuals and the company.

THE SILENT MAJORITY

INNOVATORS
Eager for change

EARLY ADOPTERS
Positive toward change

LAGGARDS
Against change

FORGOTTEN GROUP
Neither for nor against change

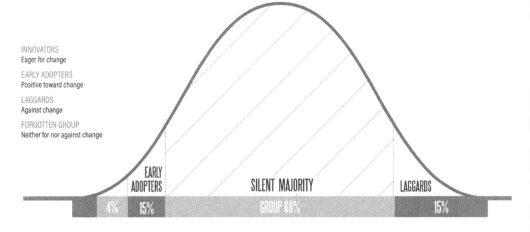

EARLY ADOPTERS	SILENT MAJORITY	LAGGARDS
4%	15%	GROUP 66%	15%

Best Case, Worst Case

WHAT THIS TOOL DOES

Best Case, Worst Case is a reminder to set out alternative scenarios at the start of the planning process. Having the discipline to do this creates more realistic and more achievable plans.

Any entrepreneur who has tried to raise capital knows that lenders want to see a best case, worst case, and most likely financial scenario. They see 'hockey stick' financial projections all the time that invariably end up as 'hairy backs'—a series of false starts and re-forecasts over time.

As insurance companies will tell you, we tend to project more favourable future outcomes than the statistics and laws of probability would suggest. Not many of us plan to build a house of straw when we're imagining a house of brick, but that's exactly what happens in many instances when resources run short or expedient measures are taken for whatever reason.

So this exercise, while not wishing to clip anyone's wings, is a sensible reality check.

Best Case
What is the best outcome you could possibly hope for? What would it look like in terms of sales, market, geography? If everything falls into place as predicted and planned, with no mishaps or corrections, this is what the outcome will look like.

Worst Case
What is the pessimistic view of the future? If everything falls 'jam side down', how would things look then? Don't dismiss the possibility before you've even started. What are the implications for your revenue forecasts? Will you be able to lower your costs sufficiently to still be able to make a profit?

Most Likely
What's the middle ground between best and worst case scenarios? What is the most probable outcome assuming not everything goes your way, but mostly it does?

The more vivid a picture you can paint of each scenario beyond financial spreadsheets, the more valuable the exercise. Timelines and key milestones should be built in to monitor progress against time. Sometimes the pattern of growth is correct but the timing of it is later than expected. And if it's sooner, well, that's a nice problem to have.

It's always good to have a plan B. When I first started in advertising, I was privileged to witness firsthand one of the historic PR disasters turned marketing coups of the times. Working at McCann-Erickson I was a knee-high-to-a-grasshopper junior account manager, just about senior enough to take coffee and tea orders for the top brass in the war room as the crisis unfolded. What was the issue? It was the launch of New Coke in April 1985.

After years of the cola wars, great rivals Pepsi had gradually been chipping away at Coke's brand share. Coca-Cola research told them what Pepsi knew — that in blind taste tests, consumers preferred the richer, more complex taste of Pepsi to Coca-Cola. That preference was reversed when the brands were revealed, demonstrating the power of emotional brand perception. Pepsi had been running the successful Pepsi Challenge campaign for years. At the same time, Coke had secretly been developing a new formula that was smoother and sweeter and that scored significantly better than 'old Coke' versus Pepsi in blind taste tests.

The decision was finally made to launch New Coke with the new formula. It was a bold move to strengthen their market-topping position and block the advancement of a competitor.

The result? All hell broke loose!

'How could you do this?' screamed the loyal Old Coke users. There was an orchestrated uprising with protest groups springing up all across America. The popularity of New Coke plummeted, with some sources reporting only 13% of Coke drinkers preferring it. (Remember, this is after research had shown a preference in blind tests over Old Coke. Again, proof that brands are perceptions.)

The President of Pepsi Cola, Roger Enrico famously said, 'After years of going eyeball to eyeball, the other guy just blinked'. He gave PepsiCo employees around the world a day off to celebrate.

The heat was intense in that bunker, I can tell you. Coca-Cola was a flagship account for the agency and what was supposed to be the biggest good news launch of the decade was turning into a disaster. After weeks of toughing it out, Coca-Cola did the right thing, something that turned a negative into a huge positive. They apologised. Publicly and sincerely. In July of that year, Donald Keough announced that Old Coke was returning. More important, that the company had made a mistake in taking a brand away that belonged to the people, not the company. They had temporarily forgotten this rule, but they wouldn't repeat the mistake.

The Coke-loving public responded to a sincere apology. The publicity surrounding the whole event was phenomenal and it drove interest levels in the cola category to a new high — and with it Coca-Cola sales and brand share. What started as a marketing nightmare ended up being a publicity coup and a huge sales success.

Storytelling

WHAT THIS TOOL DOES

Storytelling endures as one of the most powerful and effective ways of sharing knowledge between generations. The power of telling stories should never be lost on brands. Every brand has a story to tell. Told well, it becomes legend. Learning to communicate through storytelling is a skill that will help register the messages you want heard and endear you to your listeners.

'Tell me a story about when you were a boy,' my youngest son Jack asks me. The magic of storytelling is universally appealing to children everywhere around the world. Even at 13 he wasn't embarrassed to ask for a bedtime story, and I'm happy it's that way.

The young love magical fantasy, but as we get older those stories rooted in truth and real life experience take on greater interest. Parables, or stories carrying meaning, are wonderful ways of educating adults who are resistant to being told what to do.

Stories allow the listener to interpret meaning the way they want. The way that is meaningful to them. No two people will interpret a story exactly the same way.

Storytelling is a human interaction. It's proximate and intimate.

I often use Jackanory-style storytelling in my workshops (Jackanory was an old UK TV programme where a minor celebrity would read a story chapter by chapter each night from a simple wooden chair. It must have been the cheapest programming on earth, requiring no set, no other actors, and no script!). I consciously gather everyone round in a semicircle, often seated on the floor together kindergarten style, pull up a chair, and slowly open a book and read from it. The stories have a relevant message for the listeners that relates to their brand or situation. It may not always align people, but it gets them thinking and talking about a shared issue.

The magic of a good story well told never wanes. It's a bond between teller and listener in which respect is given both ways in time and 'active listening'.

"The Two Wolves" is a wonderful Native American story:

An old Cherokee grandfather said to his young grandson who had come to him filled with hatred and anger at a friend who had done him wrong, "Let me tell you a story."

I too have a fight going on inside me. At times I too have a feeling of anger and hate for those who have done me an injustice, with no sorrow for what they have done. But hate wears you down and does not hurt your enemy. It is like taking poison and wishing your enemy would die.

It is as if there are two wolves inside me in a terrible fight for their lives. One wolf is evil—he is anger, mistrust, cruelty, envy, regret, greed, arrogance, self-pity, guilt, resentment, lies, superiority and ego.

He continued: "The other wolf is good—he is kindness, joy, peace, love, hope, serenity, benevolence, generosity, truth, compassion and faith."

Sometimes it is hard to live with these two wolves inside of me, each trying to dominate me with their spirit.

The boy sat quietly, then asked him: "Which wolf wins?"

The grandfather smiled and whispered to him: "The one you feed."

The power of a short story. A better lesson for my young son in five minutes than five years of my schooling.

Stories allow adults to take learning by stepping outside of their direct situation. They disarm defensiveness. Adults resist being told what to do and tend to resent unsolicited advice even when it's well meant. Stories allow for applied learning through personal interpretation and internalisation. As long as it's not preachy or too didactic, people will take meaning and relate to it through their own personal history and filters.

Environment is important for storytelling. Your audience needs to be in a receptive mood, relaxed and with no distractions. No message can be registered without it being absorbed first. That means speaking in their language — not just literally, but emotionally too. If your audience sees your passion they are more likely to feel it too.

Conversely if you're speaking an alien tongue or in concepts that simply can't be related to, even good stories will fall on deaf ears.

Below is a real case study of mine. It demonstrates the power of storytelling to tackle a delicate topic that had been the elephant in the room for this small company for years. There were three senior executives running the company, each with different skill sets and allegiances:

"Once there were three musketeers.

Each one of them had a powerful strength and a powerful weakness.

The first had the gift of vision—he could foresee the future and envisaged a land of promise—but he had no stomach for the long arduous journey to reach it and failed to inspire others to follow him.

The second had the gift of compassion and fairness, the people would listen—but he lacked the courage to make difficult decisions—after all, the journey would be long and risky and there were bound to be many casualties.

The third had courage and tenacity in spades, enough to reach the promised land and with a band of followers behind him, but he lacked the ability to see beyond the horizon and questioned his status as a musketeer.

Each of them thought about their weaknesses and harboured doubts about their ability.

For over a decade the three musketeers worked together and became friends, adept at compensating for each other without confronting the key issues; that they worked in pairs but never all together—and consequently they never made a decision all three were united behind.

The lack of decisions and unity began to tell as their environment grew harsher.

Would the three musketeers be able to focus on combining all three of their strengths to reach the promised land?"

Relating their situation to the Three Musketeers took it away from direct personalities and added a touch of light-heartedness that allowed us to confront an issue that people had been tip-toeing around forever. The end result was a greater awareness of the issue and a commitment to constructive collaboration. Each musketeer also took a programme of executive coaching to develop individual skills to enhance their partnership skills that optimised their different attributes as a team.

The Rule of Three

WHAT THIS TOOL DOES

The Rule of Three is an unwritten law that I've found to be true and a useful rule of thumb to follow. A list of three things to do gets done. More than that and you begin to lose focus. Less than that and there's the potential to do less than you're capable of achieving.

Three legs on a stool is the minimum number of supports to create a stable platform. Three is the minimum number for identifying pattern.

I used to be presented with two great print ads of an idea, and I'd always challenge the teams to give me a third great execution before I'd be convinced this was a great idea. It was amazing how hard it was to find the third. 'Two great ads are two great ads; three great ads are a campaign', I used to say.

I like the simplicity of three. I use it everywhere, from summarising what my company does to setting objectives.

When it comes to strategic plans I encourage my clients to have at least three goals but no more than four. It's amazing how much easier it is to focus on what is important to do when you're given a smaller number of things to do. And you're not allowed to give broad 'catch-all' descriptors such as 'Satisfy customers'! They need to be specific and accountable.

Calendar planning is a good example. We're used to dealing in four quarters. I've actually found trimester planning is more effective for strategic planning. What big three things are you going to achieve this year? Give yourself four months for each. What are you going to achieve in the first trimester, the second and the third? That extra month makes up for holidays and lost time due to predictably unpredictable events.

The Impossible Triangle

WHAT THIS TOOL DOES

It seems that every client or customer out there doesn't know about the Impossible Triangle...or perhaps conveniently forgets it...so here it is to remind everyone that you can't have it all.

Good, Quick, Cheap. Pick any two, you can't have all three.

It's an immutable law of business. It should be etched in stone. Or tattooed on every buyer! If you want something good quality and fast, it's not going to be cheap. If you want it cheap and quick, it's not going to be good. And if you want it good and cheap, it's not going to be fast.

The impossible triangle is just that. You simply can't have all three at once no matter how hard the customer insists.

It's an easy tool to have ready to use the minute it comes up. If you promise to fulfill all three, you will fail. So better deal with managing expectations right from the get go. If the purchaser still insists they want all three, save yourself a lot of pain and politely walk away.

There are no exceptions to this rule.

The Three Bucket Test

WHAT THIS TOOL DOES

David H. Maister wrote about the Three Bucket Test in Practice What You Preach. *It is a five-minute exercise that can dramatically improve your own productivity and the productivity of your workforce. Don't believe me? Try it.*

Think about your work life. Break it down into individual tasks as best you can, then place each task into one of three buckets:

LOVE
TOLERATE
JUNK

Everybody can enjoy work more. Things you love to do that are productive and appropriate to the strategy, find more of to do. Things that you can tolerate, find ways to make these more enjoyable or, more likely, find ways of managing these tasks in a more efficient or rewarding way. Allocate a time of day, break tasks into achievable chunks and reward yourself once you've completed them. Start your day with the things you love doing, and it sets you up for the rest of the day.

For the stuff you simply detest doing—that is typically energy-sapping, soul-destroying, worse than mundane—junk it. Toss it in the bin. At least as much as you can without being fired.

All of us have to deal with some Junk. If it gets to be more than 15 or 20% of what you do, you need to find a solution. It is probable that what you hate doing, someone else actually loves doing (remember contrasting whole brain preferences). See if you can reallocate it.

If you find your Love bucket is empty and your Junk bucket is full, find another job. Seriously.

For leaders of people, wherever possible, your task is to energise, enthuse, and excite your teams every day. The Three Bucket Test is a quick 'finger in the wind' to assess how people feel. As a basic rule of thumb, a 60:30:10 ratio of Love: Tolerate: Junk is a good target.

Conclusion: Keeping Your Brand at the Centre

Here are eight things the Brand Centered Management process delivers:

1. A relevant and differentiating positioning to a specific interest group or tribe

2. A compelling and credible promise in a Brand DNA that combines this with purpose and culture

3. A structured 4Ds process to follow: Discovery, Definition, Direction and Delivery

4. Consistent delivery of customer experiences across all customer touch points

5. Bias-balanced leadership teams that put the brand at the centre of business strategy

6. A strategic plan that focuses on the DO before the SAY

7. Alignment of 'brands'; personal brand, corporate brand, product and service brands, brand communications and brand identity

8. Collaborative coalitions of the willing (brand teams or business units)

Brand Centered Management starts where all good marketing begins, in asking, 'who is your customer?' It challenges organisations to identify and articulate the specific interest groups or tribes they want their brand to appeal to, remembering they can't be all things to all people. It provides a template for defining your brand through a living DNA and it lays out a structured 4 Ds process to follow. It encourages organisations to deliver consistent brand experiences everywhere customers meet the brand, every time. It describes how balanced leadership teams with diversified skills can be built to lead the way. It lays out templates for strategic plans with an emphasis on delivering the substance of desired experiences or promises before the packaging of communicating them. And it encourages consistency across each aspect of the brand, delivered through collaborative teams aligned in purpose and belief.

The Brand Centered Management process is, in fact, a powerful change management process in which the brand is the central driving force. But time and again, I see clients gradually forget the lessons learned from these tools. I see organisations struggle to embrace change or bring it about effectively. So, with this last section, I have identified three valuable tools to help you successfully overcome obstacles and incorporate what you've discovered, so that your brand can continue to be at the centre of everything you do.

Done well, Brand Centered Management delivers a stronger brand, an engaged, aligned and motivated team and a richer cultural environment.

Monitor your progress against this checklist of benefits:

- A clear understanding of what you stand for

- A focused, differentiated, compelling and credible promise

- A better understanding of the current perceptions of your brand, its strengths and weaknesses relative to competitors and the category

- A better understanding of the opportunities for your brand

- A better understanding of personal leadership characteristics

- Clear, shared corporate goals and objectives

- A blueprint for determining the right brand family architecture (the number of brands and interrelationships between them)

- Effective, customer-led change management

- Marketing communications that reflect the reality of the experience and justify the intrusion

- Effective internal communications through formal and informal channels

- Increased trust, commitment and loyalty among your people, to each other and to the brand

- A detailed roadmap for leadership, management and staff to deliver on your promise

- A defining set of principles or values required to deliver your promise and stand your brand apart from competitors

- Translation of these principles into specific actions and behaviours

- A leadership team that teamworks and takes ownership of the process and results

- Personal leadership development assessment, interpretation and coaching for senior players to enhance personal and professional development in life and work

- Motivated, challenged and energised thinking-intensive employees

- An aligned workforce all pulling in the same direction toward a shared goal, who 'live the brand' and are committed to delivering your promise to customers

- Performance measures and targets required to deliver a consistent experience to your customer

- A feedback system to recognise and reward top performers and coach others to succeed

- A better understanding of the cultural dynamics of your organisation and a plan to develop effective team-working

- A culture that encourages openness, trust and challenge

- Productive, collaborative teams of specialists

- A retention strategy that keeps the right people from leaving your company and a recruitment approach that attracts the right people

Overcoming Vested Interest in Inertia (VIII)

WHAT THIS TOOL DOES

Overcoming VIII is a thinking tool that helps change agents identify and overcome the barriers and resistance to change put up by those with a vested interest in maintaining the status quo. Perhaps the greatest help is in recognising the phenomenon of Vested Interest in Inertia or VIII exists—and giving it a name.

Everyone knows Winston Churchill's famous two-finger V-for-victory salute. If you turn it around, it becomes a very rude gesture in the UK. 'Flicking the V sign' is often accompanied by an aggressive glare and an expletive or two.

That second 'V-sign' should be the symbol of Vested Interest in Inertia (VIII). Organisations afflicted with VIII will rarely give you the V-sign to your face, although they might behind your back. They'll likely demonstrate it through willful disobedience, foot-dragging, obstruction, non-compliance and sabotage. In extreme cases, it can develop into militant resistance and revolution. It's an apposite symbol for how passionately people in organisations will defend their 'old' territory from the perceived threat of 'new' change.

We are surrounded everywhere by VIII. Vested Interest in Inertia is prevalent everywhere organisations exist, private or public. Amy Sample Ward offered a clue as to why VIII persists from the world of charitable and not-for-profit organisations. She observed: *"We are creating organisations that are so vested in the social issues they are working towards ending, that they require those issues to persist."*

I've seen this phenomenon firsthand. I've been involved for a number of years in trying to get a disruptive technology in the clean-tech sector off the ground. It's a transportable biodiesel refinery that does everything a large bricks and mortar refinery does except in a design-engineered 20' sea container. It uses sustainable, renewable and waste feedstock oil to produce high quality biodiesel that can be used directly in any diesel engine. It costs a tiny fraction of a large-scale refinery but can be scaled-up to generate similar volumes. It can be shipped anywhere in the world and be operational within hours. By producing a carbon-neutral alternative fuel to fossil diesel close to the point of harvest and consumption, it eliminates costly and polluting transportation of goods over long distances to feed large central refineries. And it gives communities and commercial enterprises the energy independence they need.

Sound like a good idea? You'd think so. Unfortunately, the very organisations espousing a clean energy future (big government and big oil) have an enormous vested interest in retaining the status quo. Billions of dollars in sales, tax revenues and jobs are at stake. And a century of power and control of the rules of the game has created a maze of policies and regulations to protect the way it is.

How will it change? Most likely remote areas in Africa, Southeast Asia, and Latin America will spark the change first, where niche markets present opportunities. Or an environmental or military crisis will disrupt supply chains. Commodity pricing dynamics will change and so will the rules of the game. The law of diversification applies, and suddenly those adapted to small-scale, independent processing have an advantage.

It can take decades for even the most blindingly obvious superior advantages of a 'new, different way' to be adopted. A side-by-side comparison of Thomas Edison's electric light bulb versus a gas lamp was a clear demonstration of superiority. But it took decades to popularise electric lighting. The sheer scale of investment in the infrastructure of gas piping created tremendous vested interest in inertia.

Technology takes time to be adopted, even when the advantages are clear for all to see. They follow a predictable S-curve pattern where slow adoption by pioneers at first accelerates exponentially then rapidly, before saturation slows and ultimately reverses growth.

Resistance can be leap-frogged by those that have nothing holding them back. Decades ago when the mobile phone and texting revolution was taking place, the Philippines would probably not have been picked as the world's leading market for mobile phone uptake. But it was. And not just in urban areas, but in poorer rural, farming territories. How come? Because there was comparatively little vested interest in protecting the sunk costs of hard-wired copper cable infrastructure, because it hardly existed. Without this, telecoms companies were liberated and could leapfrog other countries by going from nothing to the latest technology, skipping fifty years of wired telephony in between.

Barriers to Exit

How many of us get frustrated that we can't talk to a real person when we call the bank? Or pretty much any large company these days? You can spend hours navigating automated call-answering systems before getting to speak to a human being.

How many of you have tried to close a bank account recently? Or open one? My bet is you'll find it a million times easier to start a new commercial relationship than it is to exit one. Like lobster pots, it's easy to get in and impossible to get out.

Why? Because marketers put up barriers to exit. This is another way in which even bad systems persist and another way inertia gains traction. Companies boast about customer loyalty. For some it may be well-founded. For many, I suspect it's indifference and the barriers to exit they've put up. No matter how bad the service is, most people assume the competitors will be just as bad.

How can this behaviour be changed?

Calling companies out on it is one way. Have them experience their own systems. James Veitch has made a business out of some very amusing TedX talks on 'unsubscribing' from unscrupulous internet spammers. He gives them a dose of their own medicine by sending them thousands of automatic responses to flood their inboxes until they are the ones trying to get rid of him!

There are elegant solutions. Edward de Bono solved the problem of industrial companies polluting river systems by having laws passed that required them to take their water *downstream* from the source (not upstream as they invariably did) and to evacuate waste water upstream. If they were not polluting, as they claimed, then why would they object to this solution?

Perhaps there should be a law that says companies have to make it as easy to exit a relationship as it is to enter one. Then, I suspect, we'd see more effort put into satisfying customers.

Why are Organisations Resistant to Change?

More importantly, what can we do about it? Organisations are only collections of people and here are some of the reasons people are resistant to change:

- 'What's in it for me?'
- Lack of understanding of the need for change and the value it brings
- Low tolerance for change (T1, T2 types)
- Poor communication, mistrust, or bad timing
- Reluctance to let go of the 'old ways' they've invested time, resource, energy in
- Loss of control, autonomy or power under 'new rules'
- Loss of job security, income, prosperity

- Fear of the unknown
- Feeling of incompetence, unworthiness, loss of purpose and value
- Benefits and reward don't match perceived effort and risk

So What Can Be Done to Counter VIII and Resistance to Change?

First and foremost, recognise the syndrome. Then call it out. Make companies aware of the issues, and the best ones will respond with solutions. If companies don't respond, maybe the public will. Individuals can change the world, sometimes overnight.

Move Around Immovable Obstacles

I like the thought that when faced with one of only two options, take the third. You often need to step outside the constraints of existing perceptions and think laterally to find creative solutions to an old problem.

The Gordian knot was so complicated it became synonymous with impossible tasks; nobody could unravel it. As legend has it, it was 'solved' by Alexander the Great. How? Not by messing around trying to untie it. He just chopped through it with his sword.

In Hong Kong there was a saying that in essence meant 'When faced with an immovable object, move around it like water moves around a rock'. Sometimes you don't need to blow up the rock; save the energy, work around it (and erode its foundation a little more every day at the same time).

Flea in the Ear

In his book *The Elephant and the Flea*, Charles Handy describes how large organisations can be made to 'dance' by small, influential advisors in their ears, in the same way a flea could in an elephant's ear.

Influencers can have a profound effect in determining the direction and behaviour of large organisations. You don't need large organisations to change other large organisations. Individuals, pairs and small teams can change huge companies.

Demonstration

When you do have a meaningful promise, demonstrating it can be extremely effective.

Demonstration works well for the rational thinkers who ascribe to the notion: "I'll only believe it when I see it".

Suspend Disbelief

Encourage people to think the upside-down way. "I'll only see it when I believe it" may sound silly to some, but it's a powerful way of overcoming resistance to change. It also encourages a positive frame of mind.

You're more susceptible to hypnosis if you believe it, for example. Remember Mary Poppins taking Michael and Jane to tea with uncle Albert? The table was suspended in air, kept aloft by them laughing. When the laughing stopped, the magic was lost.

As adolescents and adults, we lose the power of belief in magic that we held as children. I like to think it's still there and can be recovered from time to time, when we need to believe to see.

Plan Ahead

It's predictable that you're going to encounter resistance to change, so plan for it in advance.

Many of the reasons listed above for why people resist change are completely understandable. You'll rarely be able to solve everyone's issues, but timely, clear, transparent, honest communication tailored to the target is rarely a mistake.

Opportunity and Hope

Too often, change management is used as a euphemism for downsizing a workforce. Change management invariably can cause disruption and upset, but it is also about opportunity, hope, and excitement. It's a natural part of growth and evolution to be celebrated and enjoyed.

A Sense of Purpose

The most powerful driver of self-esteem is a sense of purpose.

Young offenders told they are useless, helpless and a nuisance to society will tend to continue fulfilling that role. Successful rehabilitation programmes begin with seemingly unimportant tasks such as setting tables and serving at restaurants, to re-connect with the sense of responsibility, a job well done, recognition and reward— something many young offenders will never have experienced before.

Given a sense of worth and a sense of purpose we all feel there is a place for us in the world. For those impacted by change, ensure they retain a sense of purpose — even if it isn't with the organisation.

Courage and Persistence

Above all, it takes courage to venture into the unknown.

Making a leap of faith is frowned upon in a world of risk-alleviation and compliance. Successful entrepreneurs commonly have both courage and determination to succeed. They persist in pursuing their dream despite setbacks.

Constructive Disruption

As it suggests, constructive disruption is disruption in a constructive way. It is a mindset and an approach, both at a personal and an organisational level. The opposite is destructive disruption—that is tearing things down with little regard to collateral damage—and with no intention to rebuild.

When I facilitate strategic workshops I like to cast myself in the role of constructive disruptor; that is, someone that takes the group out of their comfort zone in order to change perspectives and challenge conventions, but do so in a way that doesn't alienate participants.

It's a difficult balance to strike.

Humans are creatures of habit and disruption is often unwelcome, uncomfortable or unsettling—even if the outcome is positive. Some are willing participants; many need to be encouraged to free themselves from entrenched thought-patterns in order to embrace the new.

I've found it helps to pre-empt. 'This may be a bit confusing or painful . . . but it's necessary and it's going to be worth it in the end . . .' It's important to bring the team with you on the journey, so I use check-back mechanisms to review progress, without allowing it to derail forward progress.

As in life, you will find it is impossible to please everybody and with any disruptive process there will be some casualties. However, approaching the process with a commitment to be constructive rather than destructive is a good discipline.

Opportunity Cost

WHAT THIS TOOL DOES

Opportunity Cost is the cost of inaction. More accurately it should be called Lost Opportunity Cost. For those made aware of it, and who believe it, it is the most powerful tool of all with potential to turn the world upside down in a positive way.

I have always wondered why some people struggle with the concept of opportunity cost. It's an inconvenient notion that simply doesn't exist for some. But it's real.

Opportunity cost is the cost of *not* doing things. Of sticking instead of twisting. Of not taking that calculated risk, or indeed, of not taking a risk at all. As the Turbulence Model illustrates, many of us are less comfortable with uncertainty than we'd care to admit. As we get older our tolerance for risk diminishes too, perhaps out of respect for what limits on accomplishments we've imposed on ourselves. Perhaps it's the natural tendency to hold on tighter to what you have. The young have less to lose and more excitement in the unknown. Naivety can be a great asset in appetite for risk.

Actuaries, bankers and insurance brokers know all about opportunity cost. It's built into the premiums and interest we pay. But few others are aware of the concept, let alone manage their world this way.

Why? I don't have an easy answer, but I think it goes back to human nature. We are all wired to post-rationalise decisions we've made, good or bad. We tend to take credit for the good decisions and put the bad ones down to bad luck, fate, or changes in circumstances beyond our control.

Confronting the notion of opportunity cost *before making decisions* is one of the small ways you can exert more control of your situation. Every strategic plan should include a section on the opportunity cost. This would start with the potential cost of inaction. What would doing nothing, or retaining the status quo, likely cost?

Then it would include the opportunity cost of the course of action that is decided upon. Assuming that all of us are subject to limitations on resource, making a decision to do one thing means also making a decision NOT to do something else with that resource.

Consider Avogadro's Mule: Stuck equidistant between two bales of hay, a starving mule starves to death, not knowing which bale of hay to turn to. This is the reality of how some organisations find themselves paralysed by choice.

Choosing what NOT to do is one of the easiest ways of starting a discussion towards what you do want to do. Similarly, what you stand against helps articulate what you stand for.

Our commercial world is geared towards measuring the cost of the things we do in great detail. Corporate governance regulations, financial audits, financial forecasts, and so on are all oriented towards what has been done, or what we plan to do. Rarely is a figure attached to the cost of *not* having done something.

Partly, that's because it's impossible to go backwards and change things that have been done. We don't get that time back, and one cannot say with certainty where the other path would have led. Why dwell on things you can't change, some will say.

Opportunity cost is not about looking backwards, though. It's a tool for the present to assist in planning for the future.

Tools are about action. They help you do things. They help you do things faster, better, more efficiently, with a different outlook or perspective. The thread that binds them is that they are ammunition in the war against vested interest in inertia.

Building Your Personal Brand

WHAT THIS TOOL DOES

This tool is a reminder that the principles that build strong commercial brands are the same ones that will help you build a strong personal brand. We can all consciously shape our mindset and our behavior. We are all authors of our own story—if we take responsibility for it.

Think about your own Brand DNA. What is your role or purpose in life (deep down)? What is it that you promise and deliver to others? How does it benefit them, you and the bigger world, even in little, seemingly insignificant ways? How do you go about doing it—what are your personality traits or character?

You might feel it's a little artificial to approach building your own brand identity in a similar way to selling a product—but in many ways the process is similar—especially to those people with whom you are creating first impressions. They may have already heard about you from friends, or checked out your online profile and begun to form perceptions before meeting you. Your background, your nationality, your home town, your school, who you socialise with, how you dress, what your comments or opinions are on certain matters and how others describe you all begin to create a picture in the mind about you. Regardless how complicated we as humans are, or how we might change with time or mood—people that may have a profound impact in your life will sometimes only have a thin moment-in-time sample of you to create a perception.

So when that moment comes, it's important that the desired perceptions are created. The chances are increased with singularity of message and consistency.

Consistency is important in building and reinforcing personal brands as it is with product brands. If you are consistently seen to be upbeat, optimistic, resilient and caring it's likely these will become enduring traits that begin to define you. Alternatively, if you're optimistic one day and pessimistic the next, resilient one day and fragile the next, people will find it hard to tell what you are. Perhaps unpredictable and changeable is you? If you're predictably unpredictable (or reliably unreliable as some we've all experienced!) consistency will cement those traits.

I'm not suggesting for a moment you should, or ever could, become a planned automaton. But it may be helpful to draft a personal Brand DNA as a thought piece and a guide.

To craft it, some Discovery work would help too. Find out how others perceive you. How do you see yourself? What are traits you aspire to—and what would you like to change if you could? Remember a DNA is a desired future state so there should be some stretch goal in there.

When you craft your personal brand DNA you might find the following thoughts about happiness and meaningful lives useful.

Mindfulness has become a well-known word in the last few years, meaning being more conscious of one's feelings and thoughts, and living in the present moment. The notion has been around for centuries. As the old Chinese proverb says, 'Be careful of your thoughts, for your thoughts become your words. Be careful of your words, for your words become your actions. Be careful of your actions, for your actions become your habits. Be careful of your habits, for your habits become your character. Be careful of your character, for your character becomes your destiny.'

I would add beliefs and values in at the beginning too. Beliefs are both the product of thoughts and become primary drivers of thoughts over time—like hardened thoughts that influence other thoughts. Values are beliefs expressed through words and proven by action. To me they are like principles—they only come with sacrifice of some sort. You cannot hold on to a value if your actions betray it.

Happiness

Let me share with you the secret to a happy life.

Appropriately, it comes from the man who is credited with coining the term mindfulness. George Vaillant is a Harvard psychologist who has spent most of his adult life analyzing the data from the Grant Study—probably the longest-running longitudinal study in scientific research history, tracking 268 people over 75 years across all aspects of their lives. Vaillant has spent 40 years analyzing this study to determine which factors most reliably correlate with well-being.

He's probably studied happiness longer, and in greater depth, than any other single human being.

So, what did he conclude is the secret to a happy life?

In a sentence:

"That the only thing that really matters in life is your relationships to other people."

Of course, there are other factors you might predict such as education, a stable relationship and health (not smoking or abusing alcohol or drugs, exercising regularly and maintaining a healthy weight)—but the main conclusion is relationships with other people. Not money, material wealth or the perceived trappings of 'success'.

Purpose

Emily Esfahani Smith would agree; relationships was one of the four pillars to a meaningful life that she identified after years of studying what makes people happy or unhappy. The other three were purpose, transcendence (something that lifts you above the bustle of everyday life, such as spirituality) and storytelling (being an architect of your own story).

Her relationships were described as a sense of belonging; the feeling of valuing and being valued by others for who you are.

I pay special attention to purpose. As mentioned above in the section on VIII, I've found a sense of purpose—a reason for being—is arguably the most powerful force. It's when we lose or lack purpose and direction, things go off track; 'idle hands are the devil's tools', as the old saying goes. Smith describes purpose as 'using your strengths to serve others'. I would add, in a way that brings fulfilment and reward (emotional more than financial).

Purpose goes way beyond your job. It may even be that your job is just a means to enable you to find purpose in other ways, such as being a musician, a writer or a mother.

Keep Your Promises

Which brings me back to remind you of one of the most important maxims of this book: Keep your promises! And don't make promises you can't keep!

Brands are like people—or if you prefer—people are their own brands. We've all known people who make empty promises that they don't follow through on. You may forgive the odd uncharacteristic honest mistake, but if it's habitual you quickly realise this isn't someone you can trust and probably not someone you want to associate with. It's the same for brands as it is with people.

Givers Gain

WHAT THIS TOOL DOES

This tool reminds us of the old adage: It is better to give than receive.

When I told one of my colleagues about this book, he asked me: 'Aren't you afraid of giving away all your secrets? Isn't this the value that you bring to your clients?'

Well, yes and no. One school of thought says protecting your rights, holding things close to your chest, IP, trademarks, and so on are the best way of protecting your interests. I've found that the best way is not legal ownership, but *perceptual ownership*. Both can be abused, but it's more valuable to have perceptual ownership; and it's easier to get this when you are the authentic creator or owner. Pretenders invariably get caught in a lie at some point.

I also believe in what my mother always said: 'What goes around comes around'. The more you put out there the more comes back you to.

I've found the Reciprocity Ring to be a helpful exercise for leadership groups. Each person shares a personal and a professional goal that they'd like to achieve, that is important to them but, for whatever reason, has proven to be beyond their reach. It's a request for help. But it's not just one-sided. Everybody, including the CEO, should participate. The goals, problems or challenges get evenly shared. Someone offers to help you (even if they don't have a ready-made solution just yet) and you offer to help someone else. It often plays back to whole brain types and 'vitamin deficiencies'—what you might be struggling with, another may find easy.

Finding a person with complementary skills and thinking preferences to your own is often the answer to your problems particularly if it involves a task that doesn't play to your natural strengths.

In 2013, Adam Grant wrote in *McKinsey Quarterly* about corporate culture. The problem, he said, is that many organisations don't support a culture of information sharing. Worse, in 'taker cultures' the norm is for employees to take as much information as possible without giving anything in return. Ironically, Grant found the opposite behaviour to be the most effective. The amount of help a group's members give each other is one of the strongest predictors of effectiveness. 'Giver cultures' gain.

It's not in our nature to seek help, or often to give it freely, without some kind of trade-off. Asking for help is seen as a weakness, or admission of not being in complete control. (Perhaps that's why men won't ask for directions when they're lost...or it may be just to annoy their wives!) Organisations that de-stigmatise asking for help and reward the giving of information find they create a liberated, collaborative environment where everyone feels inclined to give more freely. Contrasting with the guarded silos of information found in many organisations, these collaborative, giver groups are more likely to enjoy success faster and build greater mutual respect at the same time.

There is a comfort too for givers confident in their own ability. We can all read how to do an appendectomy. You can even watch a step-by-step guide on YouTube if you can stomach it. But it's not the same as actually doing it.

Given the choice between the self-taught internet surgeon or an expert who's performed 1,000 appendectomies or more, I know whom I'd rather have operate on me.

That said, the tools and beliefs I've set out in this book are not brain surgery. They are, hopefully, instructive and relatively easy to practice. I encourage you to experiment with the ones that intrigue you. Take pleasure in reaffirming things you knew already. Try new things you find interesting. And challenge your beliefs with the things you disagree with.

If you find them helpful, please share them. Pass on a kindness and it will come back to you in surprising ways. Be distinctive, be relevant, compelling and credible. Keep your promises. What makes great brands great is what makes great people great too.

Acknowledgements

I wish to acknowledge my partners at The Brand Company in Hong Kong. They were all architects of the Brand Centered Management approach that forms the backbone of this book. James Stuart and Ian Henry, both exceptional minds and great fun to work with all those years ago in Hong Kong when brand consultancies were in their infancy. We had terrific contributions from our team; Young Lye Peng, sadly no longer with us, Giles Rhys Jones, Stephanie Tibbatts, Sung Hae Kim, Jennifer Chan, Amy Chau, Brenda Chan, John Lui and Wendy Lam.

Thank you to my editor-turned-publisher Dan Crissman for your professionalism, patience and sensitive advice throughout the process. You've been both the pilot and the air traffic controller in guiding this plane throughout its flight—and finally to landing it!

Thank you to the folks at Parafine Press and Belt Publishing for having faith in the book—and keeping the faith.

I'd like to give a call-out to the people at Reedsy.com, the online site for writers to connect with editors. They are wonderful catalysts and enablers that helped transform this long-overdue project into reality. I highly recommend them.

Thanks to Bruce Elbeblawy for his work on the illustrations and to Grant Pasay for proofreading.

There are always a handful of important mentors in a long career path who were kind, supportive, smart and generous with their knowledge. These include John Hackney, Richard Dowdle, John Ogden, Les Naylor, Mike Walsh, John Seifert, Ranjan Kapur, Rod Wright, John O'Shea, Francois Tiger, Ian Strachan and Neil French.

I'd like to thank people who've been kind enough to scan manuscripts and provide valuable insight, advice and comments; Margot Torres, Graham Kelly, Wayne Lotherington, Andrew Roberston and David Guerrero.

With the advantage of age and experience there is an ability to reflect on pivotal periods in your life when a few people can truly create change. David Guerrero was my Creative Partner at Ogilvy Manila during a transformational period, not just for the agency but for the industry in the Philippines. With terrific people like Tina Coscolluela, Jos Ortega, Melissa Crucillo, Jun Caranghan, Peachy Todino, Ichay Bulaong, Dickie Soriano, Leah Besa, Susan Soriano, Edel Tolentino, Angeli Beltran, Tom Trinidad, Carmen Mapa, Maricelle

Narcisso and Letty amongst many others, forgive me for not naming you all. There have been other great creative minds I've benefitted from such as Barry White, Khun Decha Tangpintansuk, and Khun Suthisak Sucharittanontta.

At Leo Burnett in Malaysia Yasmin Ahmed and Ali Mohammed brought me back into turbulent waters that we navigated together with stars like Tony Savarimuthu, Zhu and Hwa, Karthik Siva, Phyliis Chan, Tan Sio Chian and Sue D'Cruz.

I'd like to acknowledge my partners at BioCube Corporation and thank them for their camaraderie and encouragement; Laurence Baum, David Tait, Dennis Chisholm, Chris Tan, John Edwards and Ed Tycholaz of CBVL have demonstrated resilience and determination in bringing a game-changing green fuel technology to market under challenging macroeconomic and political conditions.

Then there are people closer to home now in Vancouver. Wendy Hartley and Annie Kim are wonderful friends and model professionals who have generously given me their advice and time to help promote the book. I have been blessed with many wonderful friends who say kind words of encouragement and whom can always be relied on for support; Kishore and Bindu Mulpuri, Ming and Martin Shen, Karen and Chance Lee, Priya and Gregory Baker—thank you.

I am fortunate to have pockets of friends from our travels (mostly gathered and kept through the offices of my wife, as she likes to remind me). Old school friends from Edinburgh, the Filipino colonies in San Francisco, Toronto and Vancouver, the amazing community of St George's school in Vancouver, darts friends, soccer team friends…I apologise for not calling everyone out by name…you know who you are. At the end of the day, it is these friendships that matter most and for which I am truly thankful.

Of course, I want to give thanks to my family too. They don't have a choice, but have been interested and supportive throughout, from my father (who continues to inspire aged 85, still skiing and just about to complete his third book), my sisters Julia and Jane (both much smarter than me with degrees in astrophysics, environmental sciences and other subjects I don't pretend to understand) and my brother Matthew, who is the 'Exocet Missile' and financial star of the family. To my sons Arvi, Paolo and Jack, each following their own paths in their own creative ways, thank you for being the fine young men you are, you make me a proud father. Daughter-in-law Chelsea, thank you too. To Vito and Randy, Tito and Bong and all my nieces and nephews, thank you for your inspiration and support.

And to my wife Pie, I save the biggest thank you of all. Thank you for your unwavering encouragement and belief in me through thick and thin, and most of all, for reminding me that it is better to be kind than to be right.

I dedicate this book to all the givers out there. Keep the faith.

References and Useful Readings

Aaker David A., *Managing Brand Equity: Capitalizing on the Value of a Brand Name*, The Free Press, Macmillan, 1991

Aaker, David A., *Building Strong Brands*, The Free Press, Simon & Schuster, 1996

Adizes, Ichak, *Managing Corporate Lifecycles,* The Adizes Institute, 2004

Aithchison Jim, *Cutting Edge Advertising: How to Create the World's Best Print for Brands in the 21st Century.* Prentice Hall, 1999

Ansoff, H. Igor and Sullivan, Patrick A., *Optimizing Profitability in Turbulent Environments: A Formula for Strategic Success*, Pergammon Press, 1993

Barker, Joel Arthur, *Future Edge: Discovering the New Paradigms of Success*, William Morrow & Co., 1992

Bond, Jonathan & Kirshenbaum, Richard, *Under the Radar: Talking to Today's Cynical Consumer*, John Wiley & Sons, 1998

de Bono, Edward, *How to Have Creative Ideas, 62 Exercises to Develop the Mind*, Vermillion, 2008

de Bono, Edward and Tuzcular, Ercan, *Six Thinking Hats*, Little, Brown & Company, 1985

Burlingham, Bo, *Small Giants. Companies that Choose to be Great Instead of Big*, Penguin, 2005

Cacioppe, R. 'Getting Change to Stick,' *HR Monthly*, March 1998

Caples, John, *Tested Advertising Methods*, Prentice Hall, 1974

Covey Stephen R., *Principle-Centered Leadership*, The Free Press, Simon & Schuster, 1990

Darwin, Charles, *On the Origin of Species by Means of Natural Selection or the Preservation of Favoured Races in the Struggle for Life*, John Murray, 1859

Darwin, Charles and Wallace, Alfred R., *On the Tendency of Species to Form Varieties; and on the Perpetuation of Varieties and Species by Natural Means of Selection*, Linnean Society, 1858

Donnahoe, Alan S. *What Every Manager Should Know about Financial Analysis*, Simon & Schuster, 1989

Dru, Jean-Marie, *Disruption: Overturning Conventions and Shaking Up the Marketplace*, John Wiley & Sons, 1996

Dru, Jean-Marie, *Beyond Disruption: Changing the Rules in the Marketplace*, John Wiley & Sons, 2002

Gladwell, Malcolm, *The Tipping Point: How Little Things Can Make a Big Difference*, Little, Brown & Company, 2000

Gladwell, Malcolm, *Blink: The Power of Thinking without Thinking*, Little, Brown & Company, 2005

Gladwell, Malcolm, *Outliers: The Story of Success*, Little, Brown & Company, 2008

Goffee, Rob and Jones, Gareth, 'Creating the Best Workplace on Earth', *Harvard Business Review*, May 2013

Grant, Adam, 'Givers take all: The hidden dimension of corporate culture', *McKinsey Quarterly*, 2013

Handy, Charles, *The Age of Unreason*, Harvard Business Review Press, 1991 (first published 1989)

Handy, Charles, *The Elephant and the Flea: Looking Backwards to the Future*, Hutchinson, 2001

Handy, Charles, *Inside Organisations. 21 Ideas for Managers*, BBC Books, 1990

Hart, Susannah and Murphy, John, *Brands: The New Wealth Creators*, Interbrand, Macmillan Business, 1998

Hegarty, John, *Hegarty on Advertising: Turning Intelligence into Magic*, Thames & Hudson Ltd, 2011

Hermann, Ned, *The Whole Brain Business Book: Unlocking the Power of Whole Brain Thinking in Organisations and Individuals*, McGraw-Hill, 1996

Johnson, Spencer, M.D., *Who Moved my Cheese?: An A-Mazing Way to Deal with Change in Your Work and in Your Life*, G.P. Putnam's Sons, 1998

Kapin, Allyson and Sample-Ward, Amy, *Social Change Anytime Everywhere*, John Wiley & Sons, 2013

Kaplan, Robert S. and Norton, David P., *The Balanced Scorecard*, Harvard Business School Press, 1990

Kumar, Nirmada, *Kill a Brand, Keep a Customer*, Harvard Business Review, 2003

Kuhn, Thomas, *The Structure of Scientific Revolutions*, University of Chicago Press, 1962

Lotherington, Wayne, *Flicking Your Creative Switch*, John Wiley & Sons, 2003

Lotherington, Wayne, *How Creative People Connect (Or Are They Just Dotty?)*, TimeEdge Pub, 2007

Lynch, Dudley and Kordis, Paul, *Strategy of the Dolphin: Winning Elegantly by Coping Powerfully in a World of Turbulent Change*, William Morrow and Co., 1989

Maister, David, *Practice What You Preach: What Managers Must Do to Create a High Achievement Culture*, The Free Press, 2001

McCormack, Mark H., *What They Don't Teach You at Harvard Business School*, Fontana, 1986

McKinsey Quarterly, 'Management practices that work', September 2007

Morgan, Adam, *The Pirate Inside: Building a Challenger Brand Culture within Yourself and Your Organization*, John Wiley & Sons, 2004

Morgan, Adam, *Eating the Big Fish: How Challenger Brands Can Compete against Brand Leaders*, John Wiley & Sons, 1999

Ogilvy, David, *Ogilvy on Advertising*, Crown Publishers, 1983

Ohmae, Kenichi, *The Borderless World: Power and Strategy in the Interlinked Economy*, HarperBusiness, 1990

Ohmae, Kenichi, *The End of the Nation State: The Rise of Regional Economies*, HarperCollins 1995

Patterson, Kerry; Grenny, Joseph; Maxfield, David; McMillan, Ron; and Switzler, Al, *Influencer: The Power to Change Anything*, McGraw-Hill, 2008

Rasiel, Ethan M., *The McKinsey Way: Using the Techniques of the World's Top Strategic Consultants to Help You and Your Business*, McGraw-Hill, 1998

Ries, Al and Laura, *The Origin of Brands*, HarperBusiness, 2004

Ries, Al and Laura, *22 Immutable Laws of Branding: How to Build a Product or Service into a World-Class Brand*, HarperBusiness, 1998

Ries, Al and Trout, Jack, *The 22 Immutable Laws of Marketing*, HarperCollins, 1993

Ries, Al and Trout, Jack, *Positioning: How to Be Seen and Heard in the Overcrowded Marketplace*, HarperCollins, 2001

Roberts, David, *The Secret to a Happy Life: Revealed*, Grist, 2014

Roman, Kenneth and Maas, Jane, *How to Advertise: A Professional Guide for the Advertiser*, St. Martin's Press, 1992

Smith, Emily Esfahani, *Four Pillars of a Meaningful Life that Could Be Part of Every Learning Community*, Mindshift, 2018

Snyder, Blake, *Save the Cat. The Last Book on Screenwriting You'll Ever Need*, Michael Wiese Productions, 2005

Trompenaar, Fons and Hampden-Turner, Charles, *Riding the Waves of Culture: Understanding Diversity in Global Business*, McGraw-Hill, 1997

Vaillant, GE, *Triumphs of Experience: The Men of the Harvard Grant Study*, Belknap Press, 2012